The Art of Business Process Management

BPM Strategy and Real-World Execution

Published in association with the
Workflow Management Coalition

Workflow Management Coalition

WfMC

Excellence in Practice Series

Future Strategies Inc.
Lighthouse Point, Florida, USA

The Art of Business Process Management
BPM Strategy and Real-World Execution

Copyright © 2016 by Future Strategies Inc.
ISBN13: 978-0-9863214-3-6

Published by Future Strategies Inc., Book Division
3640 North Federal Highway, Lighthouse Point FL 33064 USA
954.782.3376 / 954.719.3746 fax
www.FutStrat.com email: books@FutStrat.com

For bulk orders, resellers, academic orders and extracts, please contact the publisher.

The Art of Business Process Management:
BPM Strategy and Real-World Execution

p. cm.
Includes bibliographical references and appendices.

1. Business Process Management. 2. Organizational Change. 3. Technological Innovation. 4. Information Technology. 5. Total Quality Management. 6. Management Information Systems. 7. Office Practice Automation. 8. Knowledge Management. 9. Workflow. 10. Process Analysis

Fischer, Layna. (ed)

Table of Contents

Section 1: The Art of BPM Strategy

Section 2: The Skill of BPM Execution

Award-winning Case Studies

Section 3: Appendix

Foreword

Change the Trajectory

In a workshop for Change Program Managers at a major bank, one of the teams started their project presentation with the phrase "There's nothing like a major operational failure to get everyone's attention ..."

Think BP in the Gulf, Volkswagen the diesel cheat, RBS and their countless systems meltdowns, Standard Chartered and Iran, Barclays and Libor ... Sony or Target with their security woes. All of these represent highly visible operational or regulatory failures. They got everyone's attention and very often there were high profile casualties in the boardroom as a result. We trust large brands to do the right thing, but operationally, they are often found lacking.

The Costa Concordia - Image Source - ABCNews

If we were on a boat, we'd blame the captain for not steering the ship away from danger ... but isn't it really *everyone's* responsibility? We all need to act in the lookout role; to identify, package and prioritize the signals—to help the captain turn the super tanker, without putting the ship on the rocks or running it aground. And let's face it; most large organizations have a lot of similarities with big boats. The point is that any large, established business can suffer a similar fate. One moment, everything appears normal, the next thing you know, you're out of a job.

The captain (CEO) may know and appreciate the need for a change in direction, but the body politic of the organization, like the inertia of the super tanker, always wants to keep going in the same direction. While this sounds like a useful analogy, there is a spectrum of change:

- **Some CEOs want a fundamental "wellness program" for the organization**—a radical change that involves cultural change and true value innovation, such as pivoting the brand to focus on the long term needs of customers and their experience rather than quarterly shareholder returns. In these sorts of change programs everything is up for grabs including the role played by the organization within its ecosystem, the organization structure, the processes, the products and services. There's normally a mountain to climb in terms of the cultural change element.

- **Somewhere in the middle, the ambition is more modest**—simplifying business operations in preparation for the ravages of the digital economy, or reaffirming organizational purpose and ensuring it reflects in policies and practices. Typically, this sort of initiative follows on from an organizational merger, where multiple functions do similar things in many different countries. These sorts of changes often involve challenging the organization structure and its fiefdoms, right down to the compensation mechanisms, decision-making practices and processes.

- **Others are content with applying a "Band Aid"**—fixing a major problem within a function or dealing with some "burning platform," as if, once applied, we can all then return to normal. Whatever that is. This sort of change is often more about putting "go-faster stripes" on what is already happening—reducing the cost or speed of doing something (resource reduction). The organization structure is taken as a given. Processes and management practices might need tweaking, but nobody is seriously challenging the need for them. Everyone wants clarity around what's going to happen and how it affects them, but the underlying value proposition remains the same.

In our experience, about 80% of change programs fall into the Band-Aid category, with no ambition of radical change to the fundamentals of the organization. Very few, perhaps 3-5%, set out with a wellness program in mind. Either way, the CEO wants to achieve the goal without betting the company. Or putting it another way, he or she may want to revolutionize the business but do it with *evolutionary* techniques.

At best, our courageous CEO can describe the trajectory—the direction—and paint a picture of what that future might look like along with the perils of the status quo. They'll use this as a first step to persuade other C level executives to explore the possibilities and even appoint a seasoned exec to oversee things. But it's getting everyone else in the firm involved that will really make the change happen and ensure its sustainability.

It's at that point that most change programs run into the blockers and tacklers—the ones who have most to lose. If the change involves a challenge to the hegemony of the current functions then religious (political) warfare often breaks out. They want everything kept nicely segregated—it's *their* fiefdoms, *their* budget. They've helped create these functions and have built their careers around moving up and around them. They want everything communicated in their language. Typically, managers at the C-1 and C-2 levels want to see themselves in the new structure before they invest their time, energy and resources into helping create that new future. They'll nod at the right times and send along their representatives to the key meetings to report back. But in most organizations, it's those managers and their representatives that are the ones most threatened by the emerging new world order. You'll hear phrases like "we like working stepwise," and "building on our heritage;" or best of all, "that's not how we do things here."

With revolutionary change the need for many firms, the hard part is getting there with evolutionary methods. The challenge for the change leader is to overcome the catch 22—how do you bring the critical people along? How do you engage the key protagonists into the change program and get their commitment and support, while avoiding alienating them? That usually means couching the language in ways that the existing functions can find palatable—outlining the challenge and the implications of maintaining the status quo, highlighting the opportunity and *helping them work out the best way to get there.*

A DIFFERENT VIEW OF STRATEGY

One could argue that we are talking here about tactics rather than strategy. Indeed, by the time the change program is beginning there have already been many discussions around strategy. However, any discussion around change programs as an implementation or execution of strategy must take into account how those strategic choices were made. While there are lots of different strategy methods, we see two big buckets:

Deterministic Strategy

This view of strategy involves three (OK, perhaps six) people sitting in a room to agree what the future should look like—perhaps using some variation of Porters Five Forces, PEST or SWOT analysis. Having proclaimed the future and supported by consultants, they now decide on the tactics to get there. Then it's a case of telling everyone else how they've got to change, when to jump and how high. There are always alternative methods and techniques to substitute into the mix, but the underlying assumption is that the machine itself is fine; all they have to do is to fix or replace some broken part. At the heart of this approach is a mechanistic mental model with appropriate levers and controls for the business machine. All that's needed is a reduction in resources and increase in speed, and hey bingo, the transformation is complete!

Well, not quite. That linear dogma—a way of thinking that was born in the 17th century—has very little to do with the creative economy and the rapidly evolving disruptive forces of the 21st century. Moreover, when you need a wellness program, or the more common post-merger integration, your real challenges revolve around overcoming inward-looking, hierarchical and bureaucratic cultures. Most large organizations are crippled by their existing management practices, which, in turn, stifle any attempts at meaningful change or innovation.

Emergent Strategy

In this bucket, the future strategy emerges over time. These approaches take into account that the overall direction is usually known—the mountain in the distance that we have to climb, yet what is just around the next bend is unknown. The path to get up that mountain is unique to each traveler (organization); plans are developed to follow a particular path, and then readjusted based on experimentation and feedback. Rather than just a few people making all the decisions and imposing them on others, to scale the heights the organization engages people from the core and the frontlines, challenging them to co-create the future. While teams may have efficiency targets, their ultimate focus is on value. The goal is to evolve a set of robust "service propositions" or product/service combinations that deliver more, and better, value to customers.

Rather than the inside-out approach, where the business views itself as machine to make ever larger returns for shareholders, the principle underlying this approach is that by setting out to delight customers, the enterprise delivers more value than its competitors. The organization sets out to make an emotional connection with customers; delivering an experience that a competitor cannot easily replicate. As a result, the organization turns its customers into brand advocates—think Apple and its iPhone.

Customers are more likely to buy more, to recommend the organization to their friends, and have a far lower likelihood to decamp to a competitor. There is no single well-articulated grand-master plan. The firm continuously adjusts its service propositions and products to the environment within which it finds itself.

Rethinking change outside-in ensures a focus on the "why"—why the firm exists and how it delivers value. It means you focus on creating a wellness program rather than applying yet another Band-Aid that drives up complexity. It means engaging your people to do the right things (rather than just doing things right). This way of engaging and co-creating helps overcome the silos (politics), drives innovation, and in the end, delivers differentiated value to your customers. This style of thinking gets to the marrow of the organizational culture rather than just going skin deep. If you do it right, it becomes their change, not yours. But that means that most of you—the change agents, need to change the way you think about change.

This is an uncomfortable place for many traditional managers and executives. Many large businesses are still dominated by that inward-looking, hierarchical and bureaucratic culture. They've only got where they are today by exercising their knowledge and power; change is for everyone else, not them. They still think that better and more controlled in execution of the plan is the route to success.

Our central thesis is that the deterministic approach to change just doesn't work.

Galileo Galilei once said "You cannot teach a man anything, you can only help him find it within himself."

Too many change efforts in big businesses start with exactly the opposite; they begin with decree and diktat. The initiative risks getting derailed before it gets started.

Galileo also said "I have never met a man so ignorant that I couldn't learn something from him."

The point is that, when you reimagine change—when you refocus the trajectory—to become more of a conversation on the why rather than just the how; outside-in, building an engaged and involved workforce; *that's* when you'll get real and sustainable change.

Derek Miers
Structure Talent Ltd, United Kingdom

Introduction:
The Art of Business Process Management

Layna Fischer, Future Strategies Inc.

This book goes to the *heart* of what is driving interest in BPM today – the ability to improve and automate how we manage both our business processes and the information that supports them. The authors discuss the impact of new technologies, the mandate for greater transparency, and how the ongoing aftershocks of globalization have collectively removed nearly any trace of predictability within the business environment.

As Nathaniel Palmer points out, as a result, sustainable competitive advantage no longer comes from scale and efficiency but adaptability – the ability to process streams of information flows, make sense of these, and rapidly translate these into effective responses designed for precision rather repeatability.

In addition to the highly insightful and thoughtful white papers contributed by industry thought leaders, this book provides compelling award-wining case studies written by those who have been through the full BPM experience.

These case studies describe the skills involved to generate successful ROIs and competitive advantages gained through BPM and the writers also generously share solid advice on how to avoid the pitfalls they personally encountered– and overcame.

BPM is essential to a company's survival in today's hyper-speed business environment. The Art of BPM is to empower an enterprise to compete at the highest level in any marketplace.

Section 1: The Art of BPM

FOREWORD: CHANGE THE TRAJECTORY

Derek Miers, Structure Talent Ltd, United Kingdom

When you reimagine change—when you refocus the trajectory—to become more of a conversation on the why rather than just the how; outside-in, building an engaged and involved workforce; *that's* when you'll get real and sustainable change.

THE HEART OF BPM

Nathaniel Palmer, BPM, Inc., USA

The impact of new technologies, the mandate for greater transparency, and the ongoing aftershocks of globalization have collectively removed nearly any trace of predictability within the business environment. As a result, sustainable competitive advantage no longer comes from scale and efficiency but adaptability – the ability to process streams of information flows, make sense of these, and rapidly translate these into effective responses designed for precision rather repeatability.

THE PROCESS OF PROCESS MANAGEMENT

Dr Mathias Kirchmer and Peter Franz, BPM-D

Business strategies and operations need to consider scores of ever-shifting factors: from demographic changes, capital availability and legal regulations to technological innovations and an all present digitalization. Static business models do not keep pace with this dynamic change. Companies need a management approach that fits to this volatile environment. Organizations need to execute their strategy systematically and deal proactively with our "digital world". In effect, they must know how and when to modify or enhance their business processes, to know which processes are best candidates for intervention, and how to move rapidly from strategy to execution.

PROCESS DISCOVERY AND IMPROVEMENT

Hartmann Genrich, Process Analytica, Germany, Robert Shapiro, Process Analytica, USA

In recent years, tools have become available that can mine process logs and generate visualizations of the historical behavior of the process(es). The visualizations prove useful in process improvement. We have added to this the ability to construct an executable model consistent with the historical data and a capability to (re)construct a sub-process decomposition of this model to improve understandability and performance.

ACCELERATING VALUE BY REBOOTING ENTERPRISE ARCHITECTURE

Linus Chow, Thomas J. Cozzolino, David Grimm, Salesforce

Shifts in people, processes, information and technology are key factors in how Modern Architectures are both disrupting and providing value to Enterprises. This seismic shift is forcing a hard look at the value of traditional Enterprise Architecture (EA), and leading the demand for strategic transformational outcomes that "Modern" EA needs to enable.

We will look at how and why we need to "reboot" EA to understand specific focus areas for change. Additionally, we will discuss how to transform EA from a "noun" (artifact and meta-work focused) to a "verb" (acceleration and business outcome-focused). Finally, we discuss best practice approaches to assist EA to become both a leader of, and a partner in, building this new world.

Section 2: The Skill of BPM

Award-winning Case Studies

ADMIN RE, U.K

Nominated by Corporate Modelling, UK

Part of the Swiss Re group, Admin Re UK is a specialist in the run-off of legacy closed life business portfolios with a proven track record in the administration of life, pensions and health business and the acquisition of entire life insurance companies. Our organization continues to grow through merger and acquisitions and strategic client and third party partnerships, underpinned by solid and efficient customer servicing at a low cost that is highly compliant and low risk.

AGFIRST FARM CREDIT BANK, USA

Nominated by Bizagi, United Kingdom

AgFirst is part of the national Farm Credit System, the largest agricultural lending organization in the United States. With assets of more than $27 billion, AgFirst provides funding and financial services to 19 farmer-owned financial cooperatives in 15 eastern states and Puerto Rico. These cooperatives, operating as Farm Credit and AgCredit agricultural credit associations (ACAs), offer real estate and production financing to more than 80,000 farmers, agribusinesses and rural homeowners.

AGESIC: E-NOTIFICATIONS IN THE E-GOVERNMENT AGENCY, URUGUAY

Nominated by INTEGRADOC, Uruguay

This case study details the experience of transforming a costly paper-based, mostly manual process, to permit government entities to notify and communicate with citizens, into a highly automated, completely electronic system that achieves legal compliance. The scope of the system is extensive, with the system expected to reach every citizen, public entity and private company in the country.

BUSINESS PARTNERS, SOUTH AFRICA

Nominated by Pétanque Consultancy, South Africa

Business Partners, a $US342m+ risk finance lender, applied process design *and* a change management campaign to improve customer experience. The campaign, dubbed "The Transformers" set out to reduce approval and implementation processes, resulting in Customer Excellence; improve efficiencies and turnaround time; and increase revenue by 20 percent.

CHICAGO PARKS DISTRICT, USA

Nominated by Sofbang and Oracle, USA

The Chicago Park District (CPD) is one of the largest municipal park systems in the US. It is responsible for more than 8,100 acres of green space, including 580 parks, 77 pools, and 26 miles of lakefront and beaches. CPD implemented an integrated custom and off-the-shelf solution to streamline operations for interdepartmental efficiency across the organization, saving costs and eliminating duplication of efforts. An integrated BPM platform enables the enterprise to work within its specific applications, such as E-Business and Enterprise Project Management products, and ensures effective collaboration across these integral departments.

DELTA LLOYD, THE NETHERLANDS

Nominated by You-Get, the Netherlands

Delta Lloyd Group is an expert, reliable and accessible financial services provider. We have a single goal: to offer security to our customers, now and in the future. We operate under three strong brands: Delta Lloyd, OHRA and ABN AMRO Insurance.

Delta Lloyd has been a trusted partner for insurance, pensions, investing and banking since 1807. It is our goal to offer financial security, now and in the future. We deliver clear, reliable and contemporary products and services that meet our customers' needs and create value for them, our shareholders and our employees.

FREEDOM MORTGAGE, USA

This case study details the *Retail Title Track Rewrite Process*. Title Ordering and Review are key components of the mortgage financing process. Title ordering and the title search process reveal the financial obligations that could potentially impact the sale of the property, including such actions such as lawsuits, liens, legal claims, etc. The mortgage lender holds responsibility for the title review process. The change to this process impacted the Title department, closers, mortgage applicants, title providers, and FMCs management team. FMCs Title Process dramatically changed the once manually intensive title ordering/review process.

GE AVIO SRL, ITALY

Nominated by EKA Srl, Italy

In 2012 Avio SpA, now General Electric Avio, supplier of engine modules and components, started a new project to modernize the management and dissemination of quality procedures. Promoted by the Quality Unit, this initiative involved an interdisciplinary project team composed by several divisions (e.g. Purchase, Business, and Logistics) with the additional participation of the IT Unit and EKA Srl, in charge of IT system development. The new approach consists of a quality system that aims to map operational processes and gathers them under a unique reference tool to all procedures.

GENERALI CEE HOLDING B.V.

Nominated by Bizagi, United Kingdom

Generali CEE Holding (Generali) is a leading insurance group in Central and Eastern Europe with total assets under management of €14.8 billion and more than 11 million clients. In 2011-2014, we embarked on "Project Puccini," a large-scale initiative to significantly boost process visibility, productivity and efficiency in the area of Corporate Risks underwriting for 10 countries throughout Central and Eastern Europe.

MELITTA, BRAZIL

Nominated by Lecom S/A, Brazil

Melitta of Brazil, a unit of the German multinational coffee giant, Melitta, found operational barriers that impacted their costs and their agility. Therefore, the intention to improve their business routine was to break barriers between their locations, eliminating the circulation of papers, reduce the number of licenses used for approvals in ERP, integrating legacy systems and thus speed up the execution time of processes. After studying the scenario of Melitta, processes that met these needs were created with the resulting success in the reduction of cost and time.

SOUTH EAST WATER

Nominated by South East Water, Australia

South East Water (SEW) credited customers with $3,500,000 in allowances for unexplained high usage and leaks that occurred on their properties in the 2012/13 financial year. It was projected that it would credit customers with $4,400,000 in the 2013/14 financial year. A BPM project was launched to reduce this amount substantially. It involved 17 teams from across the organization, ranging from customer service teams to plumbing services, debt management, legal and IT. Through changes in policy and process, and with significant change management efforts, the project delivered $1,140,000 for the financial year, which equated to $1,500,000 on an annualized basis.

HOW TO SUBMIT AN ENTRY IN THE ANNUAL BPM AWARDS

The annual WfMC **Awards for Global Excellence in BPM** are sponsored by WfMC.org and BPM.com. The prestigious annual Awards are highly coveted by organizations that seek recognition for their achievements. General information and guidelines for submissions, see **www.bpmf.org**

Section 1

The Art of BPM

The Heart of BPM

Nathaniel Palmer, BPM, Inc., USA

ABSTRACT

This chapter goes to the *heart* of what is driving interest in BPM today – the ability to improve and automate how we manage both our business processes and the information that supports them. The author discusses the impact of new technologies, the mandate for greater transparency, and how the ongoing aftershocks of globalization have collectively removed nearly any trace of predictability within the business environment.

As a result, sustainable competitive advantage no longer comes from scale and efficiency but adaptability – the ability to process streams of information flows, make sense of these, and rapidly translate these into effective responses designed for precision rather repeatability.

INTRODUCTION

> **Definition**: Business Process Management (BPM) is a discipline involving any combination of modeling, automation, execution, control, measurement and optimization of business activity flows, in support of enterprise goals, spanning systems, employees, customers and partners within and beyond the enterprise boundaries.

This is the first consensus-led definition of BPM to surface since it emerged as an identifiable software segment more than a decade ago. Yet it goes to the heart of what is driving interest in BPM today – the ability to improve and automate how we manage both our business processes and the information that supports them.

The impact of new technologies, the mandate for greater transparency, and the ongoing aftershocks of globalization have collectively removed nearly any trace of predictability within the business environment. As a result, sustainable competitive advantage no longer comes from scale and efficiency but adaptability – the ability to process streams of information flows, make sense of these, and rapidly translate these into effective responses designed for precision rather repeatability.

Today we are in what many see as the third phase of BPM, marked by *Intelligent BPM Systems* or *iBPMS*, which builds upon the previous two generations, yet extends into directions previously out of reach. "Intelligent?" you may ask, "as opposed to Dumb BPM?" No, not dumb, per se, but blind. Whereas previous generations of BPM offered limited ability to make sense of business activity flows, iBPMS is distinguished foremost by a "sense and respond" orientation. This notion frames the Phase Three of BPM in terms of the synergistic combination of three groups of capabilities:

- **Phase One** – separating systems (application logic) from the processes (business logic) which they support;

- **Phase Two** – presenting a flexible architecture that supports adaptable, goal-driven process models by maintaining the intelligence for how to access information and application resources without having the bind this into a rigid process model; and

- **Phase Three** – building on the first two sets of capabilities while delivering visibility and feedback which shows what is going on within a process, as well as what will likely occur in the near future.

The first two phases of BPM have set a solid foundation for enabling adaptable systems, allowing BPM adopters to respond with far greater agility than ever before – moving away from the command-and-control structure which has defined management systems for the last 30 years.

For the first several years of the BPM market, these sorts of applications dominated. This also limited the potential market for BPM software, however, because for most firms the exception is the rule. The vast majority of business processes are dynamic, not standardized, and thus require the business systems (e.g., deployed software) that support them to adapt quickly to changes within the business environment. As a business technology, the greatest value of process management software is delivered not through automation and integration alone, but by introducing a layer between users and existing IT infrastructure to allow business systems to adapt and keep pace with the constant found in most business environments. Fully realizing the ability offered through orchestration, however, requires the 'situational awareness' necessary to adapt business systems to a changing business environment – the ability to sense and respond. By taking the lid off the black box of automation, the Phase Three of BPM offers a framework for continuously validating and refining an understanding of business performance drivers, and adapting business systems accordingly.

This will require a new level of transparency of processes and operations that is sure to present cultural and human factors challenges. But this is nothing new for BPM. At the end of the day BPM is only slightly about technology. It is, instead, mostly about the business and the people. What is indeed new, however, and at the center of the Phase Three opportunity, is the ability now to adapt systems continuously to match the ever-changing business environment. The model most frequently referenced throughout this chapter, this continuous loop of visibility and adaptability offers one of the first real leverage points for transforming business through adaptability.

THE EVOLUTION OF INTELLIGENT BPM

To understand the opportunities offered by Intelligent Business Process Management, it's helpful to consider the phases of maturation solutions have gone through over the last decade. During technology expansion of the mid- to late-1990s, the management of business processes was typically limited to the repetitive sequencing of activities, with rigid "hard-wired" application-specific processes such as those within ERP systems. Any more sophisticated degree of workflow management generally imposed a significant integration burden, frequently accounting for 60-80% of the project cost with little opportunity for reuse. Still, integration was typically limited to retrieval of data or documents, similarly hard-wired with one-to-one connection points.

These early process management initiatives often focused on integrating and automating repetitive processes, generally within standardized environments. Whether focused on Straight-Through Processing transactions or a discrete process such as Account Activation, these are applications where the flow and sequence of activities is predetermined and immutable. The role of exceptions-handling here is to allow human intervention to quickly resolve or correct a break in the flow of an otherwise standard process.

By the end of the 1990s, however, BPM had emerged as an identifiable software segment, a superset of workflow management distinguished in part by allowing process management independent of any single application. This was enabled by managing application execution instructions separate from process flows, so processes could be defined without limitation to single application, as well as through support for variable versus hard-wired process flow paths.

The first waves of BPM deployments were typically aimed at bridging the island of automation described above, such as closing gaps in existing ERP deployments. Early BPM solutions were differentiated by integration-centric functionality, such as application adapters, data transformation capabilities and product-specific process definitions (e.g., an order-to-cash process). Eventually, the introduction of standards such as Web Services and advances in the development tools within BPM suites lowered the cost and complexity of data integration. This began to shift the fundamental value proposition of BPM from discrete capabilities to enabling the management of business logic by business process managers, without threatening the integrity of the application logic (the infrastructure that is rightfully managed and protected by IT personnel).

The availability of standards-based protocols significantly lowered the burden on BPM adopters for building and maintaining integration infrastructure, freeing time and resources to focus on the process and business performance, rather than being consumed with plumbing issues. Over time this facilitated a refocus of process management software from that of automation and integration to orchestration and coordination, bringing BPM into the realm of business optimization. Business environments are dynamic, requiring the business systems that support them to be so as well. This means that systems must be able to easily adapt to changing business circumstances.

Phase Two of the BPM opportunity was presented through making orchestration a reality – the ability to connect abstracted application capabilities across orchestrated business processes, thereby transforming existing automation infrastructure into reusable business assets. What separates orchestration from automation is presented by a fundamental shift in perspective, from thinking of processes as a flow of discrete steps, to understanding processes in terms of goals and milestones.

BEYOND INTEGRATION TO ORCHESTRATION

Orchestration allows systems to mirror the behavior of the rest of the business environment (one defined in terms of objectives rather than scripts). Over the last decade, orchestration has introduced a visible shift in the axis of business computing. As firms realize the opportunities presented by orchestration, it offers (arguably mandates) a wholesale rethinking of the role of applications and information systems.

Orchestration has already had a visible impact on the direction of the BPM market, enabled by standards protocols (notably XML and the core Web Services stack of SOAP, UDDI, and WSDL), the emergence of Service-Oriented Architectures (SOA) has provided a new level flexibility and simplicity in resolving integration issues. In fact, it has to such an extent that it almost seems redundant to discuss in the context of forward-looking perspective of modern BPM.

Now we can nearly take for granted that the underlying systems of record are decoupled from how we access them – that access is enabled through a services layer rather than a programmatic interface that requires integration at the code level (i.e., "tightly-coupled"). What SOA provides for BPM and other software environments is a common means for communicating between applications, such that connections do not need to be programmed in advance. As long as the BPM environment knows where to find information and how to access it. This is critical to dynamic processes where the specific information, activities and roles involved with a process may not be predetermined but identified as the process progresses.

Of course this does require, however, that the information and infrastructure sought to be accessed is exposed as services. For example, core system capabilities can be exposed as containerized Web services with a WSDL description, able to be invoked by any Web services compliant application, or increasingly with a RESTful interface allowing integration points and data variables to be defined at design time, but resolved at run-time, eliminating the inherent problems of hard-wired integration.

LEVERAGING CONTENT AS A SERVICE: INTEGRATING UNSTRUCTURED INFORMATION

While the evolution of Service-Oriented Architecture has dramatically improved the accessibly of structured information through standardized interfaces, access to unstructured information can be far more challenging. Consider for a moment where customers reside in your firm. The answer is most likely "everywhere" – records, transactions, profiles, project data, recent news, and other sources of structured and "semi-structured" information (such as correspondence and other documents without uniform representation). For many firms it would take years to rationalize all the places where customer data might be found. But by instead knowing where to find it and how it is described, it can be left intact yet used for multiple purposes.

Following the same strategy as is presented by SOA for accessing structured information, a relatively new standard called "Content Management Interoperability Services" or more commonly "CMIS" enables a services approach to "content middleware" by exposing information stored within CMIS-compliant content repositories, both internally and externally managed sources. As content is captured or otherwise introduced to a process, it can be automatically categorized and indexed based on process state and predefined rules and policies. This presents a virtual repository of both content and meta-data that describes how and where content is managed at various stages of its lifecycle. Meta-data is exposed to the system and process nodes, but invisible to users who instead are presented with the appropriate content and format based on their identity the current state of the process.

SHIFTING FROM EVENT-DRIVEN TO GOAL-DRIVEN

The notion of orchestration has changed the role of BPM from that of a transit system designed to shuttle data from one point to another over predefined routes, to that of a virtual power user that "knows" how to locate, access and initiate application services and information sources. In contrast with more easily automated system-to-system processes and activities, "knowledge worker" processes characteristic of manual work involves a series of people-based activities that may individually occur in many possible sequences.

This transition in computing orientation can be described as the shift from *event-driven* where processes are defined in terms of a series of triggers, to *goal-driven* where processes are defined in terms of specific milestones and outcomes (goals) and constant cycles of adaptations required to achieve them. In event-driven computing, systems respond to a specific event – a request for information is received and the appropriate information is sent, or a process step is complete and so the results are recorded and the next step is initiated. In most cases, the nature of event-driven computing requires explicit scripting or programming of outcomes.

Goal-driven processes, however, are far more complex. A process that has only 20 to 30 unique activities while a relatively small number for most knowledge worker processes may present over 1,000 possible permutations in the sequencing of activities. This of course presents too many scenarios to hard-code within linear process flows in advance, or to create a single process definition, which helps explain the difficulty traditionally faced in the automation of these types of goal-driven processes. Rather, this capability is enabled through the application of goals, policies and rules, while adjusting the flow of the process to accommodate outcomes not easily identifiable.

Goal-Driven Scenarios

In many cases each subsequent step in a process is determined only by the outcome and other circumstances of the preceding step. In addition, there may be unanticipated parallel activities that occur without warning, and may also immediately impact the process and future (even previous) activities. For these reasons and the others described above, managing goal-driven processes requires the ability to define and manage complex policies and declarative business rules – the parameters and business requirements which determine the true "state" of a process. Goal-driven processes cannot be defined in terms of simple "flow logic" and "task logic" but must be able to represent intricate relationships between activities and information, based on policies, event outcomes, and dependencies (i.e, "context.")

Such a case is the admission of a patient for medical treatment. What is involved is, in fact, a process, yet the specific sequence and set of activities most does not follow a specific script, but rather is based on a diagnostic procedure which likely involves applying a combination of policies, procedures, other rules, and the judgment of healthcare workers. Information discovered in one step (e.g., the assessment a given condition) can drastically alter the next set of steps, and in the same way a change in 'patient state' (e.g., patient goes into heart failure) may completely alter the process flow in other ways.

The patient admission scenario described earlier is an example of this. What is needed to successfully execute an admission process is a super user who knows both the medical protocols to make a successful diagnosis and the system protocols to know where and how to enter and access the appropriate information. Alternatively, BPM can exist as the virtual user layer, providing a single access point for the various roles involved, while assuming the burden of figuring out where and how access information.

Yet what really differentiates this as a goal-driven system is the ability to determine the sequence of a process based on current context. For example, a BPM system can examine appropriate business rules and other defined policies against the current status of a process or activity to determine what step should occur next and what information is required.

Facilitating Better Decisions vs Mandating Actions

Often the flow and sequencing of a goal-driven process is determined largely by individual interpretation of business rules and policies. For example, a nurse who initiates a patient admitting process will evaluate both medical protocol and the policies of the facility where the healthcare services are administered. Similarly, an underwriter compiling a policy often makes decisions by referring to policy manuals or his own interpretation of rules and codes. As a result, what may be an otherwise 'standard' process will be distinguished by exceptions and pathways that cannot be determined in advance, but at each step each activity must nonetheless adhere to specific rules and policies.

PHASE THREE: INTELLIGENT BPM

The first two phases of BPM laid a solid foundation for enabling adaptable business systems, by allowing business logic (processes, policies, rules, etc.) to be defined and managed within a separate environment, as well as using an open approach to communicating with other systems (Web Services). This has provided a level of adaptability that allows BPM adopters to respond to changes in the business environment with far greater agility than ever before.

This shift towards goal-oriented computing has laid the path for Phase-Three BPM, which combines integration and orchestration with the ability to continuously validate and refine the business users' understanding of business performance drivers, and allowing them to adapt business systems and process flows accordingly. The effect of Phase Three BPM is to 'take the lid off' what has for years been a black box shrouding automation.

With the third phase of BPM, visibility combines with integration and orchestration to enable business process owners and managers to discover the situation changes which require adaptation. Phase Three of BPM offers a framework for continuously validating and refining an understanding of business performance drivers, and adapting business systems accordingly. This should represent in a new and significantly greater level of interest and adoption of BPM software, by attracting firms seeking to optimize business performance, rather than integrating and automating systems and tasks.

Part of the recent evolution towards iBPMS technology is inclusion of more sophisticated reporting capabilities within the BPM environment itself. This is both enabled and in many ways necessitated by the greater flexibility of the architectures introduced with the BPM suites that define Phase Two. With these environments, the ability to support non-sequential, goal-driven models is greatly increased, requiring more feedback (reporting) to enable success execution of this type of less deterministic process models.

With few exceptions, reporting on process events and business performance was previously done only after a process had executed, or otherwise within a separate environment disjointed from the process. This obviously prevented any opportunity to impact the direction or a process, but was based on a limitation of system and software architectures. Specifically, with regard to BPM, process models were most commonly defined as proprietary structures, and in many cases compiled into software. Thus, changes either required bringing down and recompiling an application, or were otherwise limited to discrete points in the process (such as exceptions and yes/no decision points).

BPM AND SOCIAL MEDIA

In an era when an aberrant Tweet can, within a matter of minutes, cost shareholders millions, it is the meta-context of business events across a spectrum of structured, unstructured, and semi-structured information that defines the larger perspective of business activity. The impact of mobile and social capabilities in enterprise systems, as well as external social networks is having a very real material impact on business. It has become critical (even if comparatively smaller but clearly growing) piece of the business event stream.

Most workers have access to outside information, and already no doubt incorporate this to their existing work patterns. They do this because the information available through Google, Wikipedia, and specific blogs is no doubt more comprehensive, more current, and likely more accurate than internal sources when it comes to topics and events occurring outside of the organization, and in some cases even those happening on the inside. This is because these sources benefit from socialization – the continuous scrutiny, fact-checking and updating offered by the surrounding social network.

Here trust and reputation represent the critical leverage points for the value of information, as there is no top-down governance nor authentication of information would otherwise be expected in a corporate setting. The information in question is only as valuable as the trust in and reputation of its authors – and typically not the originators but the network in place to vet.

Trust and reputation hardly play any role at all in the command-and-control world of process automation. A control flow token travels down a predefined path from one node and another, and with passes control without bias or prejudice. Often a manager sits above multiple running processes, detached from front lines, and may engage in 'load balancing' by shifting work items from one subordinates queue to another. Perhaps just as common an occurrence is circumstances where work performed on a given activity is preceded by the labor of someone else, with having no specific awareness nor concern of the others' reputation, nor any opportunity to act on it if they did. The modeled processes that provide the foundation of BPMS environments today, rarely take into account either the existence or lack of trust and reputation in the design of routing logic.

In social media, however, trust and reputation are key. It is these two factors that offer the crucial leverage point for the success of any social endeavor. Within a social network we pick and choose our partners not on firsthand experience typically, but rather on their respective positioning within a broader framework of familiar relationships. We make decisions about accepting links, becoming 'friends' and passing on information based who they know that who we know. It is highly unlikely anyone would respond favorably to a request from any individuals with whom there is no means to validate reputation or any other basis to establish trust.

Can you believe everything you read on the Internet? No, of course not. Yet this is the very point of social media – that the network of 'antibodies' represented by the crowd of linked individuals, in many cases with no more association than their affinity or membership to that particular network, will systemically attack and expunge any infection of misinformation. Through this socialization, like a well-functioning immune system, only accurate details are spared, or otherwise the infected data is sufficiently discredited such that it is immediately obvious what is credible and what is not.

The way that social computing can have the greatest impact on the execution of work is by applying the same social computing and social media concepts to business processes. Specifically, it is the ability to leverage the collective insight of a group, network or 'crowd' of individuals. In this way the network functions as an organizational immune system, not as controlled group, managed by top-down authority, but rather as a social community. The value and validation offered through this type of intra-organizational socialization can be grouped into one of three forms:

- **Social Modeling** -- leveraging social media conventions within process discovery and modeling to engage stakeholders or otherwise deliver better validated results than possible through traditional analysis.

- **Social Collaboration** – leveraging internal social networks to form goal-driven, virtual teams who collaborate and 'socialize' around a given activity or set of activities.

- **Social Chatter** – leveraging collections of events and event data from either or both internal and external networks to inform decisions or otherwise generate actionable information within a business process.

Social Modeling is one of the first recognizable instances of leveraging enterprise social software within BPM, a practice that is has been for at least a decade prior to the emergence of contemporary social media. For example, the *Collaborative Distributed Scenario and Process Analyzer (ColD SPA)* was a research project launched over a decade ago, premised on the notion that involvement of key personnel during process modeling is necessary for both model accuracy and gaining stakeholder buy-in, yet despite this models are most commonly developed by small teams due to inherent the complexity and difficulties involved in the modeling process.

Specifically, both the methods behind process modeling and the tools used to support it impose an inevitable learning curve, which either leaves out key stakeholders or otherwise requires meditation by "modeling professionals" who must interpret and explain details, thereby both slowing the process and risking biasing the result. The *ColD SPA* prototype was developed to demonstrate how a web-based tool could be used to facilitate the engagement of stakeholders directly within the modeling and discovery process.

The Cathedral and the Bazaar

It is often said that process models have three states – the "as-is," the "to-be," and "the way it is really done." When modeling is left to subject matter experts, only a limited view of potential improvements is presented. Worse yet, the reality-based view of how things actually work in practice is typically omitted, leaving only an idealized (and often naively ignorant) definition of the as-is state. Without an accurate baseline, the desired to-be state will be more difficult to win support for and likely difficult to realize in the practice.

Simply adding to the mix a rarified group of chieftains (political stakeholders versus actual end-users) to weigh-in with their opinions and observations may offer a better understanding of things, but falls short of true socialization. It is unlikely to provide for the serendipitous discovery of potential process improvements, or new processes, which arise from normal interaction (i.e., not as a part a formal discovery session) of workers within a social network. A model for this is presented in how Open Source Software (OSS) is developed, as described by Eric Raymond in his seminal work, "The Cathedral and The Bazaar." Raymond distinguishes between the traditional model of *The Cathedral*, where software is managed by a formal governance model, where access between releases is limited to discrete group of anointed stakeholders, as the case with project-led modeling efforts; and *The Bazaar* where electronically connected, yet otherwise officially unacquainted users offer continuous scrutiny and, in the case of OSS development, add periodic improvements (patches, bug fixes, et al.) as a currency for encouraging other contribution.

The result is a shift away from the centrally managed, command-economy model that governs traditional development practices, to a market-based approach where broader functionality and higher quality software is realized through many small contributions and improvements offered by the larger pool of software consumers. This is essentially the same concept pursued by the first wave of social-enabled BPM platforms, which provide not just a platform for collaborative modeling, which alone does little to transcend the cathedral model, yet also enable 'the bazaar' by connecting a much larger pool of users to connect through private and public communities.

These platforms allow users to post events in a familiar *Facebook Wall* medium, which allow other users to comment on and otherwise identify either existing or proposed process models, post documents and other information, as well as to compose working models based on 'snippets' of prebuilt software functionality.

Beyond the Virtual Water Cooler

The term "Social Collaboration" may at first appear redundant. After all, what collaboration isn't social? The answer is found, however, not in how collaboration is delivered, but how collaborating parties connect in the first place. It is in this regard that BPM offering Social Collaboration depart from other forms of Computer-Supported Collaboration (CSC) such as 'chat' and email, which require pathways to be preordained and typically lack any business process context. Today's more robust BPM environments provide the ability identify and connect with the relevant experts, not already integrated within the business process flow, but to do so within the work space of the BPMS (i.e., to enable ad hoc collaboration within the execution of a business process task.)

A business user can leverage internal social networks as well as a ranked organization chart to enlist the help of individuals outside of the standard process flow to complete a given task. This may include creating a temporary collaboration space organize individuals and related information around the completion of a given task.

Ideally, and an important distinction between BPM-enable Social Collaboration and generic white-boarding, what occurs within this space should remain as part of the permanent audit trail of the process instance, including even a virtual representation of the space itself and all accessed information saved in the form of a case folder.

This latter ability is an example of how BPM enables Case Management, with regard to both the capture of process context and information, as well as the ability to invoke guidance at any given time in the process through the identification and engagement of outside experts. The ability to recall through the audit trail individuals proven helpful in similar circumstances (but not otherwise associated with a given process task) illustrates how trust and reputation can be leveraged in the completion of a business process managed within a BPMS environment. Ideally, individuals' past performance and/or ranking by past collaboration partners is captured by the platform and represented as part of the social network hierarchy.

Divining Business Process From Business Activity Streams

A founding principal of business process management is that business activities must occur within the process itself to be manageable. This thinking originates in the Taylorist meme that *you cannot improve what you cannot measure,* and by extension you cannot measure what occurs within the ad hoc, unstructured realm outside of the process model. Yet it is a fact that much, if not most, of business activity occurs in the white space outside the boundaries of a predefined process model.

Streams of discrete activities or events collectively represent the "Social Chatter" that define backdrop of every business. Yet the ability to capture, filter, analyze and ultimately leverage collections of such events and/or associated event data to inform decisions and otherwise generate actionable information within a business process is a notable value point of BPM. This capability is premised on the "Wall" concept that was first popularized by Facebook and is now arguably the most recognized (and in demand) aspects of social computing. The event stream allows users to subscribe to events, which may be either manual (individually authored) or automated (machine generated) event entries, as well as to filter these by various categories corresponding to event tags.

The event stream represents an efficient way to quickly communicate business data to business users, typically including the ability to deliver the same format to mobile devices. Leveraging social interaction within the BPM user interface extends the reach of BPM beyond the traditional worklist metaphor and desktop environments common to previous generations of business software, supporting real-time view into business activity.

Why does this matter? Because a fundamental value point of all BPM is the ability to accelerate response time to business events. Early modality process improvement focused on the low hanging fruit of automatable activities. Yet most events today occur outside of the realm of what can modeled in advance. The next wave of performance improvement will come from generating real-time analytics from business activity streams (both internal and external) and connecting these to the type of closed-loop environment offered by BPM. Although the exact metrics vary between specific events and individual organizations, in virtually every case the value realizable through response to event declines sharply as soon as the event occurs. The faster the response, the greater the realizable value. The total reaction time from the discovery of an event to the moment that that action is taken can grouped into three categories:

✓ **Data Latency** - *delays capturing event from operations*

✓ **Analysis Latency** - *delays translating events into analytics*

✓ **Decision Latency** - *delays acting on analytics*

Traditionally, the greatest loss of value occurs in the delay in capturing the event (such as recording the event in a transactional system.) Here significant value can be preserved by capturing the event in real-time, such as by using a Social Chatter capability as illustrated on the previous page. Reducing latency here offers the greatest historic benefit, however, value is also lost in the analysis and time elapsed before action is taken.

In the context of BPM with social capabilities, an event can be actionable almost as soon as it occurs. This again involves tagging the event at the source, so that context is preserved, and as a result the need for additional analysis is diminished. The event appears within a stream on your handheld device, and with it context linked to either an individual or another point of origin that allows you to quickly assess the best response. From that event you may launch a corresponding process, or leverage Social Collaboration to enlist the support of experts within your network.

Time-based Value of Business Event Response

Regardless of the specific circumstances involved, the value of the response is greater closest to the moment of the complaint, diminishes over time and after a certain period in time, any response is going to be of little value. There is not a single set of hard metrics for all organizations, or all events, but in every case, there is predictable value gained from the ability to capture an event. It could be related to a sales opportunity, or field maintenance, or terrorist threat, in every case the faster the response the greater the value.

It can be assumed that the ability to take action on a specific event will always involve some delay. Yet there is a similar inevitability that the value lost as a result of that delay will follow a utility curve, not a straight line. Thus, the greatest source of value will always come from faster notification and actionability, rather than faster decision-making.

The value of faster decisions (automating the function of knowledge workers in the decision-making process) offers little value, particularly when compared to the cost of poor decisions made in haste. Because of the greater the delay in notification and actionability, there is greater pressure on making decisions sooner rather than losing further value. Yet the opportunity lies in reducing Infrastructure Latency. By getting actionable information into the hands of knowledge workers sooner, iBPMS systems offer a predictable source of business value and clear differentiation from passive systems (i.e., notification only, without the ability to facilitate a response.)

Yet clearly not all events by themselves alone are actionable. By using event filtering and associating metrics based on the relative trust and reputation of event originators, collections of events can be grouped into meaningful patterns which may in aggregate represent an actionable outcome not otherwise visible through the examination of events individually.

WHY BPM IS CRITICAL TO HOW WE MANAGE CONTENT

Over the last decade most, small and medium, and certainly nearly all large enterprises have invested in some combination of Electronic Document Management (EDM), Web Content Management (WCM), and/or Enterprise Content Management (ECM). As these environments are increasingly converging, we will refer to them collectively as "ECM."

ECM offers a critical tool by helping organizations keep pace with the explosive growth of unstructured information; an ever-expanding volume of content that shows no signs of letting up. ECM has become a popular source for introducing workflow management to the organization. Typically this includes document routing and approval workflows, capturing the steps involved in creating a document, or automating a basic process such as a travel request or expense report.

What ECM provides is governance and integrity of content and data. Outside of controlling access and authorization (i.e., who gets to see what), what ECM doesn't provide is *governance of work* – managing how that content and data is used in the course of business. For this reason, if you've got ECM, then inevitably what you also have is a workflow management capability, but to optimally improve and automate how you manage content and your business processes, what you need is BPM.

BPM provides the means for connecting the content from within ECM and other System of Records (SORs) to an underlying process where that content is both used and created. In this way, BPM provides a transactional thread for managing this information across processes that inevitably span different applications, and often organizational boundaries. It allows for control of not necessarily the content and information, but rather how it is used in business operations.

For example, in common business processes such as "order to cash" and "procure to pay" there is a combination of (SORs) involved. Data and information (i.e., both structured and unstructured content) define the order in terms of financial details and customer, as well as other information likely stored within an ECM repository and other SORs. Yet none of these systems alone has the complete picture, end-to-end across the process lifecycle. In contrast, what BPM provides is a consistent transactional "thread" enabling end-to-end management and visibility out of reach by any of the underlying systems.

BPM in essence is the practice of managing business operations in terms of processes, which span application, departmental, and even organizational boundaries, and which are specifically managed within a "BPMS" or "Business Process Management System". During earlier days of business computing and enterprise IT, it was recognized that the practice of managing data within the applications where it was used presented significant business risk. In particular, breaks in the continuity of data between applications, and the potential for corruption or lack of concurrency. For this reason is it was determined early in the history of IT that data should be managed separate from applications, as part of a common Database Management System or DBMS.

This notion has been fundamental to IT architecture for the last 40 years. Yet just as the notion of abstracting data from applications has defined traditional IT, modern Enterprise Information Management (EIM) understands the need to abstract processes and business logic in the same way with a BPMS layer.

BPM systems offer an ideal platform for process automation, in particular with regard to repetitive processes involved with well-defined structured data, creating *efficiency* through automation and *effectiveness* through consistent performance. These types of processes are generally characterized as rarely changing, with their integration points well-established, and often associated with existing transactional systems.

Combining BPM with existing application-specific workflow automation allows the combination of organized process structures with backend interfaces, creating a system of record for both business data entities and the content involved. From an information management point of view, the resulting fully auditable log includes the complete context and history of the evolving data flow. It is this same consolidation of elements – content, policies/rules, and information access – that distinguishes BPM from other information software systems and allows the representation of the entire process lifecycle.

In this way, BPM provides the core platform through which various information sources and repositories can be integrated. As communications have become increasing digital (or digitized) and as interaction with customers are now more often taking place within an electronic media, ensuring consistency of communication across multiple application environments and back repositories (e.g. ERP, CRM, ECM, WCM, etc.) is critical.

Again, it is not only likely you have ECM already but chances are there are multiple domain-specific SORs in place for specific business areas, such as *Procurement, HR, regulatory filings*, or discrete business areas. In addition, it is likely there are departmental and even potentially redundant ECM repositories. Across all of these, BPM offers a consistent transactional thread for teams to collaborate transparently and securely through the organization of structured and unstructured business data and content – following the process lifecycle rather than sticking within the confines of application silos. This also means having a consistent user experience, following the same transactional thread and end-to-end process with a common user interface.

BPM AND CASE MANAGEMENT

The ability to deliver a common user interface and user experience across multiple applications is a critical advantage of BPM over ECM and workflow. Further, the end-to-end process lifecycle is both information-intensive and inherently data-driven. It inevitably involves the capture of information that leads to actions being taken and decisions made that can be fully anticipated in advance.

It requires a balance between that which can and should be predefined and automated. This approach is a reflection of the increasing complexity and unpredictability of knowledge work, which is what we increasingly referred to as "Case Management." Although there is sometimes confusion of the use of this term, case management as a general notion and application type has been around for decades, however, in this case we are referring to the modern manifestation, typical called "Adaptive" or "Dynamic Case Management", which today represents an essential capability of modern BPM platforms.

Where workflow automation and even the first generation of BPM systems follow specifically a pre-defined process route, a predefined path for each item – modern BPM supports the combination of workflow automation with facilitation of ad hoc or collaborative knowledge work (e.g., not predefined or structured) that has been out of reach to work management software.

In this way BPM and Case Management enable great transparency into collaborative processes, as well as more effective prioritization of tasks when managing activities across multiple cases and workloads. BPM facilitates this by presenting a more unified interface across application silos, offering a single-access-point to information trapped within legacy systems, but needed by knowledge workers, or even customers, with modern "anywhere, any device" expectations.

The key to successful automation is to provide a balance between relieving the burden of repetitive drudgery and "busy work" (e.g., to reduce this through automation) without being overly restrictive over the aspects of work that should otherwise allow for user control and input. BPM offers the combination of offloading repetitive and predictable tasks to automation, while allowing knowledge workers to make smart choices and apply best practices in their decision-making that is the essence of the value being created.

BPM offers an opportunity for evolution and modernization in order to keep pace with rapid advances in mobile, social and cloud computing; an opportunity to build bridges between the current islands of automation by utilizing the case focus to combine isolated processes. It presents a realistic and practical "future-proofing" for enterprise IT. Below is a summary table which highlights some of the core differences between ECM and Workflow and BPM and Case Management, in particular with regard to how information is shared and capabilities are delivered.

	ECM and Workflow	BPM and Case Management
Scope	Single application, document or form; data and object model specific to application or document, not shared.	Common UI and transactional thread spanning multiple applications and process lifecycle; data structures based on process definition (process instance data) and separate from "payload" or applications where work is performed.

Security	Application-specific security, or authorization based on document-specific or form-specific processes.	Security bound to roles defined by process swim lanes and the activities they contain; role-based security applied to case folder, content, as well as fine-grain control of work items.
Analytics	Work item specific reporting, limited to a single document, repository, or application.	Advanced analytics enable identification and reuse of patterns and exceptions, operational visibility.
Data Integration	Typically data is based on form fields (specific fields within and electronic form) or otherwise application-specific data fields. Data is typically entered or viewed via these forms and not accessible as a shared service or system-to-system resource.	Connectors are provided to integrate external data into the virtual case folder and case record; Data can be manipulated (extracted and transformed or "CRUD" operations) if data structures are defined in the process or as part of external services.

GETTING STARTED

The starting point for any BPM initiative is typically the most critical event in determining the project's success. It can also be one of the most challenging and frustrating periods as teams grapple with issues such as which process to target, what politics are involved, and often simply how and where to get started in the first place. Certainly no one plans to fail. Yet with any type of project, IT-oriented or otherwise, success is by no means a certainty, and in fact for BPM in particular, it occurs less than half the time. Last year BPM.com released market research which showed that BPM-related initiatives succeeded less than 50% of the time, which is consistent with other analysts' cited failure rates.

To be clear, this should in no way detract from the potential value of BPM, nor is this failure rate necessarily higher than other business and technology areas. This is particularly true with the introduction of technologies with similarly far-reaching impact on business operations, as seen with BPM. In all such cases, providing a specific plan for success in the form of a Project Charter and mutually understood success criteria is essential. For BPM specifically, however, the BPM.com research offers further guidance for getting it right when getting started, by avoiding the common pitfalls most commonly associated with failed projects. Listed in order of frequency of mention, these are:

1. Failure to Define Realistic Boundaries
2. Resistance by End Users and Stakeholders
3. Lost Executive Sponsorship

Sponsorship can be lost through attrition or a significant change of assignment. Yet the fact is that executives have short attention spans, and if they're not seeing the results they were looking for they will move on to something or someone else.

Traditionally the most common issue dooming any new initiative is cultural resistance; stakeholders and end users don't want to participate or feel they were left out of the process and they rebel. You built it, but they didn't come. One of the critical factors for this is ensuring they are engaged from the outset. Yet the most common pitfall is found in failure to define realistic expectations and boundaries at the outset. Scope creep dooms any project. With BPM typically this is an overshoot for processes where the processes and associated rules are too far-reaching, too complex and it becomes politically intractable to reach agreement on how the process(es) should be defined and performed.

When getting started with any new BPM initiative, avoiding these common pitfalls is not simply a matter of luck, but should be a deliberate strategy – there should be a well-defined and explicit plan for success. This success place should be part of a charter established at the outset. Whether a formal "Project Charter" or simply written memo setting expectations with stakeholders and the project sponsor, the charter will set the direction and tone for the project, and should be documented in clear and specific terms, identifying how and why the project will succeed, as well as how and when success will be measured. In order to offer the best chances for success, there are **seven best practices** that should be followed when getting started with BPM.

Practice #1: Select the Right Starting Point

Selecting the right starting point is critical to project's success. Yet this less about the process itself, but rather about the momentum created by demonstrating early proof-points and benefits. As a starting point, **avoid** processes that are *already well-defined*, are *overly complex*, or are *politically-charged*.

Instead, seek out identify opportunities and processes that are characterized as *paper-intensive*, involving tasks done on a *frequent basis* (daily), lacking a rigid or controversial definition, and that offer an *immediate* and *measurably positive impact* on stakeholders and end users.

Once you have the momentum, proof-points, and the wisdom of experience from initial success, then go back and tackle the more difficult process improvement opportunities. Your starting point is the solid platform on which everything that follows will rest; it needs to make perfect sense in terms of your project aims and goals, offer a basis for the value you're looking for and (naturally) you need enough of the right resources to make it work. And as you're unlikely to be doing this solo, don't forget stakeholder engagement; the process you choose has to be compelling – if it doesn't grab the interest, it won't garner the support.

Filter your options by asking yourself a few 'reality' questions: Is this process something that is so politically impractical that you couldn't touch it? Is it something that you're going to be able to use again? Is it visible and likely to make stakeholder's lives better? Lastly, will successful transformation make heroes of those engaged in the process throughout the organization? Don't underestimate the importance of the last point. The ideal starting point will generate excitement and momentum because stakeholders will understand what's in it for them, and will work with your project team to help ensure your success. This is also why it is important to engage them in the prioritization process, as outlined below.

Rank Process Targets with Stakeholders

Work with stakeholders in a white-boarding session (or some other visual means) to identify and prioritize processes, ranking them in terms of both the impact and value they offer if addressed effectively, as well as the relative complexity involved in doing so. You're striving for a target area that is likely to generate excitement and demonstrable value, yet is not so complex that it will otherwise set you up for failure.

Consider the difficulty of each process option – but not in terms of the effort involved in performing the process, but rather how resistant people will be to changing it. Asking that will reveal aspects of how change will be implemented. Can you define the vision for how it will be different? Are there mutually agreeable metrics for improvement, such as cycle time reduction, quality improvement, greater capacity or lower resulting costs?

Ultimately the goal is to strike a balance between demonstrability and achievability. It must be clearly visible and offer real value, yet do so within a time frame short enough to keep stakeholders engaged and on board.

Practice #2: Set Process Boundaries to Control Scope

Keeping in mind that the most commonly cited pitfall was the failure to set realistic boundaries, defining the end-points of the process is critical from the outset. This is important both for the likelihood of success, as well as for the ability to demonstrate that success. It is also possible that the original target process is later determined to be excessively complex. In this case, look for ways to separate out an addressable proportion of the larger process, work with that to demonstrate proof-points for the benefits of BPM, and then use that as a leverage point to go after the other process equivalent.

Practice #3: Starting With Words Before Pictures

One of the common misperceptions of Case Management is that there is no upfront modeling involved. This is far from the truth; you will need to engage in a considerable amount of modeling of business rules, data models, and screenflows.

There will also be modeled workflows, including both automated processes for structured, repetitive tasks, and conceptual process models that may not be explicitly scripted within the system but are nonetheless an important part of the requirements definition. Of course the same is true for BPM, where most of the system's capabilities will be defined within process models.

Yet when you're trying to find the real starting point, you can't begin by drawing diagrams with boxes and lines. The starting point to the starting point is a written understanding of the target process; a written narrative. When writing your narrative, you need to answer (among others) the following questions: What are the outcomes that this process provides? What are the data and the resources that are dry in these processes? What are the specific activities? What are the roles of those who will be involved? A written narrative keeps things clear as you move forward and add the details and additional information during the decision-making process.

Identifying Goals, Outcomes, Resources, and Participants

In order to narrow down the options, it's time to break things down and draw up a list of what capabilities will be enabled by the solution as a business function. First, begin by specifying the "what" in terms of the expected outcomes and the required capabilities to achieve them. Second, establish the "why" and "how" of the system from the perspective of stakeholders and system interactions. Ask yourself the following key questions: Who's performing it? What data did they create? What data did they need and what are they actually doing with it? What are the actions—the transformations, verbs, actual performers? Differentiating the "who's" and the "what's" of specific roles and specific individuals is a vital part of choosing the right process.

Practice #4: Asking the Right Questions

The sequence of the questions that you ask is as important as the questions themselves. "What?" questions give you the facts, the realities; answer those first and then it's safe to move on to the "Why?" questions that can otherwise distract you with their baggage, drawing you towards political factors. "Why?" questions must be answered but not until you've gone into the measurable and quantifiable triggers and dependencies that the "What?" questions can give you first.

Start With What's and Who's

In the narrative, we identify the elements needed to create your own model. A crucial step is to identify the various "who's," their roles and the role details, then define and expand on those details. Once the first layer is clear, follow the trail to the next "who," their role, and so on. There is always a path of triggers, clues, and rules to be followed and it's that path that will tell you what questions to ask and in what order.

Then Ask the Why's, When's, and White Space

After the "who's" and the "what's" have been detailed, it's time to move on to the "why's," "when's," and white space. Filling in these fine detail gaps is an integral element to understanding the ins and outs of what is occurring within the process.

Practice #5: Leverage User-Centered Design

Technology is seductive and a common mistake (despite its apparent obviousness) made with BPM initiatives is to focus on the technology and its functionality as opposed to how it is used. Yet the focus on the "how" is critical to understanding the user's perspective. For the user, it's not about what the system does, it's all about how to use it and – more importantly – why they should. Creating personas which represent not just use cases but specifically a "day in the life of" perspective of actual users, will result in a solution which faces far less user and cultural resistance, leading to fewer change management and training requirements and ultimately, significantly improved user adoption rates and productivity.

Identification precedes engagement; first of all, identify the users and stakeholders for your BPM or Case Management project. There are four broad categories in any BPM project: builders, managers, participants, and customers (and in each of those groups there may exist subgroups). Of key importance is that you use this identification or mapping stage to create a unique user experience tailored to the needs of each group. The secret to keeping each group fully engaged is to present them with a 'noise-free' user experience which offers minimal distractions from their own concerns.

Practice #6: Early Involvement Reduces Overall Risk

One of the most promising approaches for introducing BPM is by leveraging the methods associated with Agile development. Agile emphasizes delivering demonstrable results quickly and in tight, measureable increments that engage business stakeholders.

The emphasis on early and on-going validation allows much greater alignment with the business than is afforded with alternative approaches. In particular, on critical matters such as prioritizing the order that capabilities are delivered, as well as the validation of assumptions made during discovery. Early involvement in the project also helps to increase user adoption, because involvement creates a sense of familiarity and shared ownership (and therefore responsibility for success).

Another hallmark of Agile methods is the notion of continuous testing, and combined with stakeholder engagement, the result is to effectively conduct usability testing at each stage, allowing usability issues to be identified much earlier and be more easily resolved. This results in more successful outcomes, as well as more cost-effective effort – not because there is less work per se, but rather less re-work because the consistent validation ensures development is closely aligned with the business stakeholder's goals and expectation. Whether your organization or project team formally embraces Agile, engage stakeholders early and often.

Conduct a Regular Stakeholder Workshops

While the notion of a "focus group" might sound clichéd, there is still no more efficient way to obtain agreement on the goals and success criteria than face-to-face discussion. Workshops should be held at regular intervals, and specifically from the outset of the initiative, to identify expectations, as well as validate findings during discovery and analysis.

Then, at the focus group, ask the stakeholders to describe to you the high level process; this will enable you to begin to map out the process. The focus group environment also can be used to explore the mission of the group that owns the process, who their customers are, what the inputs and outputs are, and – most importantly – you can begin to identify their goals and prioritize them.

Practice #7: Measure from the Start

As the old adage says: "You can't improve what you can't measure" so what better time to start measuring than the beginning? However, in order to begin to measure, you need clarity on the project specifications and the expected improvements. Put another way, you need to know how success is defined for your project. And there's the link back to Practice #2, your identified stakeholders, users and sponsors are there to help identify and (importantly) agree to the measures.

By keeping measurement in mind from the start, you ensure that you don't begin your process improvement project with a missing target. Of course, it is equally important that your chosen yardstick correlates with the objectives of the project – the business goals that prompted it in the first place.

Defining Performance Metrics and Success Criteria

The defining feature of a good metric is its objective and consistent measurability coupled with an easy comprehension by even the least technically-minded stakeholder – improvements should not only be made but be visibly made. It should be simple, elegant and effective. In fact, the more obvious the metric is, the more it effectively becomes the business case. If, by the nature of the measurement, the improvement to stakeholders' and users' lives is self-evident, no more persuasion will be needed.

Linking back to Practice #3, a key enabler in setting metrics and measurements is getting the narrative right. Part of the narrative exercise is developing a common vocabulary for all those involved in the project - a 'controlled vocabulary' or common lexicon. A single shared language is critical to project success and can give you a lateral route to consensus between different stakeholder factions. Focusing too heavily on achieving consensus on how things work can stymie the discovery process. Yet a common vocabulary lays the groundwork for agreement via the more neutral element of terminology. Along the way, as part of the discussions, you'll also be establishing agreement on the parameters of the process, the metrics, measurement techniques, and ultimately, the whole project.

Identify and Quantify Your Goals

Goal definition drives the design activity. The first step in quantifying and analyzing project goals is to list the possible improvements that can be made. What are the goals, what was the priority that the team assigned to them, and what's the current situation? Then, when you start to map out the new process, factor in the technologies available to you as well as what you can bring to bear to clean up the end user experience. Now you're starting to list your potential proposed solutions. Do so in detail and try to establish a clear picture of the impact of each possibility. To continuously improve and simplify the process, be prepared to revisit your goals and flesh-out work that doesn't not added any measurable value. An often underutilized but highly effective tool, simulation can be used as a means to sell improvements.

Simulation can be an effective sales technique for convincing stakeholders of project benefits; making them visible, demonstrable and showing how the process would be improved. It is equally powerful in the discovery phase of the project; highlighting how the process will perform under different workloads, doing well-depth analysis with processes and establishing improvement targets that may have, otherwise, been overlooked. Simulation is objective and moves the spotlight away from any particular user group or set of stakeholder requirements and effectively de-politicizes the project by focusing on design rather than individual bottleneck stages. By avoiding putting the focus on any one group of stakeholders, end users, subject-matter experts and so on, you encourage true collaboration because no one group has more to lose than the rest.

Planning is ultimately the most critical success factor. As we said earlier, no one plans to fail but it is fair to note that many fail to plan well enough to succeed and the three main factors that trip them up are: failure to define the project; end user and stakeholder resistance; and a lack of executive sponsorship. You will inevitably have a project plan, yet beyond the standard Gantt chart and work breakout structure should be a specific plan for success.

This includes having the stated (written) metrics for how and when success will be measured, agreed to and acknowledged by stakeholders and the project sponsor. As part of this plan, you should be prepared to demonstrate value within the first 90 days. Anything beyond this timeframe will be at risk of losing critical momentum, potentially even sponsorship. Your plan should involve the seven practices to counteract the common pitfalls of failing to define realistic boundaries, facing resistance by end users or stakeholders, and the loss of executive sponsorship.

THE 90-DAY ACTION PLAN FOR GETTING STARTED WITH BPM

In the first 30 days, you will identify the starting point, the scope and boundaries, validate these collaboratively with stakeholders, and define the core goals, outcomes, resources, and participants. The critical outcome of this phase is establishing scope and boundaries. You may adjust the definition of some capabilities or expectations as you proceed, and may de-scope to some degree (e.g., postpone capabilities for a subsequent development cycle) but under no circumstances should you be expanding scope beyond this phase.

Depending on the scope and goals of your initiative you may "go live" and deploy to production in 90 days, or you may be providing just the first major proof-point of a series of releases. The benefit of both BPM is that it is not a "once and done" proposition but an iterative process for rolling out a series of capabilities. Yet ensuring success for projects small or large requires identifying and sticking to what can be predictably achieved in the first 90 days.

In the next 30 days, you will engage in more discovery to develop a complete narrative, expanding this through more stakeholder workshops to develop the "look and feel" of the solution, working from the users' perspective consistent with user-centered design. During this phase you have the benefit of requirements and scope being fixed, and you now focus on realizing these within the solution. In the final 30 days, you will have the benefit of already having clearly defined expectations for what will be delivered, and focus is now on demonstrating the achievement of the defined goals and visible metrics. You will have defined when the demonstration of capability will take place and how success will be measured.

Find the right process and always, always ask yourself the right honest questions. Keep your users and stakeholders at the center of the project and have involvement as your watchword; encourage them to own their input and their influence and watch the project succeed as they buy in. Measurement is key and the right metrics are worth their weight in project gold because they will convince (and keep on board) even the most troublesome stakeholders and sponsors. Knowing what success will look like before you even begin will help you achieve it.

COMMON BPM PITFALLS TO AVOID

× ***Missing the Opportunity of Repeatability:*** *although much if not all of the business case is calculated based on a single iteration or otherwise a discrete focus of the BPM initiative, the real value comes from developing a repeatable practice area or Center of Excellence; the first phase of the project should be proof-point for future opportunities.*

× ***Following the Path of Least Resistance:*** *it is telling if a project lacks sponsors and more than likely it means more time needs to be spent on the business case. Sponsors who do not otherwise scrutinize an incomplete business case are merely setting the project up for failure.*

× ***Ignoring or Otherwise Neglecting Stakeholders When Validating Process Designs:*** *one of the best and traditionally underutilized resources for validating the process are the stakeholders themselves, not just business process owners but end users.*

× ***Letting "Great" be the Enemy of "Good Enough" in the First Pass:*** *do not fall into the trap of "analysis paralysis" in the first pass of the 'current state' process definition; get something 'good enough' out in front of the stakeholders who can tell you how it really works.*

× ***Selecting Cheap or Free BPM Technology Over the Ability to Leverage Existing Skill Sets:*** *sometimes "free" BPM is the most expensive option; look for alignment with resources and objectives over price.*

× ***Assuming Sponsorship is There When it's Not:*** *too often wishful thinking takes over and project teams assume sponsorship is committed when it is not; do whatever is necessary to eliminate ambiguity surrounding budgets and ownership.*

GAINING AND MAINTAINING PROJECT SPONSORSHIP

After nearly a decade of market research on what drives BPM implementations, the answer for what *prevents* them is consistently "lack of sponsorship" by upper management. In other words, the single largest hurdle to BPM implementation is cited as finding someone (an executive or a department) to pay for it. Often departmental teams find the opportunity but not the resources to implement a BPM project, and are unable to win management support despite what may be to them an obvious need or potential benefit.

There is no doubt that budget plays a role in whether or not sponsorship is found. Yet another factor is the perception of career endangerment. For many, any new project (particularly those which touch IT infrastructure) is seen at best as a distraction for core business, and worse as a potential career-killer. Who wants to take on another ERP project (and all the inherent risk it carries with it)? Too often, timidity and a lack of available attention span exceeds the spirit of innovation otherwise needed by senior management to spearhead BPM initiatives.

Gaining sponsorship is about building and presenting a credible business case. If sponsorship is lacking, it is almost always so because a cogent business case has not been developed. A lack of sponsorship, even in the face of such compelling benefits as described above, can be a blessing for a prospective project, as it requires its promoters to more carefully scrutinize the business case and in doing so remove much of the potential risk and uncertainty.

In contrast, one of the worst ways to begin a project is by going with any sponsor willing to fund it, but not otherwise demanding a carefully scrutinized business case. Too often, the need for sponsorship and funding forces project leaders to compromise preferred approaches and target areas, leading the BPM initiative to be setup for failure.

The right way to win sponsorship is by using short-term project wins to show proof-points and build credibility, and then to leverage this into large projects areas (i.e., leverage the **incremental** and **measurable** qualities of BPM to achieve **repeatable** success).

DEVELOPING THE BUSINESS CASE

BPM initiatives succeed or fail based on the business case. It is both the means for gaining and maintaining management support (e.g., sponsorship), and the first major test of the project's success. While it is always possible that a project may not succeed regardless, it is nearly impossible to realize success without the exercise of developing a business case. Even with project sponsorship in place, at some point it will be necessary to present the forecasted benefit anticipated through your proposed BPM deployment. This requires an understanding of the business benefits and how they will be derived. What will you present? The answer is the business case.

Developing a Return on Investment Model for BPM

The Return on Investment (ROI) model quantifies all the benefits captured in Steps 1-4, correlates them with anticipated costs, and identifies the savings potential. The goal of the ROI model is to provide quantified assessment of the anticipated value-added through the BPM deployment, specifically to estimate both the cost and net benefit expected. A secondary goal is to frame expectations for the planning and design of the BPM deployment initiative, in particular as it relates to procurement of BPM software.

ROI in basic terms is *Profit* divided by *Investment*. For the purpose of the business case, it is the total value anticipated to be returned from the BPM initiative minus the anticipated investment required (i.e., "net return") divided by the investment. For some firms *Return on Equity (ROE)* is of greater interest, as this captures the value realized from existing assets. For the purpose of the BPM business case, however, a new investment will be required and thus ROI is the more appropriate metric.

A positive ROI (i.e., when net value exceeds the cost of the investment) is any percent calculated as greater than zero (0%). Because returns and investments are made over a period of time rather than a single year (typically the business case is based on a 3- to 5-year horizon) the calculation of ROI needs to be made in terms of *Net Present Value (NPV)* or a discounted cash flow stream – although it is worth noting that actual cash flow is likely only a fraction of the value measured and you should expect the majority of the business case to be presented in terms of non-cash benefits.

Calculating NPV requires an understanding or estimation of the firm's *cost of capital*. The cost of capital is literally the cost of debt or equity required for obtaining funds and it is generally used as the minimum rate of return a firm requires for any single investment. In general, it is the rate of return that is of most interest, since the BPM initiative alone is not likely to directly involve borrowing to pay for it. Organizations use the rate of the return as the hurdle rate for determining the lowest level of acceptable ROI.

For some firms the *Weighted Average Cost of Capital (WACC)* or the average of debt and equity cost is a known and valuable factor and can be used as the driving factor. For firms where this information is unavailable, however, a conservative cost of capital can be estimated (3% is used in the examples which follow). When building an ROI model, typically two scenarios are modeled – the first is labeled as "conservative" and includes minimal projections and easily verifiable data, and the second is labeled "aggressive" and outlines the potential for greater return factoring a wider range of potential benefits and incorporates more optimistic return forecasts. In both scenarios the cost basis is the same. The difference between the two is meant to illustrate the spread of reasonable expectations.

As it would be impractical during the business case stage – that is pre-solution deployment – to analyze all possible BPM benefits, only a discrete number of project areas are factored into the analysis. These should be used to illustrate how BPM benefits can be derived, and should not be presented as the limit of potential value. It should be explained that the potential benefits of the BPM deployment can also be applicable to other project areas, as well as other benefits can be expected not otherwise identified or enumerated.

When identifying quantifiable benefits, an important caveat is to avoid the temptation of simply aggregating lots of tiny time-savings, such as 10 minutes of every employee's schedule every day. These sorts of micro productivity improvements are expected to be absorbed and of no real measurable benefit. What would you do with an extra 10 minutes a day? Probably not much compared to savings hours at a time. Instead, base ROI calculations where time-savings impact real transaction overhead, such as verifiable labor savings or reduced workload with actual redeployment of resources.

Overall, benefits should be grouped into distinct categories, such as:

- **Hard-Dollar Benefits**: fewer dollars actually being spent, therefore allowing identified monies to be allocated elsewhere; direct and measurable cash flow reductions.

- **Soft Benefits**: bottom line improvement where the impact may be challenging to quantify in dollars or to pinpoint in specific operations; improved revenue from existing operations and increased efficiency of information management functions.

- **Strategic or Operational Benefits**: which are enhanced or enabled by the BPM deployment; these are kept out of the ROI calculation but are part of the business case.

THE REAL COST OF IMPLEMENTING BPM

When presenting a business case to management, the first question is invariably "How much will this cost?" This is understandably a difficult question to answer during the early stages of a project – especially in the case of a first BPM initiative where a software solution has not yet been selected and there is no experience benchmark for estimating consulting services costs. However, in order to develop a business case, you must establish some estimate of cost. The fact that this will indeed be an estimate further supports the need for a structured yet fluid model, as cost is one of the key variables that will have to be continually refined during the discovery and due diligence process. Often, the greatest cost of BPM is not in the software license and maintenance fees but in the business resources or consulting services required.

The key to avoiding this is to establish strong communications between business users and IT staff early in the project. Process design environments offer a tool to facilitate this collaboration and they play a significant role in the success of BPM. A good graphical process design tool makes processes easier to understand and simplifies their definition, shortening the time taken to define a process while at the same time reducing the risk of misunderstandings and expensive re-work later on in the project.

Business Process Management is not new – it is an established, proven discipline that combines a focus on process with an integrated set of specialized software tools to deliver real business results. Organizations around the world and across industries have proven the value that BPM can deliver – greater efficiency, increased visibility, better control, enhanced operational agility, and measurable ROI in the range of 10-300%.

You too can realize this success, but to do so requires focus. That focus starts with learning how to implement a repeatable framework for evaluating processes, defining distinct BPM projects, and building a business case to justify the investment of time, resources, and money.

Developing the business case for the first BPM initiative will be the most time-consuming and the most important because it will include the evaluation, selection, and justification of a BPM software suite to support the implementation. It will also serve as the first proof-point for BPM in your organization. To ensure success, follow the steps outlined in this white paper and keep the tips and pitfalls in mind – the result will be a strong business case and a set of valuable metrics to monitor and measure results during the implementation.

From that point on, you will have a repeatable approach, a solid technology foundation on which to build, and a set of benefits and benchmark ROI numbers to make justifying future BPM initiatives a breeze – putting you the fast path to realizing continuous process improvement and strategic business value from BPM.

CALCULATING BPM ROI: ENGINEERING SERVICES FIRM CASE STUDY

To illustrate the type of details and calculations that should be include in the ROI model of the business case, we use an ROI assessment performed at an engineering services firm. The first example is that of a *Soft Benefit* calculation, where an identifiable qualitative benefit is developed into a quantitative cost savings. In this case, pipeline assessments are part of a fixed-price operations and management agreement, and thus represent a cost center. Because these involve a number of handoffs and data-checking activities, each cycle introduces redundant "rework" by expensive engineering resources.

The ability to automate Steps and maintain greater continuity between handoffs represents a measurable cost-savings enable by the introduction of BPM. This opportunity was identified during Steps 2 to 4 as described earlier -- based on interviews of personnel it was identified that these handoffs represented a source of process inefficiency, on average costing around 6 out of 40 hours spent on pipeline evaluations. The details for each of these areas of savings are detailed in the table below.

Areas of Calculated and Anticipated Savings

Pipeline Evaluations	Year 1	Year 2	Year 3
Number of Evaluations Per Year Per Team	6	6	6
Man-Hours Per Job	40	40	40
Rework Per Job	15%	15%	15%
Rework MH per Job	6	6	6
Total Annual Rework Reduction	36	36	36
Licensing Man-Hour Cost	$80	$80	$80
Cost Savings/Team	$2,880	$2,880	$2,880
Number of Team	8	20	50
Cost-savings Per Year	**$23,040**	**$57,600**	**$144,000**

Other areas to examine where benefits can be measured are improvements on the existing metrics such as increasing *inventory turnover* by reducing order processing time and accelerating the order-to-cash cycle. Although, as described before, this may be ambitious for first BPM initiative, this is an area where there are many handoffs involved in the process from the time an order is received to when the product is delivered.

The ability to improve inventory turnover has a direct and measurable impact on financial performance. Other performance metrics involved in order-to-cash include the *order fulfillment rate* or orders delivered to customers in full quantity at the specified time, and the *cash collection rate* or percent of cash collected within standard or otherwise contractual terms.

Based on these assumptions as well the validation of specific metrics such as labor costs and job frequency, a realistic costs savings estimate can be developed. This is not meant as an exercise in re-engineering, and inevitably while improvements will be realized, more analysis and optimization will be required before, during, and after the implementation.

Rather, this is part of the modeling exercise where metrics are defined for the business case and for measuring the success of the project as it evolves. In the business case, each calculated figure such as this should be broken out individually and explained in terms of assumptions and data sources. The same should be done for the cost side, as well as a single table should be developed so it can be view comprehensively at once.

Although BPM does not impose anywhere near the ten-to-one services-to-software ratios imposed by other technologies, it is possible that you could spend $1.20 to $2.00 in services resources for every $1.00 spent on software. This is determined largely by your ability to leverage existing skill sets versus outsourcing to external parties or attempting to hire new skill sets in house.

This is shaped largely by the ability to leverage existing skill sets, and BPM team made of programmers or analysts. Introducing a new discipline (BPM) new development model (Java, etc.) can doom both to failure, and it is a lot easier to teach or hire programming skills than business acumen. Look for solutions which leverage existing skill sets, and hire-out programmers before business experts. A model for the *Total Projected Project Costs* is presented in the table below.

Total Projected Project Costs Example

Projected Cost Summary	Year 1	Year 2	Year 3
BPM Administration	$75,000	$75,000	$75,000
BPM Development & Customization	$120,000	$120,000	$80,000
Training	$50,000		
External Professional Services			
BPM Process Consulting	$250,000	$134,800	$50,000
Application Development	$308,800	$150,000	$40,700
Integration Services		$152,400	$30,000
BPM Software			
Software License			
Phase 1 (server license)	$300,000		
Phase 2 (additional user licenses)		$75,000	
Design Tools and Developer SDK	$100,000		
Software Maintenance	$32,000	$38,000	$38,000
Hardware/Equipment			
Production Servers and Design Stations	$16,000	$26,000	
Total Projected Annual Costs	**$1,251,800**	**$771,200**	**$313,700**

One of the biggest caveats of BPM cost estimates is that "free" BPM technology can easily be the most expensive option. BPM technology that comes free with other infrastructure can introduce a great deal of operational risk to the project, starting with miscommunication between business and IT.

Another one of the (if not *the*) greatest potential points of failure is found in the transitions between business logic and application logic. Design-time environments play a significant role in the success of BPM, as difficult to understand process models lead to misunderstandings, erroneous assumptions and expensive re-work.

ROI CALCULATION

When presenting the ROI model in the business case, each cost and benefit should be broken out so that the numbers are transparent and believable, then each number should be rolled up into a single table showing the comprehensive costs and benefits. ROI is calculated as 131% here, meaning that $1.31 is returned on top of the original investment for every dollar spent, or other $2.31 comes back for every $1.00 going out (keeping mind this is not cash-flow specific but value-added through both reduced transaction costs and revenue increases).

One of the biggest sources of value in the model is *Reduction of Current Project Transaction Costs,* representing the BPM deployment's impact on the productivity involved with performing existing project work. They are productivity-based, relating to how the BPM deployment can be leveraged to perform more work with the same resources or perform the same volume of work with greater efficiency.

As such they are presented as *Soft Benefits* rather than *Hard-Dollar* savings or direct cash flow reductions. In each case specific dollar values are identified based on existing processes and validated costs and/or revenue amounts.

In contrast, the *Automation of Engineering Change Orders* led to a significant redeployment of staff, resulting in measurable Hard-Dollar savings by redeploying staff and reducing a considerable amount of outside travel.

ROI Calculation Example: Aggressive Scenario

	Year 1	Year 2	Year 3
Hard-Dollar Benefits			
Reduced Print & Distribution Costs	$21,600	$33,200	$49,500
Automation of Change Orders	$240,000	$336,000	$470,400
Elimination of Engineering Re-Work	$51,840	$72,576	$101,606
Soft Benefits			
Pipeline Evaluation Labor Savings	$23,040	$57,600	$144,000
Identified Productivity Gains	$330,000	$396,000	$475,200
Reduction of Current Project Transaction	$410,118	$706,738	$1,056,100
Revenue Improvement via Collaboration	$82,000	$127,000	$324,000
Annual Totals of BPM-Provided Benefits	**$1,158,598**	**$1,729,114**	**$2,620,806**
Total Projected Annual Costs	**$1,251,800**	**$771,200**	**$313,700**
Annual Payback	**($93,202)**	**$957,914**	**$2,307,106**

Net Present Value of 3 Year Investment Dol-	$2,296,481
3 Year Project Net Present Value	$3,013,327
3 Year Project ROI	**131%**
Year in Which Breakeven Occurs	**Year 2**

- ROI is calculated as 3 Year Project NPV / 3 Year Investment NPV
- Net Present Value (NPV) was calculated using a constant cost of capital of 3% and discounting each year's net benefit after Year 1. The discount factor is calculated as $(1 + \text{the cost of capital})^{Year-1}$

Thus, Year 2's net benefit is discounted by 3% or $(1.0+0.03)^1$ and Year 3's is discounted by 6% or $(1.0+0.03)^2$

The difference with the *Conservative Scenario* ROI model (see next page) is largely found in the *Reduction of Current Project Transaction Costs,* which is a Soft Benefit based largely on assumptions. Nothing changes in the Hard-Dollar Benefits or the Cost side of the equation, as both of these are developed from verified numbers. In this Conservative Scenario the initiative pays for itself in Year 3 and over the period three years it returns $1.39 in value for every $1.00 invested. This initiative is indeed "profitable" and earns more than 10% annually compared to an alternative investment, so even as a Conservative Scenario it should make a compelling business case.

ROI Calculation Example: Conservative Scenario

	Year 1		Year 2	Year 3
Hard-Dollar Benefits				
Reduced Print & Distribution Costs	$21,600	$33,200		$49,500
Automation of Change Orders	$240,000	$336,000		$470,400
Elimination of Engineering Re-Work	$51,840	$72,576		$101,606
Soft Benefits				
Pipeline Evaluation Labor Savings	$23,040	$57,600		$144,000
Identified Productivity Gains	$110,000	$132,000		$158,400
Reduction of Current Project Transaction	$210,118	$252,142		$302,570
Revenue Improvement via Collaboration	$82,000	$127,000		$324,000
Annual Totals of BPM-Provided Benefits	$738,598		$1,010,518	$1,550,476
Total Projected Annual Costs	**$1,251,800**		**$771,200**	**$313,700**
Annual Payback	**($513,202)**		**$239,318**	**$1,236,776**

NPV of 3 Year Investment Dollars	$2,296,481
3 Year Project Net Present Value	$885,915
3 Year Project ROI	39%
Year in Which Breakeven Occurs	**Year 3**

THE REAL COST OF IMPLEMENTING BPM

When presenting a business case to management, the first question is invariably "how much will this cost?" This is understandably a difficult question during the early stage of a project, before a software vendor has been selected and before a real assessment of consulting/services costs can be determined. Yet few organizations truly understand the actual cost of BPM initiatives, and are unwilling to share their expectations with prospective suppliers (presumably out of fear that if they over-shoot, they will lose negotiating leverage).

For the purpose of developing a business case, some estimate of cost has to be arrived at. This underscores the need for a structured yet fluid model, as costs are one of the key variables which need to be constantly refined during the discovery and due diligence process. Using estimated costs as a benchmark can help move the model along, and it is much more productive to find a starting point and develop this in a workable model than to try to get it 100% at the outset.

BPM AND THE MYTHICAL MAN MONTH

The Mythical Man-Month" is a book by Fred Brooks first published in 1975, which illustrates that adding manpower to a late engineering project only makes it later. Brooks first presented this analysis focused on software engineering, however, it has been shown to be true for other "knowledge work" requiring skilled individuals, such as claims processing or mortgage origination.

This notion, commonly referred to as Brooks' Law, holds that the productivity of any group is reduced by the number of participants in the process, and is negatively impacted by the introduction of new works. This is based on the need for "ramp up" and inefficiency of communication (thus the overhead of coordination) between individuals. This notion also presents a compelling case for the value of BPM, by leveraging the ability to streamline communication, facilitate handoffs, and embed instructions within work items.

For example, when an insurance claim is transferred from a customer service rep to an adjuster, it typically requires further research and information gathering, and then is subject to the interpretation and assumptions of the individuals involved. By managing these handoffs within a BPM suite, much of the uncertainty and inconsistency in work quality can be eliminated through data validation and skills-based routing. For this reason, Brooks' Law presents an opportunity for uncovering and identifying existing soft dollar costs wherever handoffs between roles can be found.

CONCLUSION

The opportunity for realizing business value from Business Process Management (BPM) initiatives is significant and unlike virtually any other area of software. This is due in part to the intimacy and interplay between BPM systems and core business activities within which they exist.

When done right, successful BPM initiatives (herein referring to projects involving business process analysis and the implementation of business process management software) change the entire notion of applications, by allowing core systems to respond to process context, rather than driving processes around application limited. In this way BPM changes the nature of application management and the notion of "applications" altogether.

BPM is Incremental: one of the core advantages of BPM is that it need not require boiling the ocean to deliver results. Rather projects can start small, yet still make a large impact. As management sage Peter Drucker observed in his seminal work *Management Challenges for the 21st Century*, "Continuous process improvements in any one area eventually transform the business. They lead to innovation. They lead to new processes. They lead to new business." To paraphrase, it is less important to start with the perfect process candidate than it is to establish a leverage point from which to extend into other opportunities.

BPM is Measurable: BPM is unique among technology-based initiatives in its ability to incorporate metrics and measurement parameters at the outset of the project. BPM presents the opportunity for an immediate and material impact on business performance and visibility. Ultimately, the real value of BPM is delivered through what you can gain when you have access to data you never had before and tools that enable you to change and adapt your business.

BPM is Repeatable: BPM presents a compound benefit where the skill set and competencies gained from the first process optimized can be leveraged on multiple processes through the organization.

BPM projects fail more often as a result of missed expectations than inadequate technology. Yet a greater number of BPM projects fail to launch at all due to the inability to be a credible business case. The value of BPM is realized through planning and measurement, and the business case needs to be developed with transparent success criteria and "real world" metrics. Yet any business case is only as good as the validity and trueness of the project's architecture and assumptions.

Prioritization and validation of assumptions is part process (methodology) and part tools (simulation and modeling). An iterative should be taken to enable closed-loop analysis or a "round-trip" approach for comprehensive modeling, validation, implementation and refinement or continuous process improvement.

All successful BPM initiatives require executive sponsorship, based on realistic expectations. This should be clearly defined and measurable success criteria with incremental proof-points, and should begin with clearly understood prioritization of process targets (where to begin and where to go next).

Using short-term project wins to build credibility, successful BPM initiatives start at manageable scope and are leveraged into larger projects areas, taking advantage of the incremental and measurable qualities of BPM to achieve repeatable success.

The Process of Process Management

Strategy Execution in a Digital World

Dr Mathias Kirchmer and Peter Franz, BPM-D

ABSTRACT

Business strategies and operations need to consider scores of ever-shifting factors: from demographic changes, capital availability and legal regulations to technological innovations and an all present digitalization. Static business models do not keep pace with this dynamic change. Companies need a management approach that fits to this volatile environment. Organizations need to execute their strategy systematically and deal proactively with our "digital world". In effect, they must know how and when to modify or enhance their business processes, to know which processes are best candidates for intervention, and how to move rapidly from strategy to execution.

That's where the Business Process Management-Discipline (BPM-Discipline) helps. The BPM-Discipline has become the "Strategy Execution Engine" of an organization. It delivers significant business value by converting strategy into people and IT based execution at pace with certainty.

The BPM-Discipline is implemented through the "process of process management". Organizations look for a way to systematically establish their process of process management fast and cost effectively. This can be achieved using a holistic framework and reference model. This chapter introduces the BPM-Discipline and how it is implemented through the process of process management.

THINGS ARE CHANGING

Organizations' strategies and operations are driven by scores of ever-shifting factors: from demographic changes, capital availability, legal regulations and customers who require something new every day to technological innovations and an all present digitalization. Static business models do not keep pace with this dynamic change. Companies need a management approach that makes them successful in this volatile environment. Organizations need to master a systematic strategy execution and deal proactively with the opportunities and threats of our "digital world" (Sinur, Odell, Fingar, 2013). Companies need to become "Exponential Organizations" who achieve a significant higher output than peers through the use of new organizational techniques and related technologies available in a digital environment (Ismail, Malone, van Geek, 2014). In effect, organizations need to know how and when to modify or enhance their business processes, which processes are optimal candidates for intervention, and how to move rapidly from idea to action.

That's where the Business Process Management-Discipline (BPM-Discipline) helps. It enables organizations to deal with change successfully, drive their growth agenda and create immediate as well as lasting competitive advantage. Companies increasingly invest in areas of "intangibles" such as "business process" (Mitchel, Ray, van Ark, 2015). The BPM-Discipline delivers significant business value by converting strategy into people and IT-based execution at pace with certainty to meet the requirements of a systematic strategy execution and benefit from the opportunities of digitalization (Kirchmer, Franz, 2014) (Rummler, Ramias, Rummler, 2010).

Existing approaches to BPM focus in general on one or very few aspects of process management, e.g. implementing a process automation engine or setting up an enterprise architecture. There is a need for a comprehensive overarching approach to identify and establish all process management components required to form a simple but successful BPM-Discipline in the context of a specific organization. This is the topic of the research presented in this paper.

The BPM-Discipline is implemented through the "process of process management" (Kirchmer, 2015), just as other management disciplines are implemented through appropriate business processes: human resources (HR) through HR processes, finance through finance processes, to mention a couple of examples. The process of process management (PoPM) operationalizes the concept of the BPM-Discipline. It applies the principles of BPM to itself.

This whitepaper defines the BPM-Discipline and its value. It explains how this management discipline is further operationalized through the Process of Process Management (PoPM). Then it gives an overview of a reference model for the PoPM, developed to enable a systematic application of the PoPM approach to build and run a value-driven BPM-Discipline for strategy execution. Finally the paper will share experiences with the practical application of the PoPM.

VALUE AND DEFINITION OF THE BPM-DISCIPLINE

Research involving over 90 organizations around the world of different sizes and in different industries has shown that companies who use BPM on an ongoing basis get significant value in return (Kirchmer, Lehmann, Rosemann, zur Muehlen, Laengle, 2013) (Franz, Kirchmer, Rosemann, 2011). Basically all surveyed organizations state that the transparency BPM brings is a key result. This transparency is on one hand a value by itself: It enables fast and well-informed decisions which is, in the volatile business environment we are living, crucial for the success of a company. On the other hand BPM and the transparency it provides also helps to achieve other key values and enables the systematic management of the trade-offs between those values. BPM enables four key "value-pairs":

- Quality and Efficiency;
- Agility and Standardization (Compliance);
- External Networks and Internal Alignment; and
- Innovation and Conservation.

Let's look at an example. A company wants to improve its call centre process. Only few sub-processes are really relevant for clients and their willingness to pay a service fee for them. Hence you improve those sub-processes focused on "quality" aspects. Other sub-processes are more administrative. Clients don't really care about them but they are important and need to be executed well. Hence the prime focus on those processes is on "efficiency" (mainly cost or time) aspects, using appropriate BPM approaches. BPM delivers the transparency to achieve both values and end up with the highest quality where it matters and the best efficiency where this counts most. BPM helps to identify where it is really worth thinking of process innovation and where you can conserve existing good practices. Because an organization competes only with 15-20 percent of its processes, it is key to identify where innovation pays off. This is again possible though the transparency BPM delivers. The values BPM delivers are shown in figure 1 (Kirchmer, Franz, 2013).

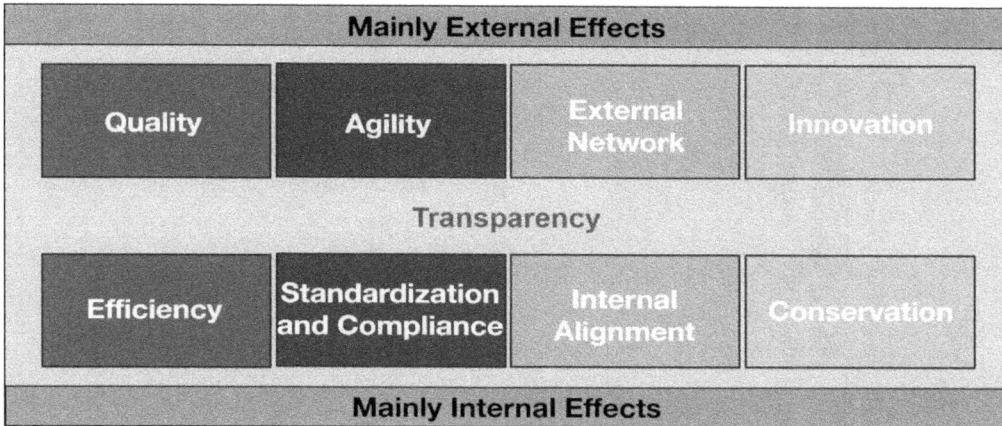

Figure 1: Values delivered by BPM

In general all those values are important for an organization. However, depending on the overall business strategy, companies focus on a subset of those values. These values and the underlying strategic objectives need to be realized across organizational boundaries within a company and beyond, while focusing on creating best results for clients.

In order to achieve those values consistently it is required to establish BPM with its infrastructure as an ongoing approach to run an organization (Alkharashi, Jesus, Macieira, Tregear, 2015) (von Rosing, Hove, von Scheel, Morrison, 2015). BPM becomes a management discipline.

We define BPM as the management discipline that transfers strategy into execution – at pace with certainty (Franz, Kirchmer, 2012). Hence, we refer to BPM as the BPM-Discipline (BPM-D). This definition shows that BPM uses the "business process" concept as vehicle for a cross-organizational strategy execution, including the collaboration with market partners like customers, agents, or suppliers. The execution of the strategy can be people- or technology-based, or a combination of both. This definition is consistent with newest findings in BPM-related research (Swenson, von Rosing, 2015). In addition it stresses the value that processes management produces and its key role as strategy execution engine.

The BPM-Discipline addresses the entire business process lifecycle, from design, implementation through the execution and control of a process. Hence, it handles the build-time as well as the run-time phase of a business process. The definition of BPM as a management discipline is shown in figure 2. We refer to it as the BPM-D Framework.

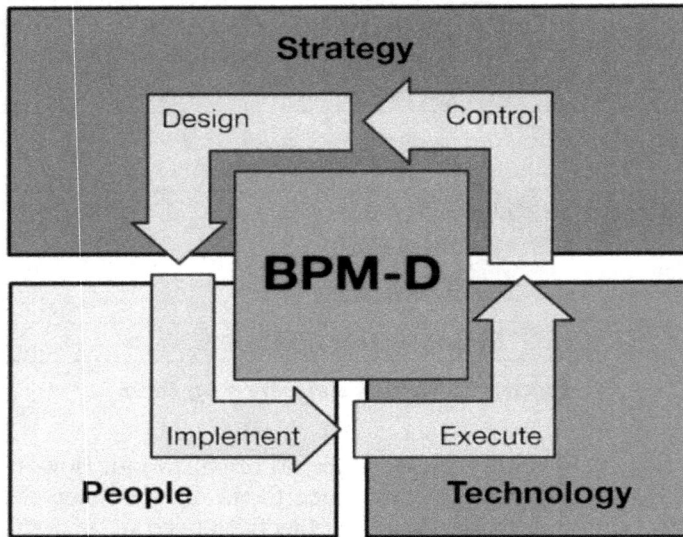

Figure 2: The BPM-D Framework

THE PROCESSES OF PROCESS MANAGEMENT

While over years many practitioners, especially executives, questioned the value of BPM, this situation has changed significantly in the past 5-7 years. Most organizations and their leadership start at least understanding the value proposition and the broader dimension of BPM. The challenge has become how to establish it in an organization in a pragmatic, but systematic way with minimal up-front investment.

In order to resolve this issue we can look at other management disciplines and how they are implemented. An example is the discipline of Human Resources (HR), as mentioned before. How do you implement the HR discipline? You introduce it into an organization through the appropriate HR processes, like the hiring process, performance evaluation or promotion process.

Consequently, you can implement a BPM-Discipline through the "process of process management", the BPM process. You address the BPM-Discipline just like any other management discipline. If you interpret the BPM-Discipline as a process itself, you can apply all the process management approaches, methods and tools to it – enabling an efficient and effective approach.

You basically implement BPM using BPM.

In order to identify and address all key aspects of the process of process management we use the ARIS Architecture (Scheer, 1998), a widely-accepted and proven framework to engineer processes from different points of view. This enables the operationalization of the framework so that it can be applied to specific organizations. Based on ARIS, the BPM-D Framework is decomposed into sub-frameworks. Result are four core frameworks describing the process of process management:

- BPM-D Value Framework;
- BPM-D Organization Framework;
- BPM-D Data Framework; and
- BPM-D Process Framework.

The decomposition of the overall process of process management as shown in figure 2 is divided into sub-frameworks based on ARIS. The BPM-D Process Framework covers both a functional decomposition and aspects of the control view of ARIS.

The BPM-D Value Framework is shown in figure 1 and has been discussed before. It describes the key deliverables (values) the process of process management (PoPM) produces. The use of this framework therefor enables a value-driven approach to BPM. This is especially important when you establish BPM as a management discipline so that you don't end up just with another overhead unit but an organization that systematically drives value by improving execution of strategy.

The previously mentioned research studies also show that organizations who apply BPM successfully have multiple different process specific roles in place. We identified over 40. The segmentation of those roles led to the BPM-D Organization Framework.

There exist two big groups of process-related roles: Core roles and extended roles. People with BPM core roles are part of the core BPM organizational unit, for example a centre of excellence (Alkharashi, Jesus, Macieira, Tregear, 2015) (Franz, Kirchmer, 2012). People with roles in the extended BPM organization are part of other organizational units. BPM roles can be centralized to achieve best synergies or decentralized to be close to operational improvement initiatives. Roles can be permanent or project-based, relevant only for a specific initiative. In most of the cases the roles are internal roles. However, in more and more organizations there is a tendency to procure administrative roles, like helpdesk activities or the maintenance and conversion of process models, externally, as a managed service. The BPM-D Organization Framework is shown in figure 4.

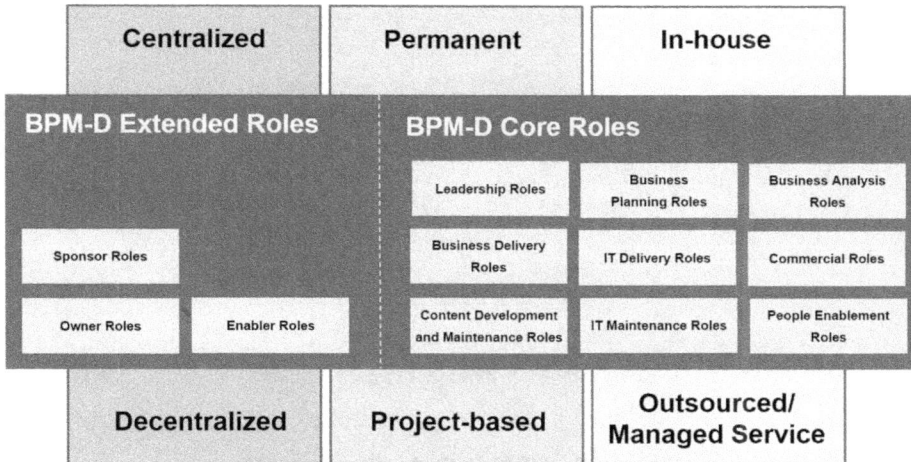

Centralized	Permanent	In-house
BPM-D Extended Roles	**BPM-D Core Roles**	
	Leadership Roles	Business Planning Roles	Business Analysis Roles
Sponsor Roles	Business Delivery Roles	IT Delivery Roles	Commercial Roles
Owner Roles	Enabler Roles	Content Development and Maintenance Roles	IT Maintenance Roles	People Enablement Roles
Decentralized	Project-based	Outsourced/ Managed Service

Figure 4: BPM-D Organization Framework

Very important is an emergent top leadership role in the BPM-D core organization: the Chief Process Officer (Kirchmer, Franz, von Rosing, 2015) (Kirchmer, Franz, 2014a). This business leader owns the overall process of process management, hence leads the overall BPM-Discipline. The empirical research confirmed the trend of such an emerging top management position. In many cases in successful BPM organizations the Chief Process Officer report directly to the board of a company.

The most important role in the extended BPM organization is the process owner, responsible for the end-to-end management of a business process. This role has to make sure things get done with the expected impact on the strategic value-drivers, using the BPM core organization as internal service group. Other groups of core and enabling roles are shown in figure 4.

In most organizations you may not have representatives for all the groups of roles immediately or some may only be part-time roles. It depends on your overall BPM agenda regarding *which* roles you need *when*. The required roles change over time, driven by the specific value the BPM discipline has to provide to execute an organization's strategy. It is important to have both core and extended roles in place to be able on one hand to execute, and on the other hand to avoid reinventing the wheel for every new initiative.

Next "ARIS view" to be addressed is the data view. The information used in or produced by the process of process management is summarized in the BPM-D Data Framework. This view helps to plan information requirements for the process of process management. This includes business strategy related information to enable the link between strategy and execution. Examples are strategic goals realized through value-drivers. But also operational information, like project-related information, enterprise architecture, organization or tool- and technology-related information. The BPM-D Data Framework is shown in figure 5 in form of a simplified entity-relationship model.

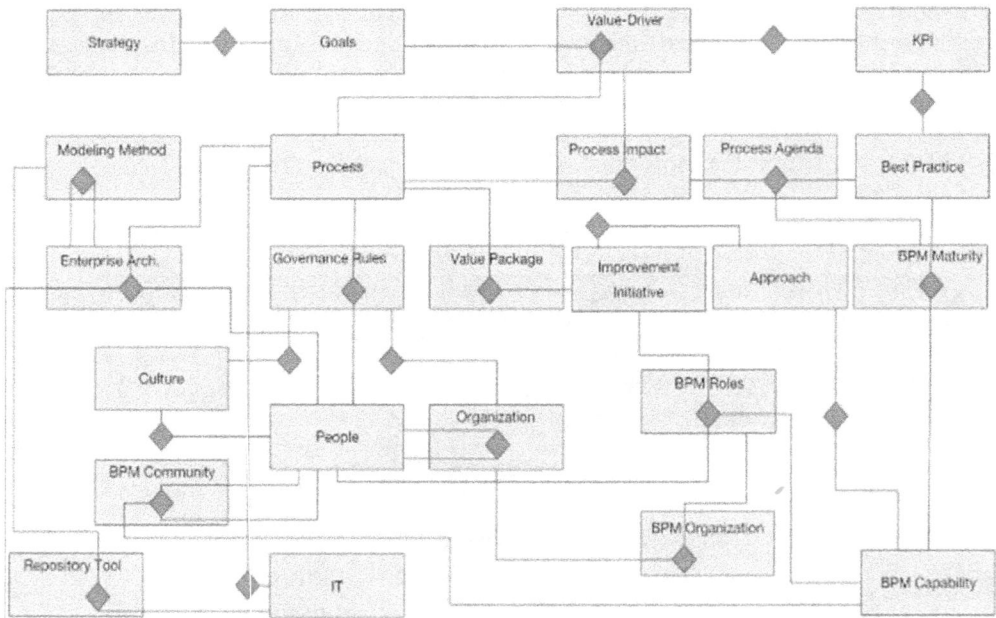

Figure 5 : BPM-D Data Framework

The most important area for the operationalization of the process of process management is the BPM-D Process Framework, covering the function and control view of the ARIS Architecture. It basically represents the first three hierarchy levels of a functional decomposition and a content related segmentation of the key activities of the PoPM.

The structure of the Process Framework is based on the principal thinking suggested in Scheer's Y-Model to segment the processes of an industrial enterprise (Scheer, 1995). In order to make the PoPM happen an organization it requires project-related sub-processes (activities), focusing on improving specific business processes. On the other hand it also needs to have "assets-related processes" in place to execute improvement projects efficiently and effectively. Both project and asset-related sub-processes require planning and execution. This results in four groups of BPM-related sub-processes.

The specific sub-processes of the PoPM were identified based on the analysis of over 200 process management initiatives. The result is shown in the BPM-D Process Framework in figure 7.

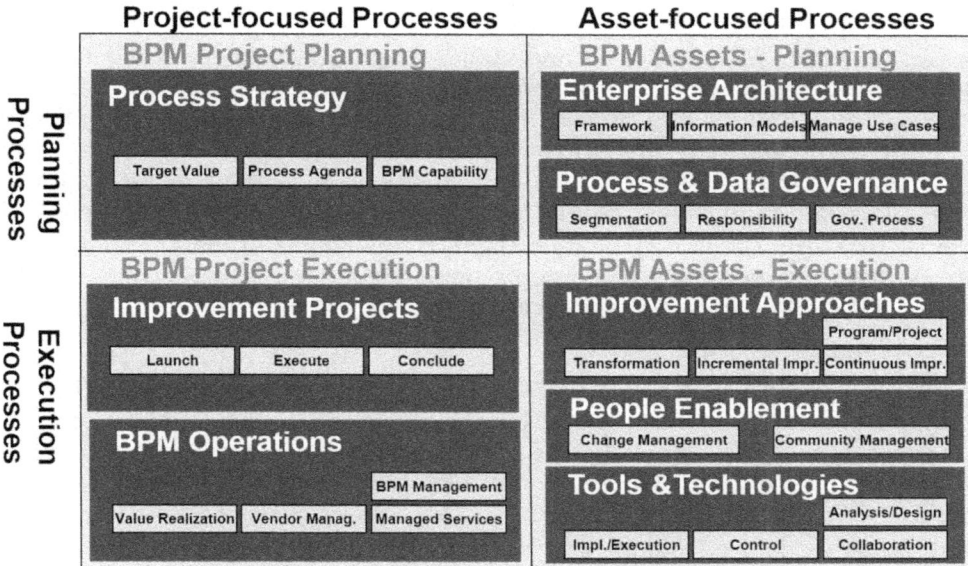

Figure 7: BPM-D Process Framework

The BPM Strategy identifies high-impact low-maturity processes, BPM capability gaps that need to be filled to improve those processes and the development of a BPM Agenda, showing *which* processes are improved *when* to achieve specific business objectives and which BPM capability gaps are closed during that specific improvement initiative. Hence, every initiative delivers immediate business value while creating lasting process management capabilities. Improvement projects follow a straightforward project approach: launch, execution, and conclusion of the project. BPM-Operations enable the execution of activities outside specific projects, for example the value realisation once a project is already concluded.

The Enterprise Architecture-related sub-processes handle all activities necessary to create and manage information models necessary to improve specific processes or keep them on track. Process and Data Governance sub-processes organize the way process management is executed, hence, grant the user power to take decisions, drive action and deal with the consequences of those actions. Important here is the integration of process and data governance (Packowski, Gall, Baumeister, 2014). Insufficient master data quality in many cases also leads to ineffective processes. An integrated governance approach aligns both aspects.

The availability of improvement approaches and of people trained in those approaches enables improvement projects which use those capabilities. People enablement is all about information, communication and training. Hence it prepares people to think and work in a process context and deal with process change successfully. Tools and technology-related sub-processes handle the technical infrastructure required for a successful BPM-Discipline including, for example, automation engines, rules engines, repository and modelling tools, process mining, strategy execution tools, social media, the Internet of Things and other internet-based approaches or e-learning applications. These are core BPM tools but also additional technology is required to increase the performance of a process to the required level.

While all the sub-processes of the PoPM shown in figure 7 can be important in a specific company context, organizations only rarely need all of them in full maturity. The specific objectives of a company's BPM-Discipline determine the importance of a specific sub-process and the required maturity level. Once the relevant sub-processes of the PoPM are selected and their required maturity level is defined, the necessary roles and information are identified using the appropriate BPM-D frameworks. All frameworks need to be configured consistently to a specific organization, its strategy and business context. The right application of the BPM-Framework and its sub-components enables companies to focus on what really matters, improve those areas efficiently and effectively as well as to sustain those improvements.

The BPM-D Framework with all its components is patent-pending. It is a strategy execution environment helping organizations dealing successfully with the challenges of the new normal in a digital world.

REFERENCE MODEL

In order to operationalize the BPM-D Framework and its components further, the framework is transferred into a more formalized reference model. Reference models are generalized knowledge, structured and documented in a manner that enables adaptability to specific situations (Kirchmer, 2011) (Fettke, Loos, 2007).

During the development of the BPM-D Reference Model the BPM-D Process Framework is further detailed and integrated with the other BPM-D sub-frameworks. The control flow logic is added to the functional decomposition. Key functions are linked to tools, templates or other job-aids supporting their execution.

The process framework is described on three levels of detail. The top level is represented as value chain diagram (VCD) and levels 2 and 3 as an event-driven process chain (EPC). The EPC notation was selected since it is focusing on the description of the business content and has less formal requirements than other methods like the business process modelling notation (BPMN). It is in general easily understood by business practitioners. Also people accustomed to working with other modelling methods can usually quickly adjust and understand the EPC notation. In order to support a potential automation of some of the sub-processes of the process of process management, level 3 processes are also available in BPMN (simple model conversion). These BPMN models can be used as starting point for the specification of application software supporting the PoPM. While this redundancy needs to be managed we feel that at the current point of time it helps to achieve both ease-of-use of the content by process practitioners and by software developers.

The reference model is developed in a web-based process repository tool. This enables the easy access from all relevant locations and reduces tool maintenance to a minimum. It can be easily transferred into all leading modelling and repository applications. The reference model currently consists of 67 individual information models.

The implementation and execution of the level 3 processes is further supported through the link of the models to execution tools, templates and other job aids. The sub-process "BPM Capability" of "Process Strategy" is, for example, linked to a BPM maturity assessment tool, based on the BPM-D Framework. The "Responsibility" sub-process of the "Process and Data Governance" is linked to job aids supporting the establishment of a BPM Center of Excellent with its different roles and the introduction of process and data governance to a specific end-to-end process. The reference model includes over 20 tools, templates and other job-aids.

LESSONS LEARNED

The BPM-D Framework and Reference Model or components of it have been applied in 23 organizations of different industries and sizes over the last two years to implement the process of process management or components of it. This has been done through a combination of consulting, coaching and educational activities, combined with appropriate research activities to continuously improve the process of process management reference model.

Let's look at a couple of examples: The CEO of a medium-size consumer goods company has, for several years, focused successfully on a small niche market. The company offers their products at a high price, enabling high revenues and profits – in spite of a relatively high cost level. Competitors have now entered that niche market and offer similar products at a much lower price. The CEO decided to adjust strategy, reduce their prices in the current market and enter new market segments with new products. However, to reduce prices they need to reduce cost. None of the functional executives see significant cost-reduction potential in their own areas. They blame other departments for the cost issues. Additionally, the innovation-related processes are not performing at the level required. A process repository with its process models did not really help: the models are outdated and inconsistent regarding semantic content as well as modelling format. The only person who is somehow familiar with the models and the repository has left the organization. There is no cross-functional management in place with responsibilities beyond department boundaries. It is very difficult or even impossible to identify focus areas for cost reduction or a consistent approach for the development and launch of new products.

The situation is addressed through a combination of defining and establishing an appropriate BPM-Discipline through the according process of process management, combined with the immediate application of the new capabilities to "no regret" processes. Additional improvement targets are defined when all high-impact low-maturity processes are identified by the new BPM-Discipline. Key areas of the PoPM addressed in this initial BPM-Discipline launch are the development of a process strategy (high-impact low-maturity process to focus on and capability development plan), introduction of a simple process and enterprise architecture approach, definition of a basic process governance, outline of a straight forward model-based improvement approach and some targeted training.

Another typical example is a large financial organization. They have, over the last four years, invested significant amounts of money into what they call "BPM". However, none of the top executives has seen any business impacts or usable results after all that time and money spent. A stakeholder assessment and BPM maturity analysis showed that almost all BPM-related initiatives focus on tools and technologies – for all business units in parallel. There is, for example, a process repository in place with over 1000 models – how to get value out of them is unclear. A flexible process automation is in the works – but business changes faster than the technology can be adjusted. And it is impossible to focus on just one area because business priorities are not or not well-enough defined.

The introduction of a value-driven BPM-Discipline, led by a top manager as Chief Process Officer and its use for a simplification of processes with known issues as preparation for a more focused and business-driven automation is used here to address the current issues. Key areas of the PoPM addressed are the value-driven process strategy with its prioritization approach, process and data governance, a process model based simplification and standardization approach and several people enablement initiatives. Existing capabilities are linked to specific outcomes to achieve step by step a value-driven approach to BPM.

The experience with the first 23 organizations shows that organizations looking for the systematic implementation of a BPM-Discipline through the process of process management fall into three groups:

- Organizations that have launched one or even multiple process improvement initiatives but the results are not sustained. Every new improvement initiative starts from scratch, not using existing knowledge about business processes systematically.
- Organizations that put in place many components of a BPM infrastructure (e.g. process execution environments) but have not achieved real business value through their BPM activities.
- Organizations that launched some improvement initiatives and built some BPM infrastructure but both do not really fit together, it is unclear what the next steps and priorities are. The resulting business value is limited.

Organizations of the first group establish the "project-focused" sub-processes of the PoPM but forget about the activities and infrastructure necessary to keep the improved processes on track and to be able to create synergies between different initiatives over time. In those cases "asset-focused" sub-processes need to be addressed. In most of the cases this results in a combination of governance, enterprise architecture and people enablement processes, combined with the development of an appropriate value-driven BPM agenda.

The second group of organizations gets lost in all the available methods, tools and technologies but forgets to identify how to create business value through them. The link of BPM activities to strategic value-drivers and the launch of initiatives affecting those value-drivers is key here. Hence, the "project-focused" sub-processes of the PoPM need to be addressed. The launch of a process strategy initiative is here most important: identifying high impact low maturity processes, the required BPM capability and based on those the development of the BPM agenda. This needs to be combined with the launch and execution of improvement projects and the consequent value-realization. BPM capabilities can be adjusted according to the requirements identified in the BPM agenda.

Most organizations belong to group three. They have some BPM capabilities and improvement initiatives in place but the BPM journey is missing direction, focus and clear business impact. They don't have a BPM-Discipline in place but know how to apply a number of methods and tools, e.g. Six Sigma. Instead of strategy execution, BPM activities result in operational fixing of symptoms. Here a combination of a real outcome-focused process strategy, the management of the process knowledge in an enterprise architecture and a well-defined (but simple) governance approach are good starting points to move towards a value-driven BPM-Discipline.

Here are some key lessons learned from first practice experiences:

- Get top management support. Establishing a value-driven BPM-Discipline requires the top-down support, best for the entire company, but at least for the business unit in scope.
- Identify business processes where you can deliver immediate benefits while building the required lasting BPM capabilities. Otherwise sponsors will lose patience.

- Set clear priorities, don't try to "boil the ocean". Organizations who launch too many initiatives at once often fail.
- Keep things simple, "less is often more". This is especially true for the use of tools and technologies.
- Encourage innovation and creativity instead of punishing people for making mistakes.
- A value-driven BPM Discipline is an enabler of growth and strategic agility, not just a cost reduction engine.
- People are key for success. You need to treat them accordingly.

A value-driven BPM-Discipline and its leadership recognizes the business value potential of technology and digitalization and makes it transparent to the organization. It enables real business value from digital initiatives.

The first experiences with the BPM-D Framework and the reference model of the process of process management have demonstrated the business impact of the approach and enabled the continues improvement of the reference model. The reference model allows identification and establishment of the appropriate BPM capabilities in the company-specific context quickly and at low cost while applying them immediately to achieve fast business benefits.

A company can use the adjusted reference model as basis for the definition of the company-specific BPM processes. The process of process management is transferred into an operational business process. It becomes part of the enterprise architecture of the company. The owner of the process of process management, the Chief Process Officer, manages this process.

BPM has become a value-driven management discipline that transfers strategy into people and technology based execution – at pace with certainty. This management discipline is implemented through the process of process management. It enables an organization to execute its business strategy systematically in a digital world.

The process of process management enables companies to create an end-to-end *value network* around the existing organizational structure. This is the basis for sustainable performance and productivity.

REFERENCES

Alkharashi, Jesus, Macieira, Tregear, 2015: Establishing the Office of Business Process Management, Leonardo Consulting Publication, Brisbane.

Fettke, Loos, 2007: Reference Modelling for Business Systems Analysis, ICI Global, London.

Franz, Kirchmer, 2012. Value-driven business Process Management – The Value-Switch for Lasting Competitive Advantage, McGraw-Hill, New York, e.a.

Franz, Kirchmer, Rosemann, 2011: Value-driven Business Process Management – Which values matter for BPM. Accenture / Queensland University of Technology BPM Publication, London, Philadelphia, Brisbane.

Ismail, Malone, van Geest, 2014. Exponential Organizations – Why new organizations are ten times better, faster, and cheaper than yours (and what to do about it). Diversion Books, New York.

Kirchmer, 2015. The Process of Process Management – Mastering the New Normal in a Digital World. In: BMSD Proceedings, July 2015. (in publication)

Kirchmer, Franz, von Rosing, 2015. The Chief Process Officer: An Emerging Tope Management Role. In: von Rosing, M., Scheer, A.-W., von Scheel, H.: The complete Business Process Handbook – Body of Knowledge from Process Modeling to BPM, Volume 1, Amsterdam, Boston, e.a., p. 343-348.

Kirchmer, Franz, 2014a. Chief Process Officer – The Value Scout. BPM-D Whitepaper, Philadelphia, London.

Kirchmer, Franz, 2014b. Targeting Value in a Digital World. BPM-D Whitepaper, Philadelphia, London.

Kirchmer, Franz, 2013. The BPM-Discipline – Enabling the Next Generation Enterprise. BPM-D Training Documentation, Philadelphia/London.

Kirchmer, Lehmann, Rosemann, zur Muehlen, Laengle 2013. Research Study – BPM Governance in Practice. Accenture Whitepapers, Philadelphia.

Kirchmer, 2011. High Performance through Process Excellence – From Strategy to Execution with Business Process Management. Springer, 2nd edition, Berlin, e.a.

Mitchel, Ray., van Ark, 2015.: The Conference Board – CEO Challenge 2015: Creating Opportunity Out of Adversity: Building Innovative, People-driven Organizations. The Conference Board Whitepaper, New York, e.a. 2015.

Packowski, Gall, Baumeister, 2014. Enterprise Process and Information Governance – Integration of business process and master data governance as competitive advantage – Study Results, Camelot Whitepaper.

Rummler, Ramias, Rummler, 2010: White Space Revisited – Vreating Value thorugh Processes.Wiley, San Francisco

Scheer, 1998. ARIS – Business Process Frameworks, Springer, 2nd edition, Berlin, e.a.

Scheer, 1995. Business Process Engineering – Reference Models for Industrial Enterprises, Springer, 2nd edition, Berlin, e.a.

Swenson, von Rosing, 2015: What is Business Process Management. In: von Rosing, M., Scheer, A.-W., von Scheel, H.: The complete Business Process Handbook – Body of Knowledge from Process Modeling to BPM, Volume 1, Amsterdam, Boston, e.a., p. 79.88.

Sinur, Odell, Fingar, 2013: Business Process Management: The Next Wave – Harnessing Complexity with Intelligent Agents, Meghan-Kiffer Press, Tampa.

Von Rosing, Hove, von Scheel, Morrison, 2015: BPM Center of Excellence. In: von Rosing, M., Scheer, A.-W., von Scheel, H.: The complete Business Process Handbook – Body of Knowledge from Process Modeling to BPM, Volume 1, Amsterdam, Boston, e.a., p. 217-240.

Process Discovery and Improvement

Hartmann Genrich, Process Analytica, Germany
Robert Shapiro, Process Analytica, USA

INTRODUCTION

In recent years, tools have become available[1] that can mine process logs and generate visualizations of the historical behavior of the process(es). The visualizations prove useful in process improvement.

We have added to this the ability to construct an executable model consistent with the historical data and a capability to (re)construct a sub-process decomposition of this model to improve understandability and performance.

The sub-process decomposition can also be applied directly to human-authored models to improve maintainability and performance.

From a business perspective, Process Discovery reveals the actual way work is carried out and a starting point for improvement based on the discovered process model, using simulation and cost/benefit analysis.

These new capabilities address two key process improvement challenges: accurately understanding the current state of affairs and designing optimal solutions.

Capturing the current "as is" process is an important, albeit costly, time consuming and notoriously error-prone task – so error-prone that many projects are inclined to skip the activity altogether. Process Discovery overcomes these difficulties by automatically capturing actual events from information system logs and synthesizing them into formal process models with execution statistics based on historical information.

In this paper we describe the basic concepts and show examples of automatically constructed models and sub-process decomposition.

1. Sequential Processes

At a minimum, a log event contains four pieces of information:

1.   Trace ID
2.   Task name
3.   Start time
4.   Stop time

Focusing on a single trace[2] for a process that has no parallelism, paths between tasks are deduced by matching the Stop (completion) time of a task with the Start time of another task.

Here are two patterns in the ten traces. The first pattern occurs seven times. The second pattern occurs three times.

---

[1] bpmNEXT 2013: Process Mining: Discovering Process Maps from Data

[2] A history for one work item, e.g. an order.

HISTORY (ARRIVAL 0 - 1 OF 7)

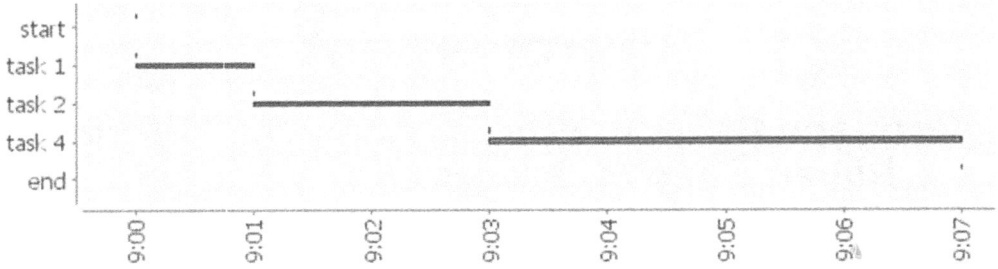

HISTORY (ARRIVAL 2 - 1 OF 3)

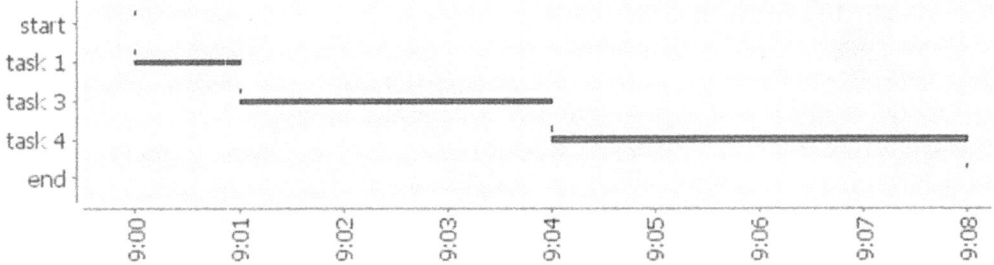

The task durations in the histories may be different!! They do not affect the number of patterns. They will determine the task durations in the discovered model, possibly requiring a statistical formula for defining duration.

Discovered Process:

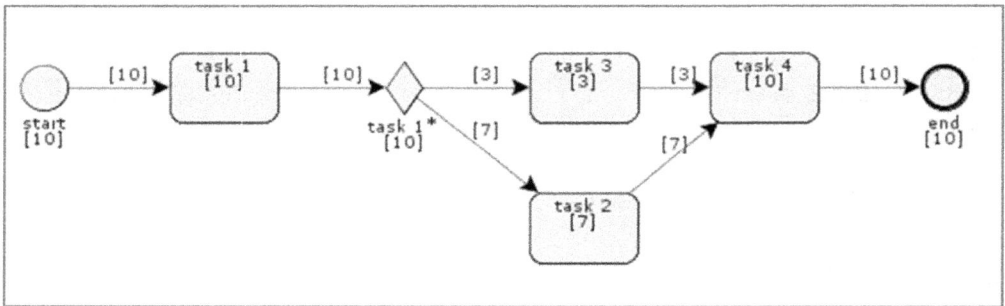

Discovered Rule:

This rule determines the route out of the decision 'task 1*. An attribute of the work item is used to decide which way to go.

```
task 1*/OD-0
logic: expressions
OD-0.ID-8: Pick task 2="YES"
OD-0.ID-9: Pick task 2="NO"
```

2. Processes with Parallel Constructs

A trace with parallel tasks.

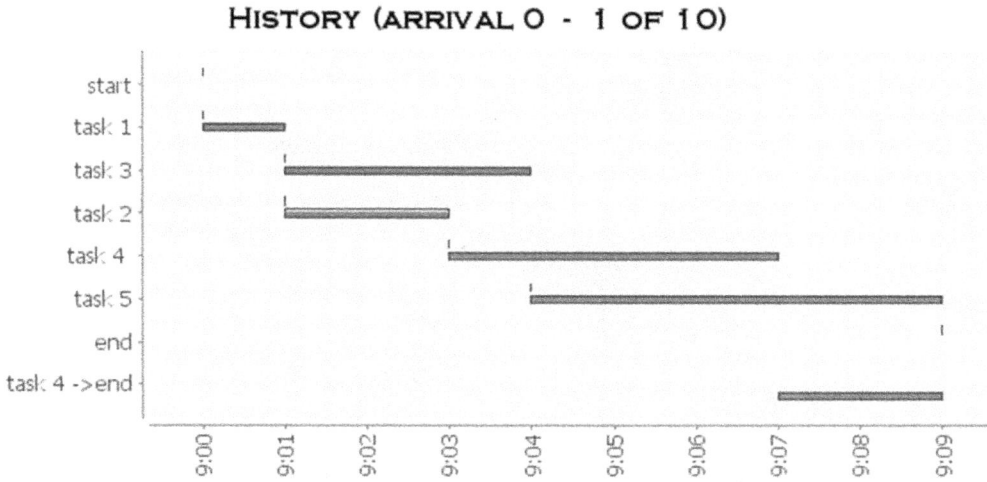

HISTORY (ARRIVAL 0 - 1 OF 10)

In this example it is still possible to use time stamps to arrive at the following model:

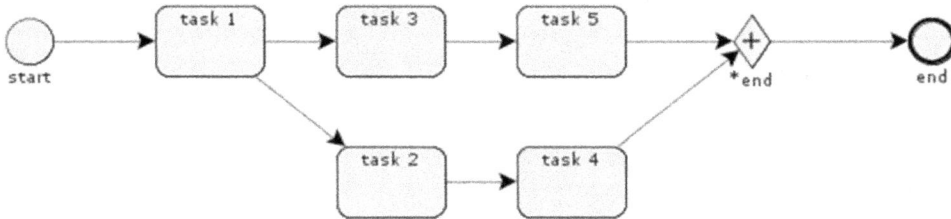

However, if task 2 and task 3 had the same duration, we would have the following trace:

HISTORY (ARRIVAL 0 - 1 OF 10)

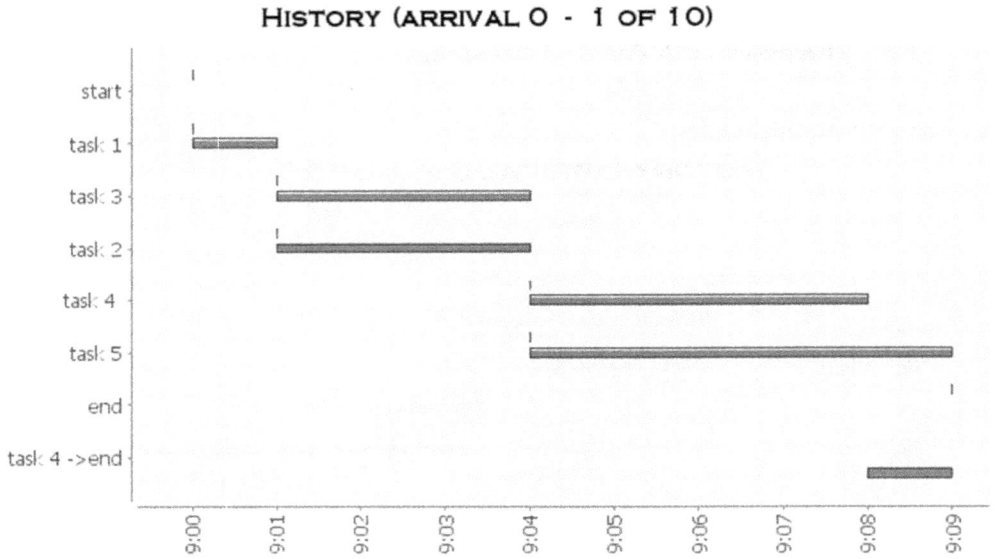

In this case there is no information to decide the connectivity to task 4 and task 5. The time stamps cannot in general resolve the problem if two or more stop times are identical. To do this work item information (which distinguishes between the different paths in a parallel split) is required in the log events.

3. Complex Processes

HISTORY (ARRIVAL 8 - 9 OF 10)

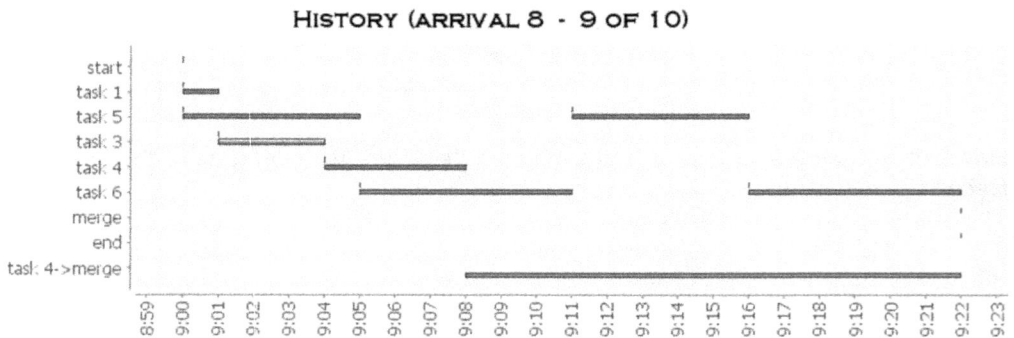

This example includes both choices and parallel constructs. The discovered model, before application of structural rules for introducing sub-processes looks as follows:

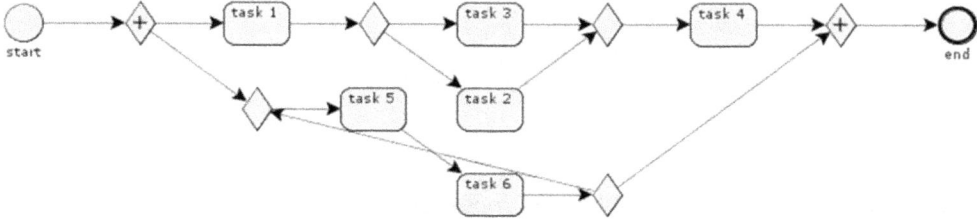

A flat process: no sub-processes

The restructuring results in the following:

Note there are three types of structures. Only two are used in the example.

- **CHN**: a 'chain', linear sequence of nodes;
- **BLK**: a 1-in/1-out acyclic 'block' or clause;
- **SCC**: a 'strongly connected component', that is: a loop structure

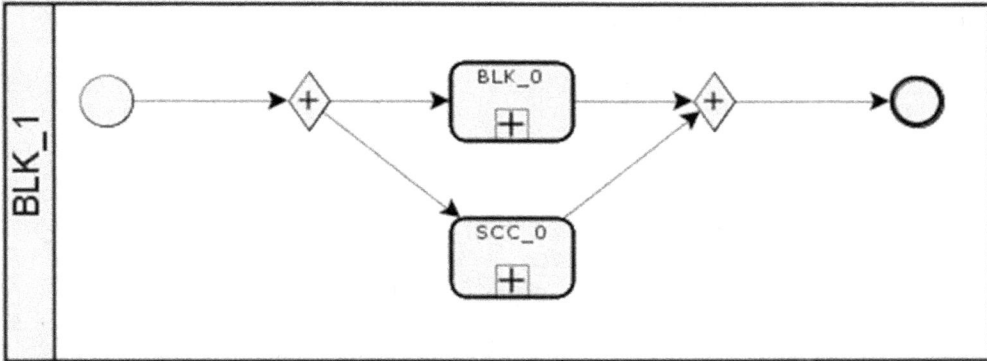

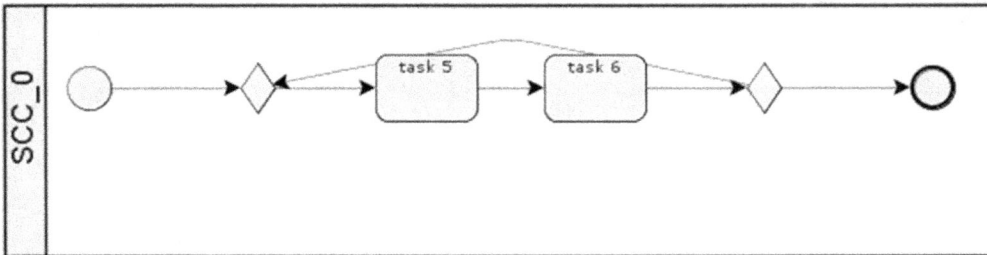

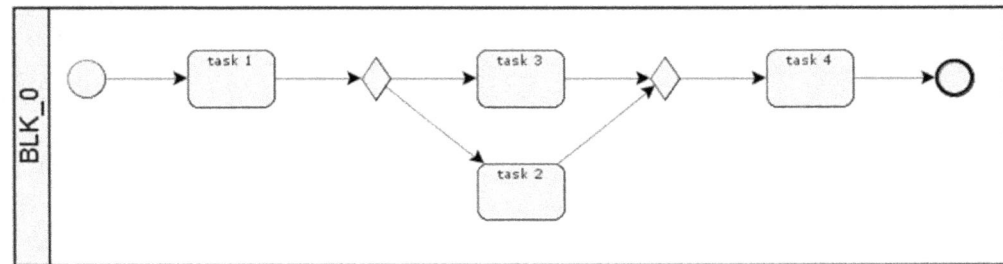

Of course the restructuring can also be applied to process models that were not discovered from log events, e.g. processes drawn by people.

CONCLUSION

Applying this approach in Healthcare Process Improvement has been illustrated in papers presented at the 2015 Health Care and Process Improvement Conference[3] and at the *bpmNEXT 2015 Conference*[4]. The example was a hospital Supply Order process.

Process Discovery analyzes actual events from information system logs and generates a formal process model with execution statistics based on historical information. Restructuring makes this model more understandable. Simulation of the 'discovered' model supports cost/benefit analysis of alternative process improvement proposals.

In the context of Healthcare Process Improvement we have described an enhanced capability for fact-based decision-making that balances clinical desirability, technical feasibility and financial viability.

---

[3] Process Improvement for Healthcare Systems: Some New Tools and Techniques
[4] Process Discovery and Analytics in Healthcare

Accelerating Value by Rebooting Enterprise Architecture

Linus Chow, Thomas J. Cozzolino, David Grimm, Salesforce[1]

ABSTRACT

Shifts in people, processes, information and technology are key factors in how Modern Architectures are both disrupting and providing value to Enterprises.

This seismic shift is forcing a hard look at the value of traditional Enterprise Architecture (EA), and leading the demand for strategic transformational outcomes that "Modern" EA needs to enable.

We will look at how and why we need to "reboot" EA to understand specific focus areas for change. Additionally, we will discuss how to transform EA from a "noun" (artifact and meta-work focused) to a "verb" (acceleration and business outcome-focused). Finally, we discuss best practice approaches to assist EA to become both a leader of, and a partner in, building this new world.

INTRODUCTION

Our world is changing. Fast. In the accelerated world of business growth, what started as a whisper is now a scream for a disruptive approach to Enterprise Architecture.

No longer is it possible to construct a technology-only system from the bottom up, built to stand static for decades. The business of technology—of the now, near, and distant future is evolving at a rate that will only increase.

IT leaders need to fundamentally reconsider the way they approach, design, communicate, and ultimately deliver systems that provide business outcomes to match and exceed the demand of flexibility. Of course, all of this must occur through a set of trusted, robust and resilient solutions that can stretch and morph in unforeseen new directions.

Enterprise Architects, CIOs, CTOs and other IT leaders understand how threads of information are woven throughout internal systems, the cloud, partners, devices and numerous other entities that are connected to their organizations. The question is, however, do they approach their *current* set of applications and ensure that it is truly ready to evolve to these "Modern Architectures"? This paper introduces a process to think through the Business and IT plan and also presents a pragmatic way to create, manage, and begin the journey towards a truly flexible, future-proof architectural strategy.

WHY DO WE CARE?

The technological revolution that started back with the Web has broadly impacted people, processes, information, technology and the complex relationships between each. For businesses and organizations, this is a double-edged sword creating both opportunities and threats. Roughly 20 years ago, Enterprise Architecture was born to try to bring some order to the chaos by addressing two major challenges:

1. System complexity—the cost, pain, and ongoing effort to maintain an ever-expanding number of systems and toolsets

---

[1] Note that all materials contained herein are subject to Salesforce's Safe Harbor statement (see Appendix).

2. Business and IT alignment—the ongoing relation between Enterprise business goals and technology enablers (and constraints)

In short, EA has had to evolve due to the ever-increasing cost and complexity of IT systems. This is coupled with the increasing expectation gap between business and technology. Recent rapid changes in the market forces are forcing a rethinking of the outputs of the entire EA effort across these dimensions:

- People: Consumers expectations are rapidly changing, and skill sets are challenged to keep up
- Information: Creation of massive amounts of new data is becoming increasingly hard to manipulate
- Technology: Adoption rates of key trends including cloud, mobile and IoT are stressing application portfolios almost to the breaking point

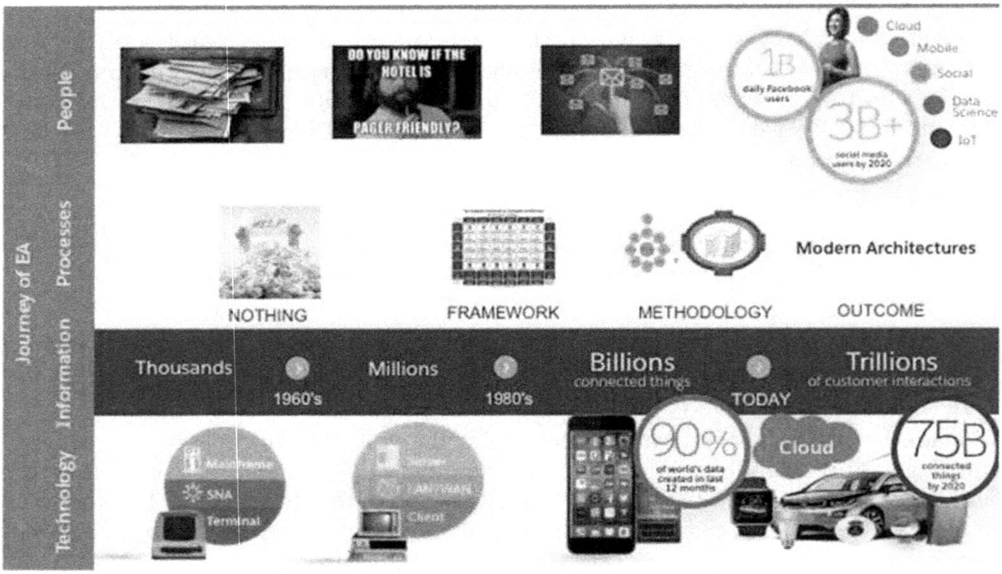

Figure 1: The Journey of Modern EA [2]

This pressure on IT leaders is clear. In IDC's CIO Magazine's "State of the CIO 2015"[2]. CIOs say their job is getting tougher and more important, as they juggle innovation and operational excellence – plus a new journey to what is commonly called "the digital enterprise." But 20 percent of CIOs feel like they're going in the wrong direction, or "sidelined" in the business.

The good news is that the "sidelined" segment is down eight percentage points from last year. The bad news is that IDC found that even more business peers (37 percent) see the CIO as sidelined (see below).

---

[2] (CIO Magazine 2015) http://www.cio.com/article/2862760/cio-role/2015-state-of-the-cio.html

STATE *of the* CIO 2015

Vital Signs
The CIO role is becoming:

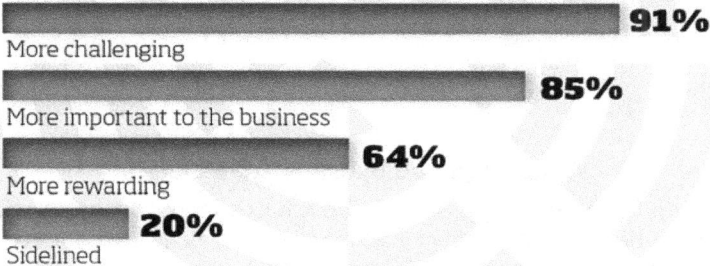

91%
More challenging

85%
More important to the business

64%
More rewarding

20%
Sidelined

MULTIPLE RESPONSES ALLOWED

Figure 2: Pressure is Building on IT leadership[3]

Clearly, while the job of the CIO is becoming more valuable in the business overall, the complexity, challenge, and pressure are mounting. Couple this with the fact that Enterprise Architecture is one of the Top 5 skill shortages, and the picture zooms into focus: the success of the CIO is intimately tied to effective EA and technology management. But there is more.

STATE *of the* CIO 2015

Top 5 Skills Shortages
Expected in 2015

1 — Big data, business intelligence, **analytics**

2 — **Security**, risk management

3 — Application **development**, programming

4 — **Mobile** technologies

5 — Enterprise **architecture**

Figure 3: EA is a Top Skill Shortage[3]

[3] (CIO Magazine 2015) http://www.cio.com/article/2862760/cio-role/2015-state-of-the-cio.html

STATE *of the* **CIO** 2015

C-Suite Perception Gaps

Business colleagues take a harsher view of the IT group's status in the organization than CIOs do

Agree with the following statements	CIOs	Line-of-business Executives	Gap (percentage points)
Non-IT departments view the IT group as an obstacle to their mission.	33%	54%	21
The CIO is being sidelined in our business.	20%	37%	17
The CIO is fighting a turf battle with at least one C-suite peer.	36%	47%	11

SOURCES: CIOs: State of the CIO 2015 survey, 558 respondents; LINE-OF-BUSINESS EXECUTIVES: C'3 CIO sentiment survey, 304 respondents.

STATE *of the* **CIO** 2015

The Balancing Act

It's challenging to find the right balance between business innovation and operational excellence

- Agree — **74%**
- Disagree — **24%**
- Not sure — **2%**

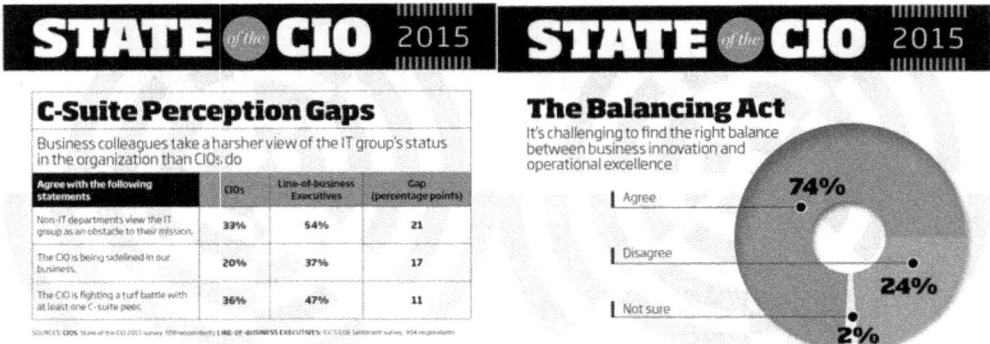

Figure 4 (a and b): CIOs are struggling [4]

"Business leaders increasingly expect the CIO to lead corporate-wide innovation projects and to help develop new products and services." But instead, "a third of CIOs acknowledge that IT may be viewed as an obstacle by other departments" and more than half (54 %) of those other departments see IT as an obstacle to their mission. And as the C-suite gets crowded with C-level titles, "turf wars are arising with peers in the C-suite. Non-IT business execs are seeing more of this phenomenon than the CIOs themselves are aware of."[4]

CIOs need Enterprise Architects to lead strategic innovation and address this perception gap. This means the "Traditional EA" focusing on the as-is state of what an organization does has to change to a "Modern EA" focus on what value and business outcomes are being provided to the organization. Thus, it is time for EA to fundamentally change.

THE CHALLENGES WITH TRADITIONAL ENTERPRISE ARCHITECTURE

Most Enterprise Architects have strong backgrounds in one or more architectural methodologies. However as Business and IT Leaders further consider Modern Architectures, there are a few uncomfortable, but true observations about traditional IT architectures and how they typically come to life:

Historical Enterprise Architecture methodologies (TOGAF, Zachman, FEA) were effective ways to approach first and second-generation architectures. However, they are a challenge to adapt to agile, Modern Architectures, and sometimes do not always resonate with Business stakeholders, who are more focused on business outcomes than diagramming and repositories, and other mapping exercises. Furthermore, the focus on artifacts rather than partnership and alignment with business goals is often a challenge to reconcile.

"Fit for purpose" approaches typically cannot capture the continuum of legacy applications through emerging technologies with any resiliency. Often, such application architectures stumble forward and remain technology-driven and not capabilities-driven. In addition, such bespoke approaches lead to solutions that are all too breakable and hence short-lived.

Traditional vendor technology "stacks" are oftentimes brittle, tightly coupled, or require so much custom integration (along with a large amount of code and maintenance) that they are virtually unsustainable. We live in a hybrid, heterogeneous world – and the Holy Grail of a single-vendor solution continues to be both unrealized, and unrealistic.

---

[4] (CIO Magazine 2015) http://www.cio.com/article/2862760/cio-role/2015-state-of-the-cio.html

All of this is leading us to a fundamental architectural pivot.

WHAT IS MODERN ARCHITECTURE?

Consider the notion of "Modern Architecture"—a fresh look at how Enterprises shift toward this future using both new and existing technologies, specifically cloud technologies. Such architectures are rooted in a number of basic realities:

- smart "hybrid" application design: the data locked in on-premises and legacy systems needs be quickly "surfaced" to the cloud through lightweight integration, API-first thinking, and in-memory analytics—in some cases cutting delivery to hours instead of months.
- agility as a way of life: rapid prototyping, effective product owners, and visible, defensible backlogs must be supported by the next wave of practitioners.
- future-proof by design: changing process automation requirements, IoT, and other data-intensive trends are forcing applications to evolve rapidly. Metadata-driven platforms provide the right flexibility to allow Architects to pivot and act instead of react. Also, support for both model-driven and elastic approaches are critical to success.
- developer democratization: conventional development approaches are giving way to "composability" – ranging from drag-and-drop component assembly to functional components that can be "snapped into" the ecosystem. Tooling needs to continually move up the "food chain" resulting in rich palettes from which to compose and assemble (vs. craft by hand).
- event-driven as a design point: the combination of the mobile revolution and the coming IoT tsunami of big data shows a clear trend towards "apps" and the supporting ecosystem becoming much more event-driven and less procedural and pull-focused. Truly, the very nature of now we meet such business demands will cause disruption to the Enterprise portfolio.

This change in focus to speed and change allows Modern Architectures to:

- doing more with less by refactoring systems and skills
- adding value vs. containing costs (one of the traditional goals of both EA and IT)
- pivoting into core competencies (and away from an infrastructure focus)
- gearing up for transformation
- releasing "Minimal Viable Products" (MVPs) early and often

This allows Modern Architecture processes to "think big, start small, and move fast," and in so doing enable the Enterprise to more easily embrace the fastest growing forces affecting organizations today: the cloud, mobile, data and IoT revolution.

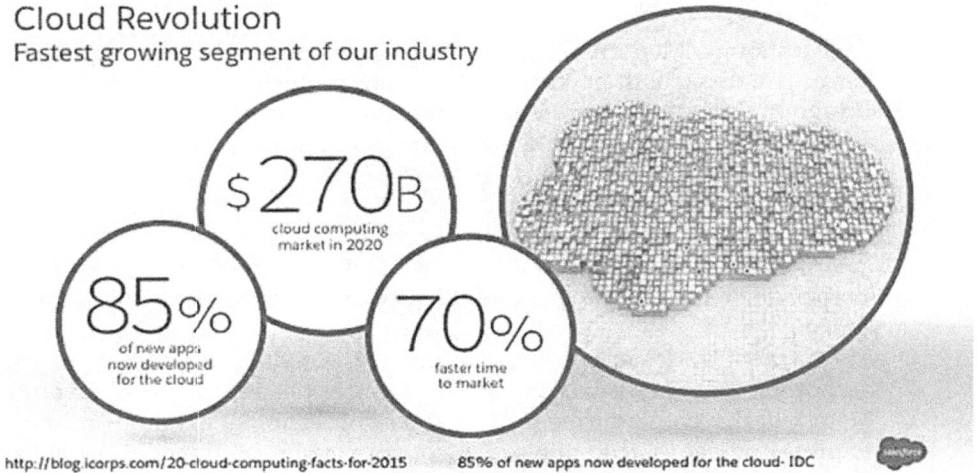

Cloud Revolution
Fastest growing segment of our industry

$270B
cloud computing
market in 2020

85%
of new apps
now developed
for the cloud

70%
faster time
to market

http://blog.icorps.com/20-cloud-computing-facts-for-2015   85% of new apps now developed for the cloud- IDC

Figure 5: the Cloud Revolution

SO HOW DO WE REBOOT OUR EA?

In many Enterprises, architecture planning processes are fragmented, siloed or even non-existent. Application portfolios are typically large, duplicative, and often-times managed purely from an operating cost perspective vs. a TCO and go-forward business value perspective. Also, while many Enterprise IT functions create "blue-prints" or "roadmaps" as part of their annual planning cycles, these often become snapshots that quickly lose relevance and are neither regularly updated nor sustainable. To effectively "reboot" EA, we propose the following 3 steps:

Using the backdrop of Modern Architecture presented earlier, consider this set of design points, or a Modern Architect's "Manifesto":

1. **Collaborate (or Perish)**: the need for EA to collaborate with both Lines of Business (LOBs) and Developer teams has never been more critical for success.
2. **Run with Scissors:** while EA needs to operate at higher speeds throughout the entire planning and deployment lifecycle, prototyping needs to be balanced with the resiliency of business continuity and risk management.
3. **Use It or Lose it:** EA is encouraged to suck every penny out of existing systems, via surround strategies and other methods. Using a rigorous portfolio planning process also accelerates the sunsetting of legacy systems where and when it makes practical sense.
4. **Lose the Hammer:** technology managers need to be willing to consider that their current toolset may not be complete. Consciously using the right tool for the right job, whether it be new or old, is indicated here.
5. **No Meme for You:** security and compliance continue to be top-of-mind for all, so Modern Architects must consider the ever-increasing "attack surface" of the Enterprise to maintain trust.
6. **Play it Where it Lies:** moving data is still too hard; new approaches leverage data-by-reference to reduce complexity and raise data quality. Further, considering "good enough" approaches to data can provide immediate benefits while other data efforts are mobilized.

7. **No More Heroes:** truly, laziness can be a virtue; IT leaders should strive to automate everything, starting with the SDLC. It is a plain fact that heroism does not scale.

8. **Think Big**: Modern Architectures (Cloud, Mobile, Big Data, IoT, and Microservices) will test any ecosystem's capacity to scale. EAs need to plan for elasticity and scale from day 1. Cloud should be considered as *"when"* and *"how much, how fast,"* vs."*if*".

9. **Be "Not Wrong" and Survive:** In the new world flexible interfaces and platforms will continue trump top-to-bottom thinking, as requirements will change in unknowable ways. Here being "directionally correct" is a critical goal.

Adopt a Reference Architecture that actually works—We have observed that reference models tend to be either very high-level (and generic) or too specific (and hence brittle by nature) and present the "fabrics" model.

Consider the idea of "fabrics"; hierarchical groupings of technical components that directly enable the Modern Architectures. Fabrics are:

- Intuitive: they make sense to non-practitioners so Business and IT can understand and easily discuss them
- Intelligent: they can filter and react to events and also massage data and execute business rules
- Flexible: they are resilient and scale / stretch as needed (too many fabric layers lead to unmanageable complexity; too few lead to generalities and architectural chaos)
- Component-based: they support API-first, Microservice, and object-oriented concepts including abstraction, isolation, and independence.

Fabrics are not:

- Products: in the real world of hybrid applications, no single vendor provides a complete solution—fabrics by design will blend a number of technologies and providers (both planned and current).
- Rigid: instead of stacks of components, think firm in the middle and malleable on the interfaces. Fabrics represent distinct functions per level, but will flex based on use cases, patterns, and emerging capabilities.
- Static: instead of tightly coupled end-to-end chains, they will change over time, with a manageable impact on the rest of ecosystem. Think loose coupling with interfaces that are "plumb able".

Fabrics are the manifestations of the deployed and evolving portfolio, and are supported by Governance processes (specifying the portfolio) as well as DevOps (caring for the portfolio) as shown below:

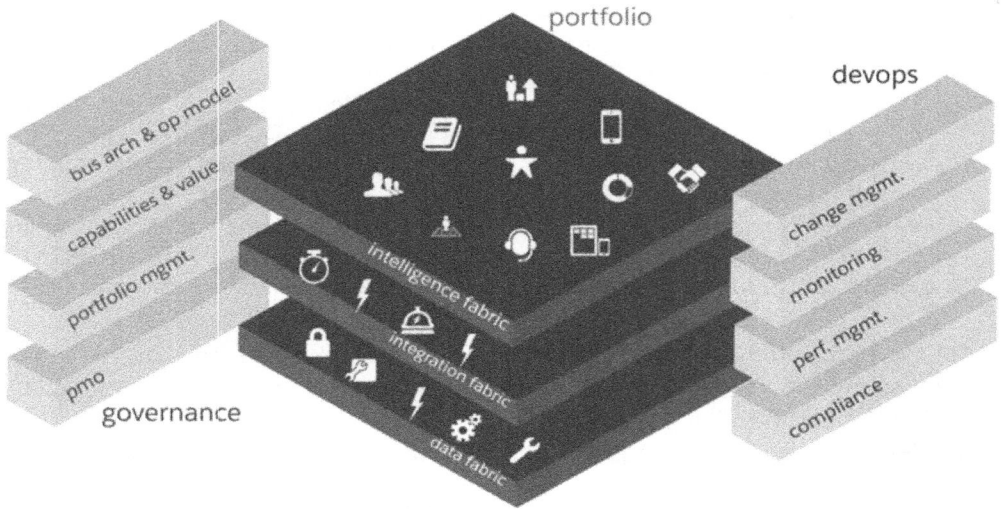

Figure 6: Fabrics Reference Model

FABRICS APPLIED TO "TWO-SPEED" ARCHITECTURES

A more detailed view of the fabrics-based reference model is shown below. Bear in mind these important distinctions across the model:

- Some of the components are "slow," meaning that they are subject to longer update cycles. In such cases, architects need to plan for less rapid change and reduced agility, but consider ways to unlock the value in these components, including data-by-reference, APIs, and Event-Driven Architectures.
- Other components are "fast," meaning that they can be "composed" or deployed rapidly (often in days or weeks). These components are built to be iterated upon (or even discarded) as the LOBs request new features and outcomes.
- The fabrics model is designed to start a conversation: it is a way to categorize components and functionality and drive to understanding between Enterprise Architects and LOB stakeholders.

Modern Architects can map their current and planned portfolios to this model, identify integration or process gaps, and then set priorities based on the combined Business and IT Roadmap. What is liberating about Modern Architectures is the Enterprise can realize value immediately, build initial momentum, and accelerate applications and services while effectively managing budgets.

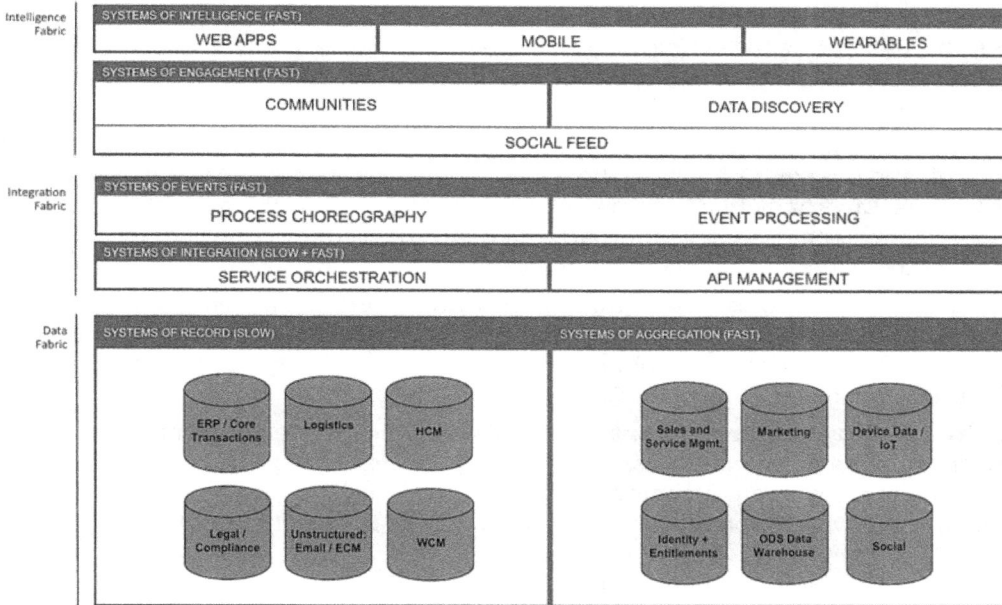

Figure 7: Detailed fabrics Reference Model (sample)

Application Portfolio as "Forcing Function"—Take a hard, value-based look at the current/planned application portfolio—this, combined with the Operating Model and Business Value Mapping (see below), form a pragmatic but future-facing roadmap for the transformation.

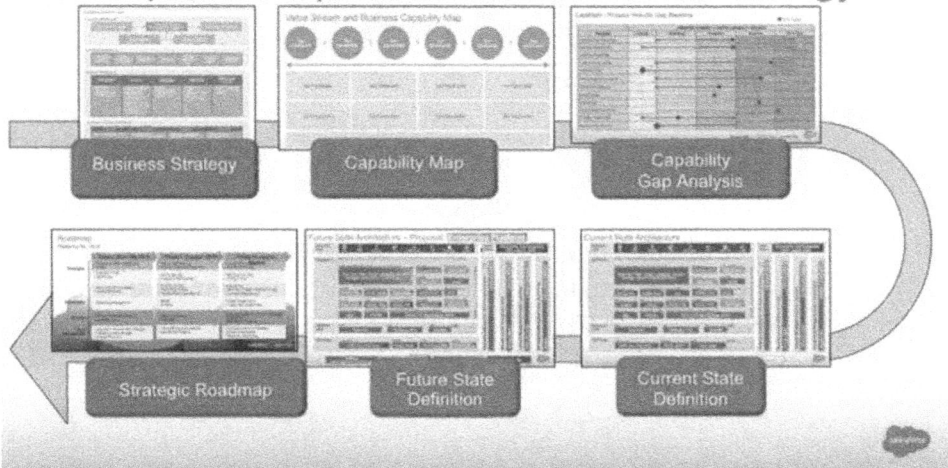

Figure 8: Enterprise Architecture Methodology Artifact Summary

Taken together, these steps offer a complete but lightweight methodology that balances the current state, future state, and a laser focus on business collaboration, all with a manageable set of artifacts designed to drive value and ongoing discussion.

CODA: HOW DO WE KNOW WE'RE READY?

As the business and technical transformation continues, many Enterprises find that their IT staffs are challenged for the migration to Modern Architectures. A few critical topics are presented below, along with best practice considerations.

New / Modified Roles: As Enterprises accelerate cloud adoption, classical IT roles morph and change. Other roles that will clearly be in flux include Database Administrators, Environment Management Engineers, and Developers. Sifting key resource concerns (via CoEs and partnerships with Human Resources) is a critical part of the planning and adoption process.

Training / Education: What training, education, certification efforts are required for each key role? This includes Architects, Developers, QA Testers, and others. Shrewd Enterprises use initial projects as incubators to extract best practices and identify gaps in cloud providers' overall capabilities.

Initial vs. Ongoing Investments: Tactical or strategic System Integration (SI) Partners are often leveraged to assist in initial projects. Enterprises need to find the right balance between outsourcing and in-house efforts to meet budgets and timelines, and have a vision of what core competencies they truly want to focus on.

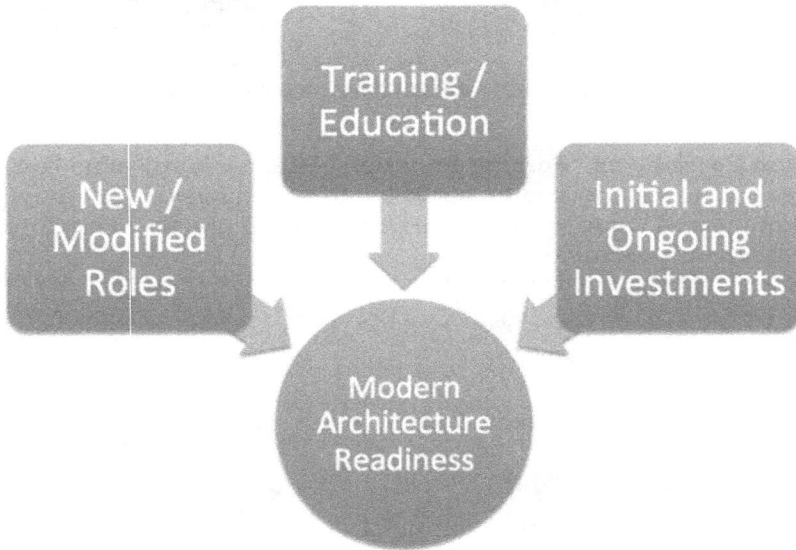

Figure 9: Getting Ready for Modern Architecture

Additionally, a key consideration in enabling and maintaining an organization's ongoing ability to execute on Modern Architecture is the ecosystem of support. Today's open standards-based, crowd-sourced paradigm provides ample opportunities to leverage collaboration.

Figure 10: the Salesforce Ecosystem

The support ecosystems can range from free training to collaboration through communities of interest. Examples include:

- Ignite—Innovative Organizations are already executing Modern Architecture processes. Ignite is Salesforce's unique collaborative approach to help businesses design their Customer Company vision and execution roadmap. Through carefully designed interviews and workshops, an innovation team works with key individuals with organizations to rethink processes and reengineer how Enterprises engage employees and customers. It is business outcome driven to produce a complete business vision, execution plan, business case and app prototypes in 9 weeks. http://www.salesforce.com/ignite/
- Trailhead—over 65,000 registered users from Business Users to Developers, to Admins leverage free hands-on training paths (ref: https://developer.salesforce.com/trailhead).
- Blogs and Discussions—continually-updated technical writings, best practices, and more (ref: https://www.salesforce.com/blog/2014/08/enterprise-architecture-function.html)
- Architecture Community—interactive community including customer and Salesforce EAs sharing challenges, solutions and dialog (coming soon)

CONCLUSION

Leaders of Enterprises readying to adopt Modern Architectures need to understand their internal business and technical goals and also consider their own maturity and ability to absorb change. An Enterprise armed with this self-knowledge can move more effectively and build the required readiness for to quickly move forward.

Rebooting the Enterprise Architecture strategy renews the fundamental LOB / IT relationship and will help position both the Business and the IT function for sustainable success.

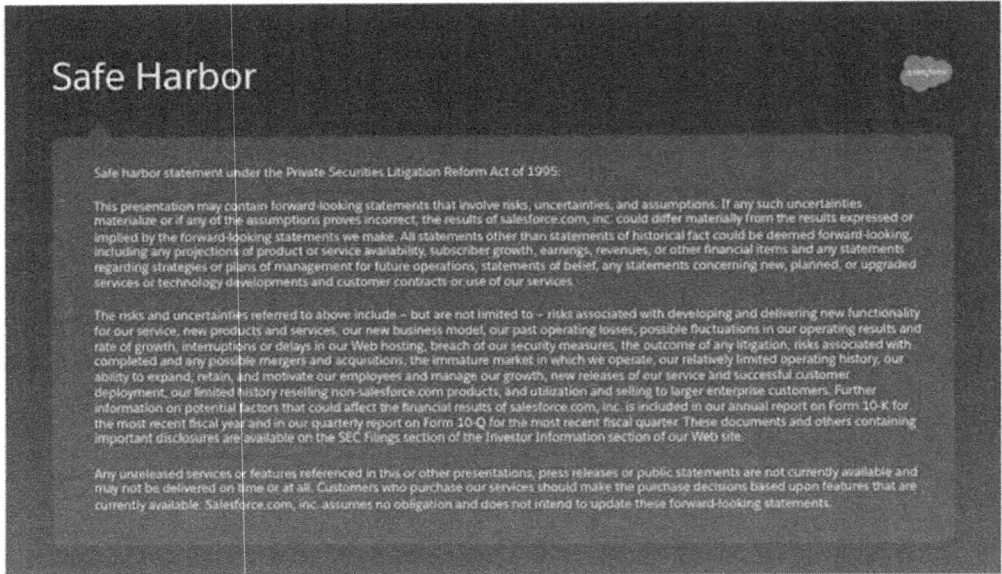

Safe Harbor

Safe harbor statement under the Private Securities Litigation Reform Act of 1995:

This presentation may contain forward-looking statements that involve risks, uncertainties, and assumptions. If any such uncertainties materialize or if any of the assumptions proves incorrect, the results of salesforce.com, inc. could differ materially from the results expressed or implied by the forward-looking statements we make. All statements other than statements of historical fact could be deemed forward-looking, including any projections of product or service availability, subscriber growth, earnings, revenues, or other financial items and any statements regarding strategies or plans of management for future operations, statements of belief, any statements concerning new, planned, or upgraded services or technology developments and customer contracts or use of our services.

The risks and uncertainties referred to above include – but are not limited to – risks associated with developing and delivering new functionality for our service, new products and services, our new business model, our past operating losses, possible fluctuations in our operating results and rate of growth, interruptions or delays in our Web hosting, breach of our security measures, the outcome of any litigation, risks associated with completed and any possible mergers and acquisitions, the immature market in which we operate, our relatively limited operating history, our ability to expand, retain, and motivate our employees and manage our growth, new releases of our service and successful customer deployment, our limited history reselling non-salesforce.com products, and utilization and selling to larger enterprise customers. Further information on potential factors that could affect the financial results of salesforce.com, inc. is included in our annual report on Form 10-K for the most recent fiscal year and in our quarterly report on Form 10-Q for the most recent fiscal quarter. These documents and others containing important disclosures are available on the SEC Filings section of the Investor Information section of our Web site.

Any unreleased services or features referenced in this or other presentations, press releases or public statements are not currently available and may not be delivered on time or at all. Customers who purchase our services should make the purchase decisions based upon features that are currently available. Salesforce.com, inc. assumes no obligation and does not intend to update these forward-looking statements.

APPENDIX AND REFERENCES

All materials in this paper are covered under this Safe Harbor.

REFERENCES:

(US Government 2012) A Common Approach to Federal Enterprise Architecture https://www.whitehouse.gov/sites/default/files/omb/assets/egov_docs/common_approach_to_federal_ea.pdf

(The Open Group 2011) TOGAF: https://www2.opengroup.org/ogsys/catalog/g116

(Gartner 2009) Collaborative Enterprise Architecture by Uwe Bombosch; Shailendra Langade; Stefan Bente, Published by Elsevier Science; Morgan Kaufmann, 2012 https://www.safaribooksonline.com/library/view/collaborative-enterprise-architecture/9780124159341/xhtml/ST0045_CHP004.html

(Zachman 2008) JOHN ZACHMAN'S CONCISE DEFINITION OF THE ZACHMAN FRAMEWORK™ https://www.zachman.com/about-the-zachman-framework

(Microsoft 2007) "A Comparison of the Top Four Enterprise-Architecture Methodologies" from Microsoft: http://msdn.microsoft.com/en-us/library/bb466232.aspx

(Gartner 2012) http://www.gartner.com/newsroom/id/1923014

(CIO Magazine 2015) http://www.cio.com/article/2862760/cio-role/2015-state-of-the-cio.html

(iCorps 2015) $270B Cloud computing market 2020 http://blog.icorps.com/20-cloud-computing-facts-for-2015

(Society3 2013) 3B+ Social Media Users by 2020 http://www.society3.com/2013/01/social-media-2020-long-term-prediction/

Section 2

The Skill of BPM

Admin Re, U.K

Nominated by Corporate Modelling, UK

1. EXECUTIVE SUMMARY / ABSTRACT

Part of the Swiss Re group, Admin Re UK is a specialist in the run-off of legacy closed life business portfolios with a proven track record in the administration of life, pensions and health business and the acquisition of entire life insurance companies. Our organization continues to grow through merger and acquisitions and strategic client and third party partnerships, underpinned by solid and efficient customer servicing at a low cost that is highly compliant and low risk.

Our operations include:

- Three main UK sites and one offshore site.
- 2,000 employees, including 1300 customer services staff.
- Servicing approximately three and a half million policies for a number of major UK Life Assurers.

In 2012, as a response to a challenge to reduce our operating costs and to improve service, we began a journey of Operational Excellence to deliver rapid reductions in operational costs and an ongoing ability to control costs, whilst at the same time improving service through Quality, People, and Productivity (which we refer to as QPP).

Operational Excellence consists of three foundations:

- Back to Basics — putting best practice at the heart of our operation to improve customer experience, reduce customer timelines and deliver more for less.
- Model and Improve — introducing a new workforce and process management technology; "OPUS" to more effectively track and manage workloads on an individual or team basis against expected measures.
- Integrate and Grow — implement the new operating model into future acquisitions.

The programme of change aimed to achieve these benefits and change the way the organization worked. Recognizing the importance of managing the change in a controlled manner, Operational Excellence was firstly delivered through process development and changes to hearts and minds; it included a focus on *right first time* and a movement to next-day processing and the status of service levels next working day, before implementing any technology solutions.

The workforce and process management solution (OPUS) would support:

- Next-day processing through a strict *First-In – First-Out* (FIFO) process regime.
- Providing real time Management Information (MI) for queue and work management ensuring delivery to agreed service levels.
- Providing real time MI and performance management to recognize over and under achievers.
- Enable multi-site processing to work share and load balance.
- Replace our existing workflow solution as the source of work.

In the first fifteen months, through a staged delivery to 1,300 users across four sites we have already seen more than a 15 percent increase in work output and an associated reduction of 15 percent in operational costs, far exceeding previous projects in operational improvement. We have also benefited from improvements in quality, customer satisfaction, and customer response times providing us confidence to enhance and look to new opportunities in QPP and the OPUS platform.

These savings reduced our cost base allowing us to be more competitive and seek opportunities to gain market share. We are now further utilizing the OPUS technology to integrate with other new technology solutions such as our new letter production system to achieve further savings.

2. OVERVIEW

Over the last 18 months we aimed to make our business more competitive, reduce operating costs per policy, reduce complaint levels, increase customer satisfaction and develop a scalable and repeatable operational blueprint.

This was done through a three stage company-wide Operational Excellence strategy, creating a shared vision with common goals:

1. **Back to Basics:** putting Best Practise at the heart of our operation to improve customer experience, reduce customer timelines and deliver more for less.

2. **Model and Improve:** introducing a new workflow and process management technology; "OPUS" to more effectively track and manage workloads on an individual or team basis against expected measures.

3. **Integrate and Grow:** implement the model into future acquisitions.

Stage one of our strategies sought to deliver the philosophies of Operational Excellence through process development and changes to hearts and minds and included movement to next day processing, where the internal service levels are next working day, and a focus on *right first time*.

In order to progress to the second stage of our Operational Excellence strategy, Admin Re sought a provider that could deliver a workforce management solution consisting of workflow and process management.

A full tender process was undertaken resulting in the selection of Corporate Modelling as the provider who most understood our challenge and the most likely to enable our strategy and deliver against tight deadlines.

In just six months, the two organizations worked collaboratively to implement the first phase release to the first 100 customer service operators on a single site in Telford.

To achieve the required model and to achieve the necessary increases in productivity, utilization and throughput, we were keen to implement the process changes ahead of the technology delivery, to create a "soft landing" and to ensure the technology remained an enabler.

This focussed on delivery of:
- New roles and responsibilities where required.
- Performance measurements.
- Next-day processing.
- Strict FIFO work management controls.
- Daily team huddles to manage daily work position and achieve next-day processing.
- Daily staff "sit-by" to discuss prior day results.
- Checklists to ensure processing compliance.
- Team leaders focusing on QPP (Queue, People and Performance management).

The project itself was required to deliver technical support or delivery of the above plus:
- Resource utilization across all four sites.
- Routing of work to the right people with the right skills.
- Real time Management Information.
- Straight through processing.

Ownership and configuration of the system should be with the business and not with IT.

Delivery of each phase should be enabled within six months and should support future new business migrations.

3. BUSINESS CONTEXT

Admin Re UK is a specialist in the run-off of legacy closed life business portfolios with a proven track record in the administration of life, pensions and health business and the acquisition of entire life insurance companies. Our organization continues to grow through merger and acquisitions and strategic client and third party partnerships, underpinned by solid and efficient customer servicing at a low cost that is highly compliant and low risk.

It operates on three main UK sites and one offshore site, with 2,000 employees, including 1300 customer services staff who service approximately three and a half million policies for a number of major UK life assurers.

Prior to the delivery of the Operational Excellence strategy, we had a number of challenges creating additional cost within the organization and restricting our ability to deliver customer excellence such as:
- Work managed on four different sites without an ability to move work across these sites.
- Staff managed their own work queues resulting in "juggling" up to 150 work items at any given time, and the ability to "cherry pick" easy work.
- Difficulty in managing SLAs and the oldest item of work due to archaic Management Information.
- Working to agreed service levels of five days and ten days.

The Operational Excellence project was aimed to deliver a massive change for the organization in how we work on a daily basis. It was critical we designed an end to end development programme that covered all aspects of people, process and technology to achieve a positive customer experience at Admin Re.

The drivers behind Operational Excellence were:
- Creating a robust, cost effective model for existing customers, whilst also ensuring that this can be maintained for further acquisitions.
- Ensuring all administration is started the day after receipt, thereby reducing timelines for customers.
- Reducing, targeting and minimising the amount of rework being done in customer services, through process improvement and targeted up-skilling.
- Ensuring that customer enquiries are dealt with in date order in the most efficient way, regardless of complexity of the case.
- Real time MI capabilities to improve workload management, staff motivation and forecasting.
- Assessing staff skills and putting the right work with the right people with the right skills.

- Improving rates of customer resolution at first point of contact (e.g. through our contact centres).
- Identifying opportunities for continuous improvement.
- Enabling supporting functions to also be a part of the Operational Excellence initiative.
- Improving staff morale, retaining talent, and recognizing high performers.

4. THE KEY INNOVATIONS

Delivery of a Workflow and Process Management technology solution (OPUS) that supports the business in its delivery of Operational and Customer Excellence:

- Enabling the utilization of resources across all four sites, thereby maximising load balancing opportunities across all four sites.
- Next-day processing.
- Daily team and individual meetings, focusing on real time, team progress against incoming work, and individual assessment of productivity, utilization and time management.
- Implementation of quality controls including checklists to monitor and support process adherence and the "factory model".
- Introduction of "Get Next" to pull next oldest piece of work that an individual is skilled to complete thereby stopping cherry picking.
- Powerful MI suite to enable real time management, and visibility of work from receipt to response.
- Movement of queue management from staff to team leaders, moving accountability to appropriate level.

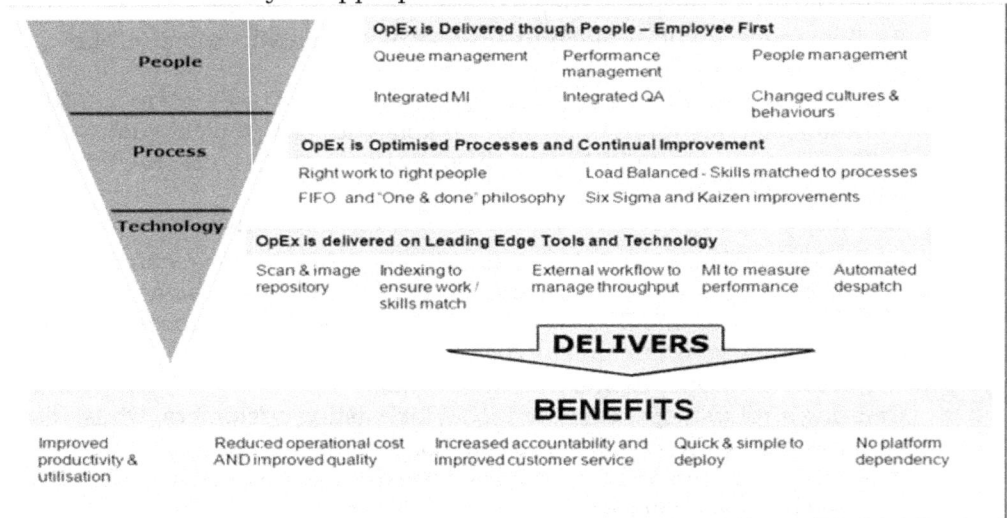

Figure 1 – OPUS overview: OPUS is about the people, the processes and the technology

4.1 Business

OPUS provided Admin Re with a new way to optimize its working practices, many of which were a legacy of manual processes, a plethora of product types and process steps that are abundant in the financial services. The project has enabled the organization to focus on factory model processing and to follow "best of breed" processes across its multiple books of business. The project has resulted in a huge demonstrable increase in productivity, utilization and throughput, resulting in increased service quality for our clients and their customers at a lower cost to ourselves.

The solution is user friendly and easy to understand. In addition, the business now has a common platform capturing key business metrics necessary for achieving its service level agreements internally, to the clients and to the regulatory bodies.

The OPUS platform delivered a multi-sited queue management capability, clear responsibility for task based processing, uniform metrics and clear benchmarking capabilities and is able to manage high-volume processing and continues to aid the elimination of inefficiencies and non-value add, costly activities.

Through data analysis, we are able to continually meet the changing regulatory and economic world, drive further enhancements and most importantly grow our business.

4.2 Process

The original Admin Re model was heavily built on an organizational tree structure, hindered by client centric processes and a dependency on key persons. Our underlying administration system workflow was based on the ability to "choose" cases to be processed from an ordered workflow queue and the user then being able to "own" this case through to completion. It did not consider prioritization, effort, resource or competence, and required line leadership to manually collate and distribute work types. The concepts of get next, one and done and no case ownership did not exist.

OPUS is intelligent and works in conjunction with our staff. It is built on the basis of FIFO (first in first out) processing requiring staff to select the next available piece of work. With the introduction of business rules as evidenced in the slide below, the work is ordered into queue based structures built and owned within the operation.

OPUS incorporates contractually agreed KPIs, skills and competencies of the person, product specifications and a host of other attributes. It actively uses this information when capturing a new work item to then push it to the workforce user who has skills to process the work. If for any reason they can't perform the work, they can refer the case to their superior or a specialist process team all managed by data setup.

The work is captured in queues and is grouped under owners who actively manage the clearance of their daily target. They are able to access all resource, managed capacity planning and update competence in real-time.

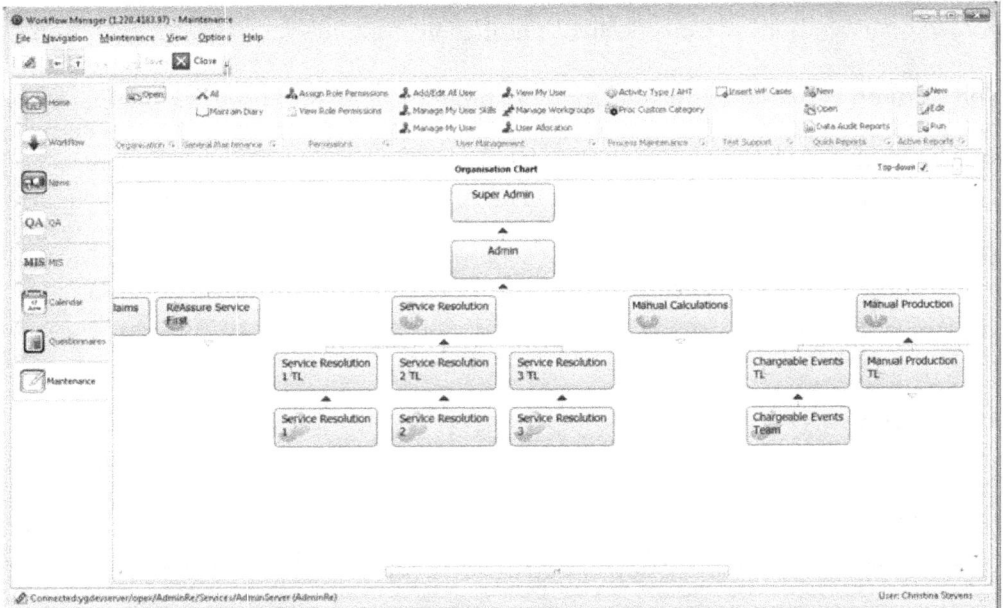

***Figure 2 - OPUS has data-driven filtering, ordering and
skill definition in its work allocation***

The organization is defined in an organizational chart painter and then the processes' and activities' ownerships are assigned to one or more organizational chart department(s). Similarly, roles and responsibilities are also painted and used to define permissions, reporting authority, MIS templates and many other features.

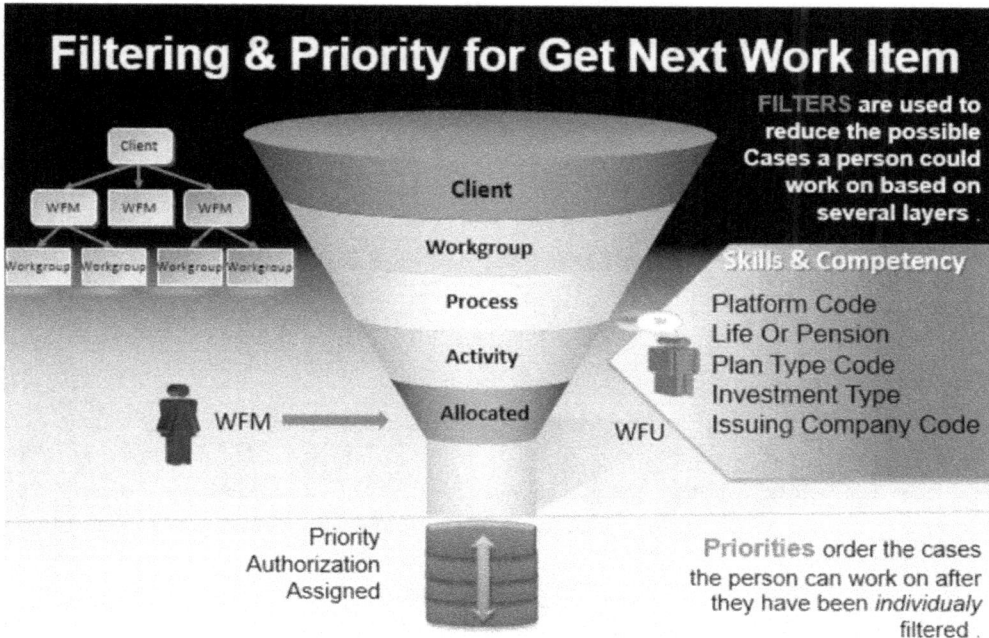

Figure 3 - OPUS allows users to paint their operational organization and process allocations as well as change these real-time through simple "drag and drop" functionality.

As stated above OPUS is based on a "*get next*" philosophy where the system knows what's best for the workforce user and what's best for the company. Team leaders can adjust priorities if needed, based on emerging business requirements as well as who has access to which queues of work associated with the process activity. This ensures the right work is allocated to the right person all the time.

Generally, the system works on a FIFO basis as this relates best to a queue driven process mentality. OPUS supports multiple role definitions, such as:

- WFU: a workforce user
- WFTL: a workforce team leader, who manages a team of WFUs
- WFM: a workforce manager who manages a team of WFTLs

All have real-time dashboards showing outstanding work, completed work and estimates for the resource required to complete the work governed by the prevailing service delivery model. Key business metrics include performance management reporting (average and actual handling times for an activity and class of case which are part of the continual improvement process), quality (right first time), straight-through processing and customer satisfaction. OPUS statistics are used as part of the business case for changes in underlying systems, processes and procedures.

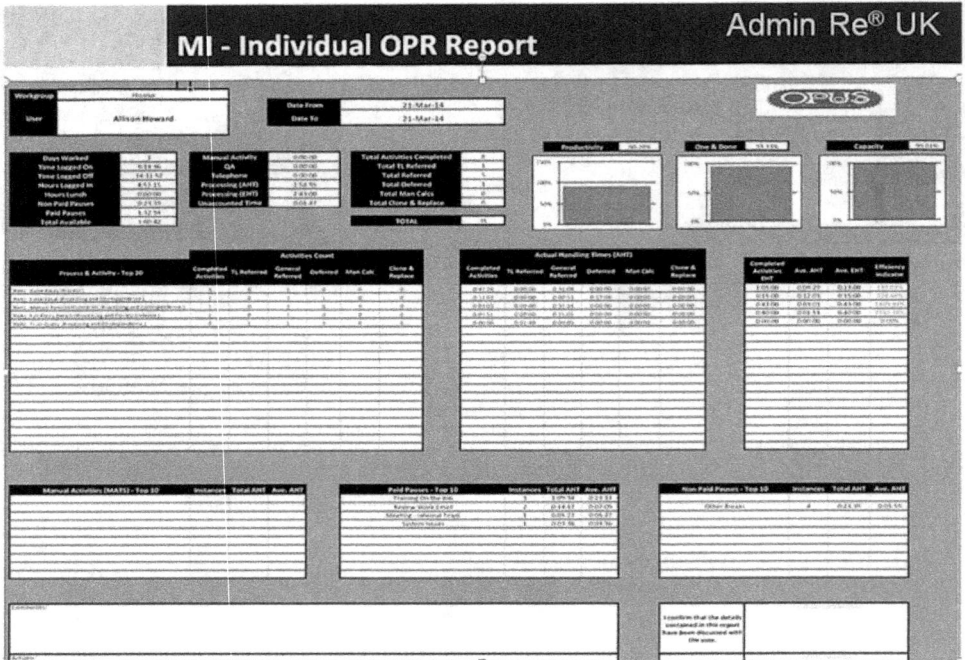

Figure 4 - OPUS has real-time sophisticated end-user reporting –
Individual performance report

Real time, individual, team and work reports enable the line manager to manage their Queues, People and Performance (QPP) throughout the day or for any specified period.

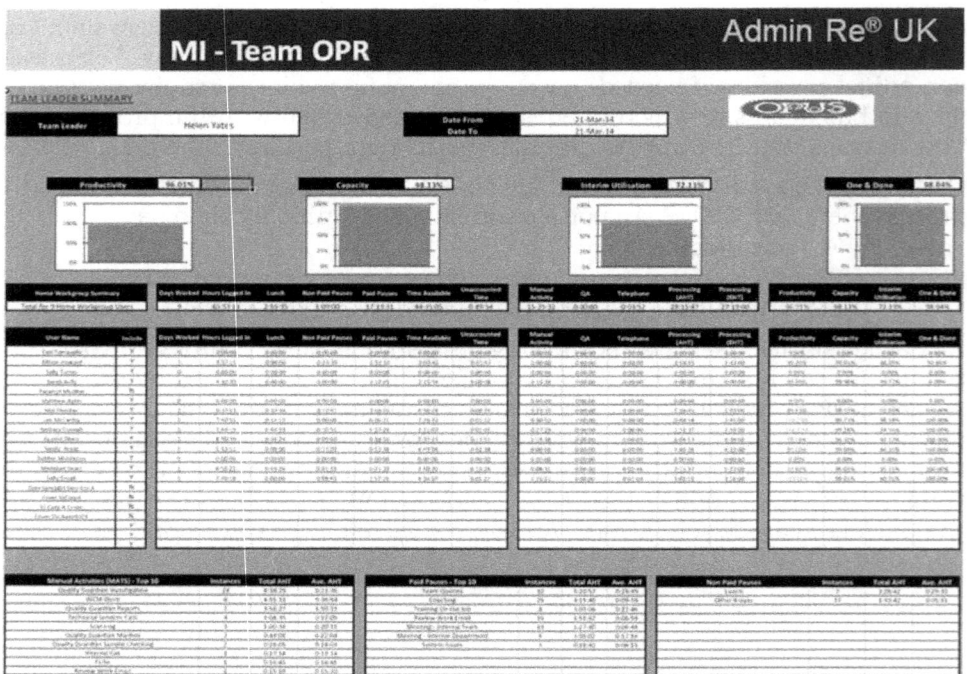

Figure 5 - OPUS has real-time sophisticated end-user reporting –
Team performance report

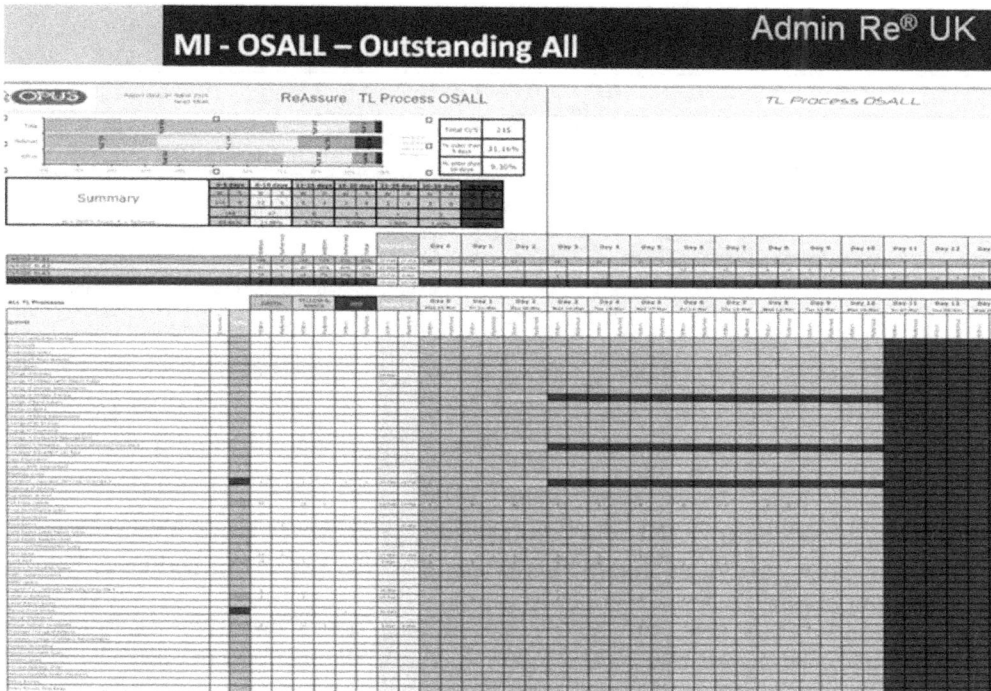

Figure 6 - OPUS has real-time sophisticated end-user reporting – Outstanding work

OPUS uses properties of the case payload as skill identifiers. In our case we hold:
- Relevant platforms (our back-end systems).
- Life or pension: a class of policy.
- Plan type: the type of policy.
- Investment type: how the insurance plan is dealing with assets.
- Issuing company: who issued the policy with the client group

These are held against the payload, as well as against the workforce users who need to be skilled and authorised in these as well as authorised for the process and activity.

Processes are developed with activity based steps to enable the delivery of an end-to-end model. The process is built within a BPM tool and loaded to OPUS. This was delivered to the business and was built with a clear understanding of procedural requirements, business interactions and all touch points.

BPMN

OPEX STP

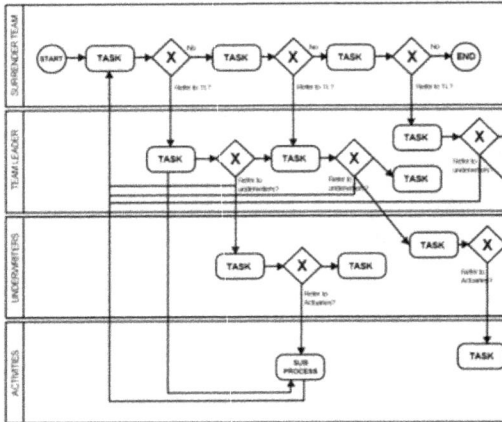

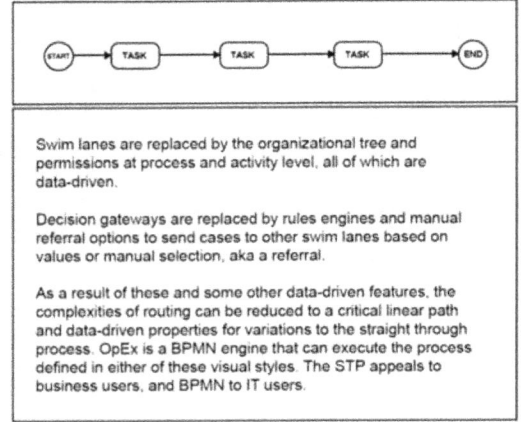

Swim lanes are replaced by the organizational tree and permissions at process and activity level, all of which are data-driven.

Decision gateways are replaced by rules engines and manual referral options to send cases to other swim lanes based on values or manual selection, aka a referral.

As a result of these and some other data-driven features, the complexities of routing can be reduced to a critical linear path and data-driven properties for variations to the straight through process. OpEx is a BPMN engine that can execute the process defined in either of these visual styles. The STP appeals to business users, and BPMN to IT users.

OPUS reports and dashboards are *user-aware* and adjust to show the information on the processes, activities and WFUs relevant to the individual's role. OPUS reports support multiple formats including:

- Calculation sheets: similar to a spreadsheet, these calculate using real-time data, driven by end-user defined parameters and formula.
- Quick reporting: end-user reporting wizard to extract key datasets for analysis.
- Advanced reporting: as above, but allows end-users to create traditional reports with headers, footers, charts etc.
- Charting: a set of manager or MIS charts that can be created into dashboards by the end-users or administrators.

4.3 Organization & Social

The Operational Excellence strategy is a three stage company-wide initiative to ensure a shared vision with common goals:

1. **Back to Basics:** putting best practise at the heart of our operation to improve customer experience, reduce customer timelines and deliver more for less.

2. **Model and Improve:** introducing a new workflow and process management technology; "OPUS" to more effectively track and manage workloads on an individual or team basis against expected measures.

3. **Integrate and Grow:** implement the model into future acquisitions.

This Operational Excellence initiative enveloped the entire organization, aiming to raise its performance and customer outcomes, and continually reduce its operating costs.

We designed an end to end development programme to up-skill and accredit our staff on the new system (OPUS), and the cultural aspects of operational excellence.

From representative level through to senior management, we led them through a massive cultural journey, resulting in a positive customer experience at Admin Re and an environment where people are measured, developed and lead much more proactively.

As part of our communication, training and engagement strategy, video messages from the CEO and project sponsor were recorded to:

- Set the context. Relay specific messages to the trainees on the company goals and the reasons for the change, and to communicate the progress the company has made so far.
- Top and tail each session showing the united approach from "the top down".

The learning solution ran continuously for the length of the initiative. This had the following results:
- The design of twelve new learning solutions; eight face to face sessions, two self-managed storylines, two videos.
- 100 percent accreditation of staff in time for OPUS being deployed to the business.
- 168 training sessions were delivered in nine months with 97 percent attendance rate.
- 1,459 staff were trained through face to face and self managed elements to their course, totalling 3,336 face to face training hours.

Results from staff training surveys further supported the project success
- How would you rate the quality of delivery of the course? - 94 percent gave a positive response.
- How would you rate the quality of content? - 89 percent gave a positive response.
- I understood the learning objectives for the session? - 99 percent confirmed yes.
- How would you rate the session overall? - 87 percent rated the session positively.

Results from staff opinion surveys also improved, following the OPUS delivery
- Do you have access to the tools you need to do your job? - increased by 13 percent.
- Does the training and development you receive help you effectively deliver in your role? - increased by six percent.

Operational Excellence and the OPUS system are seen as the beginning of the journey, and our people are fully engaged and equally committed to the organizations goals and success and additional improvement opportunities.

5. HURDLES OVERCOME

5.1 Management

Our key issue related to the high degree of change impacting our first line managers (team leaders). Much of the change depended on them understanding the new principles of Operational Excellence which were based upon the principles of QPP:
- Queue Management
- People Management
- Performance Management

Underpinned by a need for compliant control in a regulatory environment.

Using OPUS provided a different set of challenges from the way team leaders previously worked and it relied upon them pulling information daily to discuss their current work position, through daily huddles, with their line manager, to ensure they remained on target for next-day delivery, as well as having brief daily chats with staff in relation to their performance.

Additional training was provided to this special group to ensure Operational Excellence was fully understood, and this included not just training on system understanding, but included training in motivational delivery to ensure daily team huddles were inspirational.

All levels of operations management were given time to invest in the principles of our Operational Excellence model, and through new real-time information engaged staff each morning, held daily team huddles and shared regular targets and achievements. All management displayed the right behaviours, led by example and supported continued improvement in the operating model.

Operational Excellence and OPUS have enabled a shift from management to a leadership approach, based on taking ownership and having the right information to lead their people, and deliver high performance and to agreed targets.

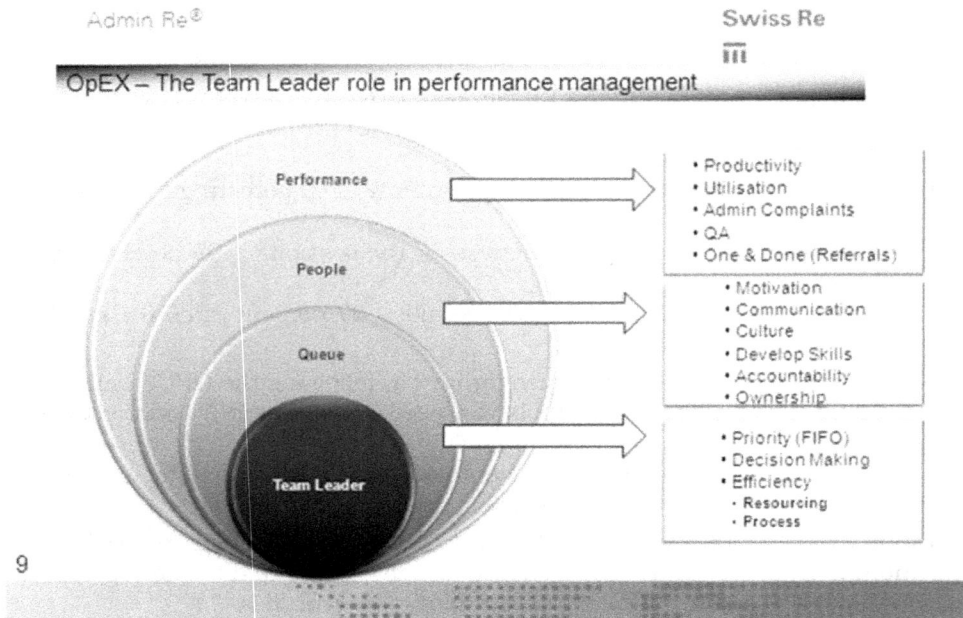

Fig 7 – Key activities underpinning QPP

5.2 Business

With a new CEO and executive management team driving the Operational Excellence strategy, the key area of challenge related to internal and "parent" sign off.

The workflow and process management solution was a key enabler of the delivery, and required significant investment in the technology and the associated costs of getting the business ready to receive a large change project.

Many support services including training worked full time on the project, and a separate "OPUS" team was set up to manage the transition into the organization.

A full tender process was also undertaken to ensure the right partner was selected to deliver the solution.

Corporate Modelling brought the perfect level of expertise, support and flexibility but this still required full governance to obtain sign off.

It is fair to say that despite the sign-off challenge, the first pilot delivery was delivered within five months of sign-off (July 2013) and complete role out has been achieved within fifteen months (May 2014) and has already gone some way to delivering the required benefits.

5.3 Organization Adoption

The OPUS project is recognised at Admin Re as a high profile project and top business success of 2013.

Operational Excellence, as a way of working, was adopted prior to the technology solution (OPUS) being implemented, thereby reducing the impact of the system implementation and instead producing an enabler to support it.

By going back to basics, all our processes have been reviewed to a detailed level, making any necessary changes to the process, and breaking it down to make the end to end process more efficient. Next day processing has been achieved through the motivation of teams to get to, and maintain this position for our customers. Both of these have resulted in the excellent service levels currently being experienced by our customers.

The effective transfer into business as usual and our induction programmes, ensured that this change was not only achieved but maintained. This target was met due to the extensive project planning which took place, development of a robust communications plan, continued consultancy and collaboration with the business.

The implementation of the OPUS system was phased, this minimised the impact to the customer, and allowed for staged improvements between phases. Following the training programme for each phase, full accreditation of staff took place within Model Office environments, which concentrated on scenario based accreditation.

Fully accredited staff were upskilled on the whole change picture, achieving their engagement. This was achieved in a few ways; firstly, the blended approach of the learning media and flexibility for them to take control of their own learning. Not only did they have access to the twelve learning solutions, they also had a robust communication plan and a replica database that could be used at any point to refresh knowledge or receive coaching. Floor walking support was also provided at each delivery to embed the learning, during and after implementation.

A pilot approach was undertaken, with three further deliveries over the fifteen month period, thereby reducing the impact to manageable levels, and ensuring an ability to learn from the prior release.

The initial pilot enabled us to get the technology infrastructure right at outset and have a solid base on which to build. "Learns" and improvement opportunities were canvassed throughout to fine-tune the following delivery.

6. BENEFITS

6.1 Cost Savings / Time Reductions

We have benefited from more than a 15 percent increase in the number of transactions processed per person (FTE). This has been a key enabler to delivering more for less.

The improved throughput of work together with an increase in *"right first time"* processing means fewer delays - a major source of customer dissatisfaction and complaints.

As a result of the Operational Excellence and introduction of OPUS, Admin Re has seen improved Treating Customers Fairly outcomes and levels, increased efficiency for customer contacts, with next-day processing being 99 percent achieved. This underlines our focus on customer service, whilst also meeting our regulatory objectives.

In addition to this there have also been the following attributable benefits:
- Breach volumes have reduced by 62 percent over the last two years
- Over the last year Admin Re achieved:
  - 53 percent reduction in complaint referrals for our third party business.
  - Satisfaction with complaint handling had risen to 98 percent.
- Between the end of 2012 and the end of 2013:
  - The propensity to contact has reduced by 11.7 percent, which we have attributed to the achievement of next-day processing and *right first time* cultural messages which our change programme has enacted.
  - The propensity to complain has reduced by 58 percent.
  - A six percent increase in customer satisfaction achieved.
  - Our call centre customer satisfaction score has consistently been over 95 percent for the whole of 2013/2014.
- In addition to this, Life and Pension complaints logged with the Financial Ombudsman Service by ReAssure Ltd customers fell by 23 percent between June 2013 and December 2013.

Consideration was also given to the customer impact of the development programme, with such a large proportion of the business being involved. The above improvements and benefits to customer service were gained and maintained whilst training was being delivered due to a flexible upskilling programme. 24 percent of all face to face training was done out of hours, minimising the impact to the customer service we provide, particularly in our front office department, as well as demonstrating the engagement of staff to attend training outside of their usual hours. Where training was done in hours, many staff still offered to do overtime to ensure service standard was maintained.

Within the first 12 months, we realized a progressive reduction in overall operating costs of around15 percent. These savings have enhanced our competitive standing and reputation allowing us to profile new opportunities to gain market share.

6.2 Increased Revenues

As a business process outsourcer in the closed book marketplace our revenue on existing contracts reduces over time. As such, our revenue has not directly increased as a consequence of OPUS; however, the cost reductions we have achieved have increased profitability and are now allowing us to compete more effectively for new business with market leading pricing models, which we could not have previously done without both the system and the metrics to back up the complex bid processes we undertake.

Our reduced costs and positive customer delivery both support and underpin our ability to land new deals; which, once migrated to our policy administration system, will also sit on the OPUS platform enabling us to identify improvement and efficiency opportunities.

6.3 Quality Improvements

OPUS is built to deliver quality assurance controls through various internal mechanisms. Peer review is developed and available to all required processes. It is dynamic within the linear model using competence and resource alignment to ensure correct allocation of work with no manual intervention.

We capture peer review volumes, effort and outcomes each available to engage root cause and process improvement initiatives, in addition to process and performance management.

Key improvements include:
- Reduction in rework.
- Improved learning and development plans for staff that meet business priorities.
- OPUS' trend analysis provides actual data for changed business cases.

Checklists have defined "pop-up" screens within each process and activity. These capture user-agreed activities and approvals necessary to drive straight through processing.

We have developed these further to ensure process adherence which support our factory model as well as accommodating procedural and audit controls.

G&S Change of Address ⊗

Have you checked:

	Yes	No
The policyholder address on the correspondence matches with Alpha?	⊙	○
If the PH has any other policies including any under another group by completing a DOB search?	⊙	○
The policy number matches the policyholder?	⊙	○
You are dealing with an authorised person? (Letter of authority relevant)	⊙	○
You have suitable authority from all policyholders? (Joint Life, Trustee/Assignee)	⊙	○
For any relevant warning flags/relevant WCM notes or policy notes? (What has gone on before)	⊙	○

Page 2 of 10

G&S Change of Address ⊗

If the request is for a Company/Trustee:

- ☑ a) Is there sufficient auth to change in line with procedures? (IFA authority is acceptable)
- ☑ b) Is the request on company headed paper?
- ☑ c) Does the request contain the necessary signatures?
- ☐ d) For PIM policies, have you logged a Trustee query where there is a named trustee at the recorded address?
- ☐ e) Updated the address at scheme level through group level?
- ☐ f) Address not in respect of a Company / Trustee.

Page 4 of 10

Fig 8 & 9 show checklists for Change of Address, built into OPUS

Key improvements include:
- Reduction in internal and external audit findings.
- Accountability enforcement.
- Improved learning opportunities.
- Less time to achieve staff competence on multi-platforms and products.

Independent Quality Assurance routes all activities to our internal quality system for open QA (captures right-first-time and potential customer detriment information), allowing in-process QA to be carried out efficiently.

Key improvements include:

- Ability to capture and analyse a customer's journey.
- Actions and outcomes traced and evidenced.
- Improved staff interaction with quality associates.
- Personal/unique staff development plans.
- Increased end to end handling times.

7. BEST PRACTICES, LEARNING POINTS AND PITFALLS

7.1 Best Practices and Learning Points

✓ *Ensure clear vision and goals are outlined, communicated and understood.*
✓ *Invest in the people.*
✓ *Keep processes linear and track any hand-offs.*
✓ *Deliver work to single business functions to ensure ownership of completion.*
✓ *Provide clear and measurable performance metrics.*
✓ *Show everyone real-time data.*
✓ *Use peer statistics to motivate laggards.*
✓ *Use real team leaders to manage the system and their people.*
✓ *Capture business re-engineering and improvement opportunities in the project and in the live environment.*
✓ *Allow the system to evolve as this is more likely to deliver the most effective and efficient outcome.*
✓ *Enable the business to own the solution and change it without the need for IT delivery.*

7.2 Pitfalls

✗ *Don't underestimate the size of the project.*
✗ *Consider the benefits of moving towards the final outcome in small steps – this relates to both the phasing of technology delivery and also the changing of culture and process prior to technological delivery.*
✗ *Consider the need for business readiness and how that can be practically managed.*
✗ *Ensure all requirements are fully specified and signed off.*
✗ *Don't use existing or pre-built MIS. Ensure business requirements are understood and develop accordingly.*

8. COMPETITIVE ADVANTAGES

Admin Re has created a dedicated UK-based service company to improve customer service, operational stability, regulatory compliance and cost efficiency. Buying a closed book not only involves taking in policies and assets; we are also inheriting the relationship with the seller's customers. Our business model is focused on keeping costs low, and equally recognising the critical importance of our obligations to be consistent and fair with policyholders.

By implementing the OPUS platform and the Operational Excellence culture into the operation we are able to focus on generating additional value to our customers, and creating a lower cost base to win new business, thereby creating a virtuous cycle of growth and value.

9. TECHNOLOGY

The technology used is an enhanced version of the Corporate Modelling Workforce Management solution OPX. This consists of full BPMN process modelling and deployment tool, a highly scalable workflow engine and an embedded rules engine.

The solution is built around Microsoft .NET web service technologies and uses SQL Server as the database. The system is deployed in Admin Re on Windows clusters running on VM Ware and also runs across Citrix to our offshore teams in India.

Two applications are used; one used by team leaders and administrators, and one used by our back and front office user teams (customer services). Both of these applications utilize numerous applets and menu items that are data driven and activated by role.

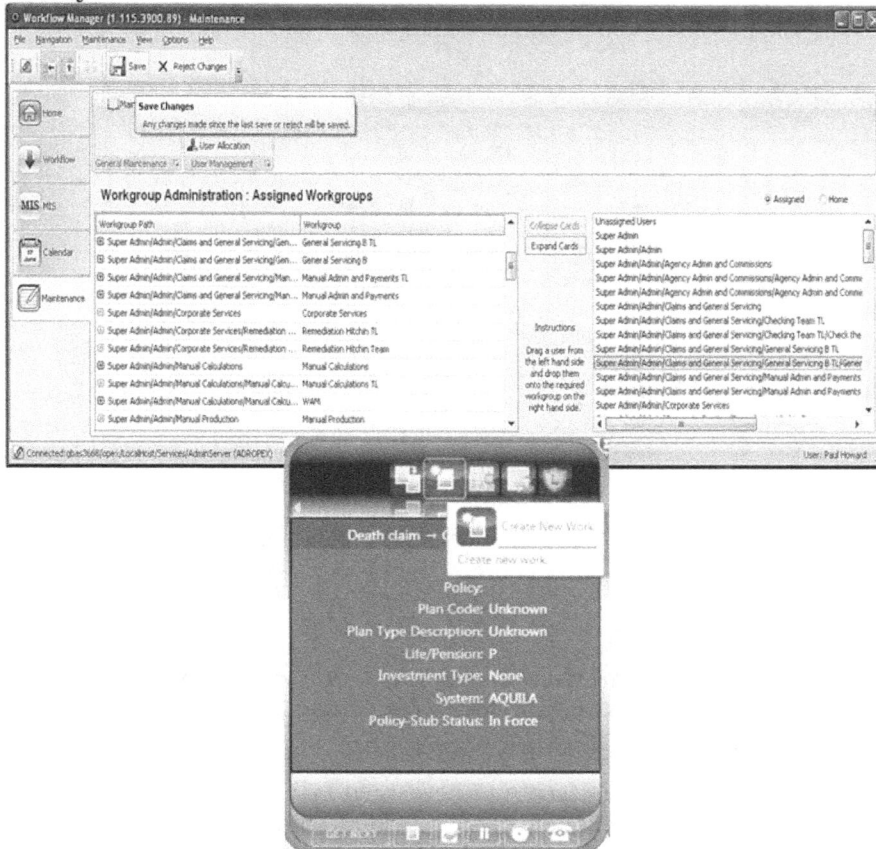

Figure 10 - an OPUS manager interface with quick reports and administrator with a work item

OPUS is used in tandem with our administration platform ALPHA. In essence, OPUS sits on top of ALPHA to provide the core workforce management functionality. Customer Service (CS) representatives use the OPUS tool to GET-NEXT, a piece of work that ensures the requirements of the organization structure, skill sets and FIFO are met. Once a piece of work is communicated to the CS representative via the OPUS tool, they then go to ALPHA to execute and complete the work on the policy administration system.

There is no policy administration work done in the OPUS product as there is limited information contained about policies and agents. The overall strategy is to manage and measure the sequencing of the work, allocation of the work and accurately record the amount of time it took to complete it, allowing for continual monitoring and real time scheduling to take place.

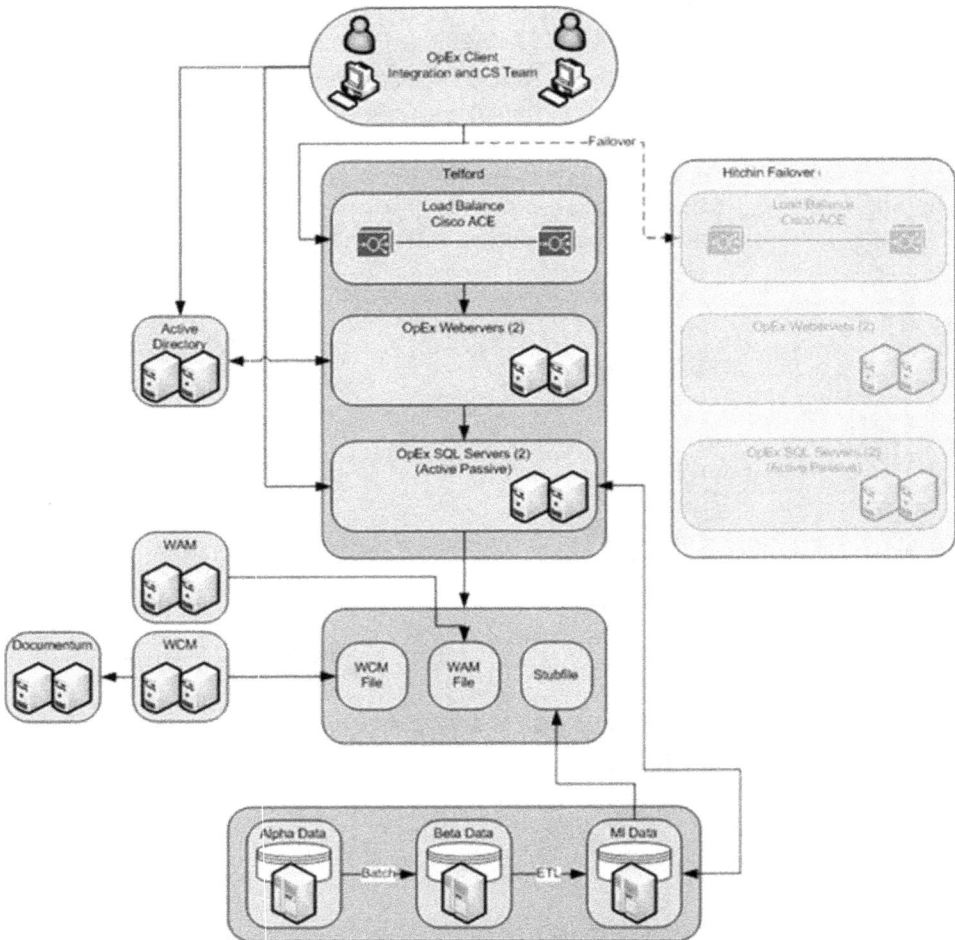

Fig 11 shows an Overview of the OPUS application and the interfaces for Phase 1

10. THE TECHNOLOGY AND SERVICE PROVIDERS

The OPUS technology was devised and developed by Corporate Modelling Services Ltd. HCL a previous customer of CMS provided some implementation services. However the vast majority of the implementation was carried out by Admin Re business staff, a key driver of the overall project.

AGESIC e-Notifications in the e-Government Agency, Uruguay

[Agencia para el Desarrollo del Gobierno de Gestión Electrónica y la Sociedad de la Información y del Conocimiento - AGESIC]

Nominated by INTEGRADOC, Uruguay

1. EXECUTIVE SUMMARY / ABSTRACT

This case study details the experience of transforming a costly paper-based, mostly manual process, to permit government entities to notify and communicate with citizens, into a highly automated, completely electronic system that achieves legal compliance. The scope of the system is extensive, with the system expected to reach every citizen, public *entity and private company in the country*.

The project was executed by the AGESIC, the Uruguayan Agency for the Development of Electronic Government and Information Society and Knowledge. This agency depends on the Uruguay Republic's Presidency, although it has technical autonomy.

The Electronic Communications and Notifications system is intended to eliminate paper in the communications between government and citizens. Every citizen, private company, and public entity will have one centralized electronic address ("inbox") to receive electronic communications and notifications over the Internet, with legal compliance, from all public entities. This replaces the need for people to visit government buildings to receive paper-based notifications or communications.

In 2013, INTEGRADOC was selected as the document-centric Business Process Management (BPM) suite to implement the system; the project began in April. The project team was required to address a strong restriction: every government entity has its own particular business processes (users, rules, flows, document types), but the citizen should have only one electronic address ("inbox"), in a single system that unifies all communications and notifications, regardless of their origin. The system would also need to scale to the entire country.

By the end of 2013, six government entities were digitally signing and sending electronic notifications and communications. In 2014, the plan continues to expand the system to other public bodies, with the long-term goal of eliminating paper in every communication and notification.

Key benefits are unifying received notifications and communications from diverse sources in one convenient location; reducing the risk of loss or delay when moving papers; reducing paper-related costs; reducing environmental footprint; and achieving the ability to meet the particular needs of each notifier, thereby facilitating adoption of the system.

2. Overview

This case study details the experience of transforming a costly paper-based, mostly manual process to permit government entities to notify and communicate with citizens, into a highly automated, completely electronic system that achieves legal compliance. The scope of the system is extensive, with the system expected to reach every citizen, public entity and private company in the country.

AGESIC is the Uruguayan Agency for the Development of Electronic Government and Information Society and Knowledge. This agency depends on the Uruguay Republic's Presidency, although it has technical autonomy. It aims to ensure improved services to citizens through the use of information and communications technologies.

In 2012, AGESIC decided to implement an Electronic Communications and Notifications system (which will hereafter be referred to as "e-Notifications"), to eliminate paper in communications between government and citizens. The project requires that every citizen, every private company, and every public entity will have a single centralized inbox to receive electronic communications and notifications over the Internet from all public entities, with legal compliance. This replaces the need for people to visit notifier building to receive paper-based communications. Uruguay was the first country to implement the One Laptop Per Child plan (Plan Ceibal), ensuring that the majority of the population has access to a computer and the Internet. This broad-based access to technology is essential for the e-Notifications system to reach the entire population as planned.

In 2013, INTEGRADOC was selected as the document-centric Business Process Management (BPM) platform to implement the e-Notifications system. The project began in April.

There were some major challenges: every government entity has its own business process for notifications and communications (their users, business rules, document types, and so on), but all of this must be transparent for the recipient, who should have a single electronic address (also called "inbox"), in a single system, unifying communications and notifications from diverse origins. Another major challenge was that the system should scale to the whole country, with a 99.99 percent guaranteed uptime.

Forming the project team was also a challenge. We established an interdisciplinary team that included process analysts, legal staff, trainers, organizational change experts, programmers and software architects. In each subunit of team members, it was necessary to add staff to address several needs.

The system was implemented in 2013. By the end of the year, six government entities were digitally signing and sending electronic notifications and communications. Citizens began to receive them at home or at work, without being required to visit government buildings as they had one year before. In 2014, the plan continues to expand the system to other public bodies, with the long-term goal of eliminating paper in every communication and notification.

The key benefits are:

- Unifying in a single point all received notifications and communications, regardless of their origin.
- Communicating easily and securely, without risk of paper loss or delay
- Reducing the cost associated with paper use (printers, supplies) and requirements for people to travel to visit government buildings.

- Reducing the environmental footprint by minimizing CO2 emissions due to absence of physical transfer of paper and people, as well as the energy needed to print and store papers.
- Accomplishing specific processes for each governmental notifier, with a graphical tool to rapidly define these flows, which is fundamental to gaining support and achieving widespread system adoption.

3. BUSINESS CONTEXT

Until now, whenever any public entity communicated with or notified a citizen, private company or another public entity, it was necessary that a person on behalf of the notified would visit the notifier building, to read and take action on this notification.

The e-Notifications system is part of the Digital Agenda of the country of Uruguay. "We are in a position to make life easier to people, let's do it. There have been many advances. The greater effectiveness and efficiency has to have concrete results," asserted Jose Clastornik, CEO of AGESIC, when presenting the new regulation for e-Government. He added, regarding the new e-Notification system: "This is a citizen-centered logic. We want a unique mechanism that allows the citizen to centralize all their electronic communications."[1]

In this context, the e-Notifications project was launched in 2013, as a key objective of the Uruguay Digital Agenda[2] for 2011-2015, with its own domain and web site: www.notificaciones.gub.uy.

e-notificaciones
Sistema de Notificaciones
y Comunicaciones Electrónicas

Illustration 1: e-Notifications logo, using the colors of the Uruguayan flag.

4. THE KEY INNOVATIONS

4.1 Business - One system fits all needs

As shown in Illustration 2, the new system integrates the following components:

- Notifiers: public entities that produce communications and notifications using their own particular workflows to elaborate and approve every document before it is sent to the recipient.
- Recipients of these documents: citizens, private companies, or other public entities. They receive the electronic documents in their "inbox", where they acknowledge the reception.

---

[1] [http://www.agesic.gub.uy/innovaportal/v/2842/1/agesic/un_tramite:_se_presento_nuevo_marco_normativo_de_gobierno_electronico.html?menuderecho=13]

[2] http://www.agesic.gub.uy/innovaportal/v/1443/1/agesic/mapa_de_ruta:_agenda_digital_uruguay_2011-2015.html?menuderecho=11

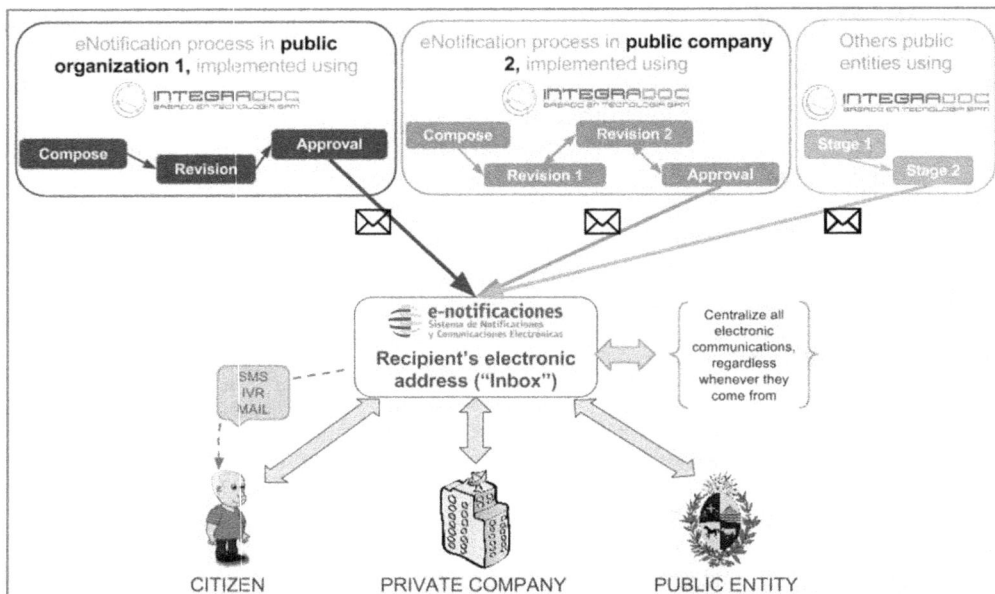

Illustration 2: Business context of the e-Notification process, including notifiers and recipients.

Please note that each notifier entity has its own particular communication process. It was very important to recognize and accept that each entity had its own work-flows, to avoid forcing the use of one system for all processes, in order to support adoption. This ability to accommodate multiple agencies was possible due to the use of a flexible BPM suite, and would have been impossible to implement by hard-coding the system.

It is relevant to note that independent of where the documentation originates, the recipient accesses only one personal electronic address ("inbox"). This is central to the intended government agency strategy of facilitating the relationship of users interacting with public entities.

4.2 Process

The e-Notifications process is not very complex, but it has several temporal con-straints and communicates with other systems using Web Services. It is also im-portant to note that different entities may have different flows, so in Illustration 3 we present the standard process, which is adjusted to the particular requirements of each entity.

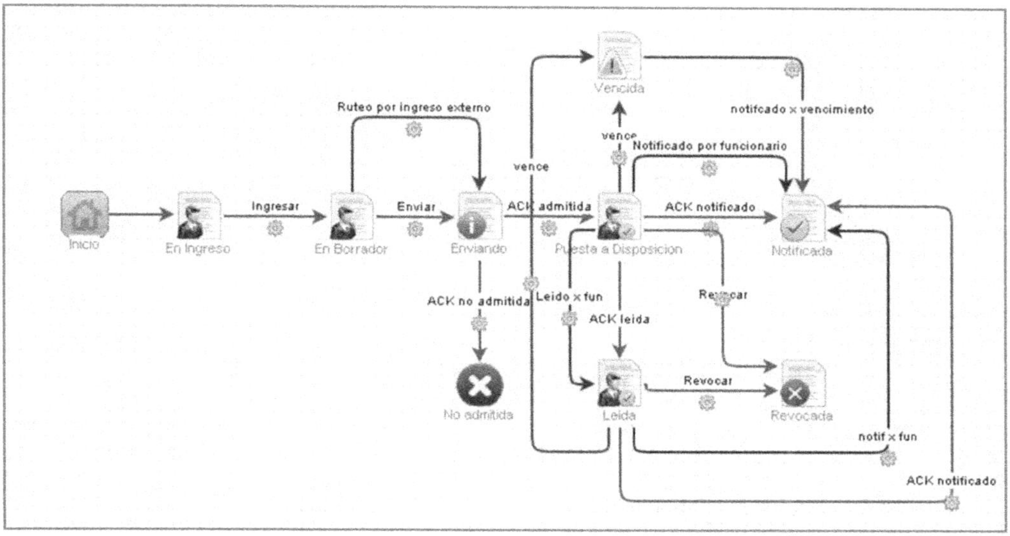

Illustration 3: Standard notification process including "compose", "approve" and final states.

The process has a basic set of main states:

- Composing the communication or notification ("En Ingreso", "En Borrador")
- Approving the communication or notification ("Enviando") to be sent to the recipient
- Sending the communication to the recipient inbox and waiting for him to read it ("Puesta a Disposición")
- Assessing the permitted terminal states: Read ("Leída"), Notified ("Notificada"), Revoked ("Revocada"), Expired ("Vencida")

Please note that there are several time constraints that could cause the process instance (i.e. the communication or notification) to move between the stages without a user interaction. This characteristic is useful to facilitate the law behind the electronic notifications: for example, if the recipient does not open the notification, the user is nevertheless considered to have been notified after a few days have elapsed.

When composing, the user can write the communication or notification in the system as shown in Illustration 4, or attach a file containing the information. Before sending the document to the recipient, it must be digitally signed using their own certificate and an applet provided by AGESIC (developed to support digital signatures in any e-Government application). This applet was integrated into the system.

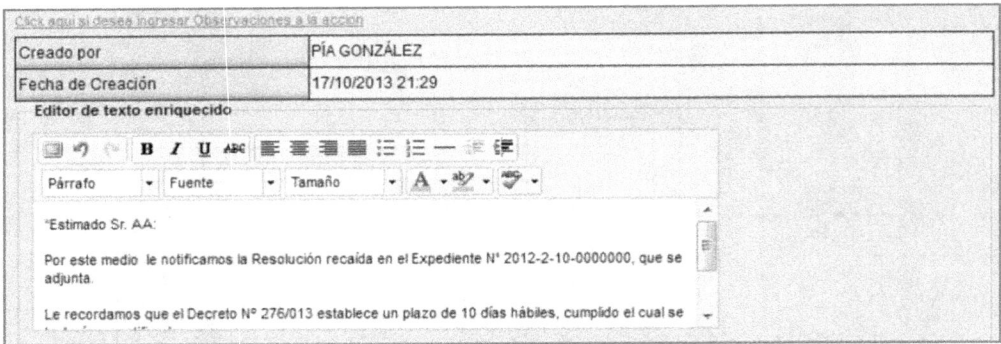

Illustration 4: Writing the communication or notification.

Once the communication or notification has been sent, the recipient can access the system through the Uruguayan government portal, as shown in Illustration 5.

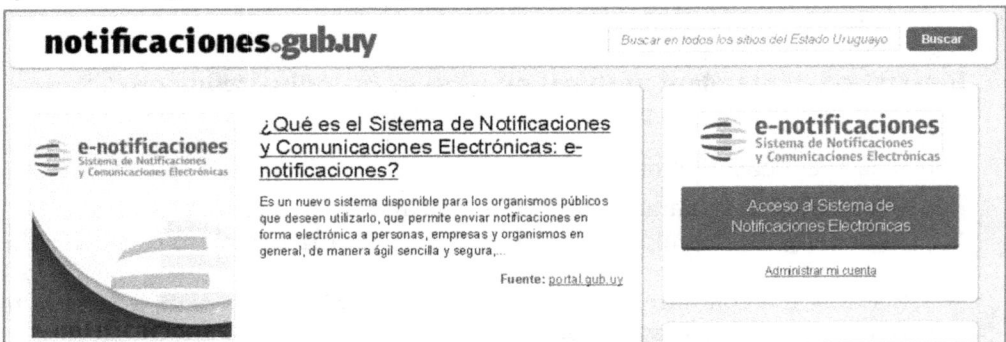

Illustration 5: e-Notifications portal at the government website.

At this point, another challenge was faced. The recipient (a citizen, private company, or any public entity), has a user account for the e-Government portal (not the e-Notifications system), so we were required to integrate with the government Centralized Access Control System, in order to minimize requirements for users' time and effort.

When the recipients access the system, they view an inbox called "My Notifications," and another called "My Communications," both featuring an interface similar to any standard e-mail application, which was designed to maximize usability.

When the user accesses a communication or notification, information is displayed about the sender, the subject, and the information communicated, in a digital signed PDF as shown in Illustration 6. If it is available, the system also displays the receipt of the message (or "Acknowledge").

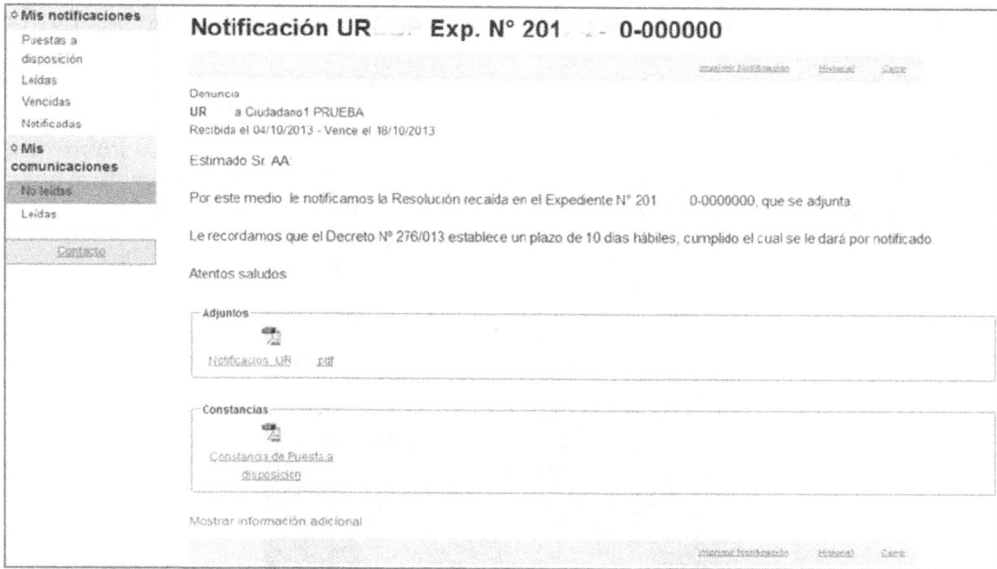

Illustration 6: An electronic notification accessed by the recipient.

The process could have different flows, depending on user actions or time constraints. Every step has associated deadlines, so the process instances could move without user interaction.

4.3 Accessibility & Usability

Given that the system is available to every citizen in the country, it has to be very easy to use. A usability expert team defined the system interface and several tests were run, providing a solid, clear, standard-based user interface.

Accessibility is defined as a set of properties built into the system, enabling it to be usable by people within the widest range of abilities and circumstances. For example, blind people should be able to use the e-Notification system. The system was designed and tested to comply with Web Content Accessibility Guidelines (WCAG) version 2.0.

4.4 Entity & Social

A Center of Excellence was formed with the aim of:

- Minimizing the impact of the notifiers and managing the changes in how these entities do their work. Notifiers are closed groups: they consist of only the people within the entity that notifies.
- Maximizing adoption of the system by recipients (citizens, private companies, and public entities). Recipients are an open group: it includes any citizen in the country.

The team involved:

- Experts in organizational change management
- Experts in communications, both inside the entity and with the general public
- Trainers for the personnel of the notifier entities, for the Help Desk team, and for the Operations and Administration teams

- e-Learning experts, who designed the videos, manuals and courses for the recipients
- Process Analysts, who understood the particular needs of each entity and configured the process accordingly

Illustration 7 displays the focal poster of the project, which was used to inform the public about the new system and its core benefits. The poster reads: "An agile, simple and secure way to send electronic communications and notifications."

Illustration 7: Focal poster to communicate the new e-Notifications system and its core benefits.

One important component that facilitates system adoption on the recipient side is the ease of access to a computer and Internet in our country. Uruguay was the first country to implement the One Laptop Per Child plan ("Plan Ceibal"), and accordingly, the majority of the population has access to a computer and the Internet. This is essential to reach the entire population, as the new communication system requires.

5. HURDLES OVERCOME

As a system designed to be used across an entire country and potentially by every citizen, the e-Notifications system presented several challenges that the team had to overcome.

5.1 Management

There were several managers, and we needed them to work in a coordinated and cohesive manner. The management team included a project manager selected by AGESIC, as well as a project manager hired by the contracted firm. Both of them used a formal methodology for project management based on the Project Management Body of Knowledge of the Project Management Institute (PMI).

Inside AGESIC, there were several specialized teams (including communications, organizational change management, etc.), each of them having their own managers. And inside the contracted firm, sub-managers for each team also participated. Moreover, in each public entity implementing the system, there was a person responsible for its success.

The strategy to deal with this complex reality was first to obtain high-level commitment of the authorities of each entity (AGESIC, contractors, and notifier entities).

Common objectives were defined to the team (and not particular to each sub-team). Project success was defined as an "all or nothing" objective, in order to eliminate divisions and create a cohesive team.

Several team-building activities were developed, such as alternating meetings between the locations of each team, thus deepening the members' familiarity with each other.

Finally, we adopted a dispute resolution mechanism based on the principle that the team always acted with good will for the success of the project.

5.2 Legal and regulatory

The legal framework had to be adapted to support the legal validity of the new system and, in particular, to give electronic notifications the same validity as paper-based notifications. The lawyers, with the support of involved authorities, did a commendable job to achieve this change without delaying the project timeline.

5.3 Entity Adoption

There were three main aspects regarding the adoption of the system by the notifiers:

1. The validity of the new system when sending relevant information to the recipient, and avoiding their refusal of such electronic notification. The team had to demonstrate that the legal framework was suitable and sufficient for a diverse range of notifications and communications.
2. The particularities of the workflow in each entity. The team had to slightly adapt to the business process to attend to specific needs, and not force compliance using a process that does not perfectly fit each entity's needs.
3. Training several different roles in each notifier entity: the notifiers themselves, the help desk team, the administrative staff, etc.

In addition to these considerations, a gradual strategy was adopted, beginning with controlled implementations with a small number of recipients, and then scaling to larger numbers of users.

6. BENEFITS

5.3 Quality Improvements

The main objective in this project was to simplify and facilitate the communication between citizens and public entities, in order to achieve one of the goals of the national digital agenda.

In this context, unifying in a single point all received notifications and communications regardless of their origin, is a great benefit for every citizen, private company, and public entity.

The security of the electronic process is another relevant point, given that it is less vulnerable than the paper-based process, without risk of paper loss or delay.

Reducing the environmental footprint is another benefit, minimizing emissions related to the physical transfer of paper and people, and the energy needed to print and store papers. In a five year span, it is estimated that we will avoid printing 150 million sheets, which entails preventing the emission of 200 tons of CO_2, and saving one million liters of water and 1,000 trees[3].

5.4 Cost Savings / Time Reductions

Using the new system permits a significant cut in the costs of communications:

- There is no need to use paper printouts.
  - o In a five-year span, we will have approximately 30 public entities using the system, saving an estimated one million sheets per public entity per year.
  - o This will prevent printing approximately 150 million sheets in this timeframe, saving about US$ 15 million[4].
  - o This saving should increase in subsequent years, as the system continues to be adopted by other public entities.
- There is no need to move papers and people.
  - o In the five-year window, we will avoid 150 million personal trips (by bus, car, and so on), with the subsequent savings in time, energy and emissions.

7. BEST PRACTICES, LEARNING POINTS AND PITFALLS

7.1 Best Practices and Learning Points

✓ *Authorities' explicit support and participation to overcome challenges.*
✓ *Several teams collaborated thus creating one large team. Success is achieved by the whole team.*
✓ *Gradual strategy, starting with public entities having a small number of recipients in a controlled scenario.*
✓ *Use a document-centric BPMS suite to facilitate the mapping between paper-based notifications and electronic notifications.*
✓ *Adapt the process to each public body, attending to their individual needs to gain approval and adoption.*

7.2 Pitfalls

✗ *Avoid postponing the integration of external systems; try to achieve integration at the very beginning to mitigate risks.*
✗ *Avoid postponing legal issues; prioritize these issues at the very beginning due to the time usually required to solve them being much more extensive than with IT issues.*

8. COMPETITIVE ADVANTAGES

This system is being pioneered in Uruguay and Latin America, unique in its characteristic of being a single integrated system for the entire government and all citizens. Technologies and methodologies used in this project have been refined to the point that it is now possible to add one public entity in less than a month.

---

[3] Using widely-accepted formulas for paper production.
[4] We use the standard and widely-accepted cost of US$0.10 per page.

This project is replicable in other countries, especially in Latin America, where governments are engaged with e-Government initiatives.

9. Technology

Given the documental nature of the process, a document-centric BPMS suite was preferred in the open and competitive procurement process. INTEGRADOC was the selected BPM suite, mainly because it is specialized for document-based business processes, including a powerful Document Management System (DMS) that integrates transparently with the automated business processes. The company also has extensive experience with automating business processes in government.

The selected BPM tool is coded in Java/JEE running over open source software (Linux + JBoss + PosgreSQL). The administration tool, process designer and web client are all web applications that could run on Linux. These characteristics were important to comply with governmental guidelines about IT infrastructures.

The system is highly stable and scalable, both essential requirements for the solution. It has been installed in one of the main data centers in the country, with fault tolerance and a strong security policy.

The new system had to integrate with several other existing systems: Centralized Access Control System, e-Mail servers, the applet for electronic signatures, etc.. Standard technologies (i.e Web Services) and protocols (i.e SMTP) were used to integrate these diverse systems.

10. The Technology and Service Providers

The Uruguayan government contracted a firm to implement the project. This company, INTEGRADOC, is the same company that develops the BPM suite, also named INTEGRADOC (www.integradoc.com).

INTEGRADOC is an innovative document management system, allowing the modeling of document-based business processes, automating and analyzing them for improvement. It manages electronic documents and their associated workflows and electronic transactions, integrating documents, people and processes, increasing the efficiency of the organization under the paradigm of Business Process Management (BPM).

The company has implemented its product in several countries in South and Central America (Uruguay, Panamá, Chile, Peru and Colombia, among others), being the leader in its country in this field. In 2010, INTEGRADOC received the Uruguayan National Award for Innovation, a very important recognition by the National Research and Innovation Agency (ANII). In 2012, the Uruguayan National Development Corporation won the National Transparency Prize using INTEGRADOC. And in 2013, INTEGRADOC received the "Environmental special mention for the development of an innovative document management product aimed at reducing the use of paper," granted by the Uruguayan Ministry of Housing, Planning and Environment (MVOTMA).

AgFirst Farm Credit Bank, USA
Nominated by Bizagi, United Kingdom

1. Executive Summary / Abstract

AgFirst is part of the national Farm Credit System, the largest agricultural lending organization in the United States. With assets of more than $27 billion, AgFirst provides funding and financial services to 19 farmer-owned financial cooperatives in 15 eastern states and Puerto Rico. These cooperatives, operating as Farm Credit and AgCredit agricultural credit associations (ACAs), offer real estate and production financing to more than 80,000 farmers, agribusinesses and rural homeowners.

Every Association has independent governing processes and business rules, based on its respective product portfolio. So while much of the processes are similar, there are key differences in the data they collect, and the rules they follow.

As the premier technology service provider for its affiliate Associations, the AgFirst technology division is often tasked with developing custom solutions to automate key business processes. Historically, the Microsoft InfoPath platform has been used to develop these solutions. Examples of these solutions include:

- Loan transmittal
- Loan treatments
- Loan accounting
- Task management and tickler systems

However, in 2012, it was apparent that the InfoPath platform was no longer sufficient to handle the growing complexity of business processes. Additionally AgFirst's challenge was not to build 19 different systems, but to deliver a solution based on the core business logic that could be quickly adapted to the needs of other Associations.

As a result, AgFirst launched an effort to select an enterprise class platform to replace its legacy InfoPath solutions. After an in-depth selection process, that included onsite proof-of-concepts, AgFirst chose a BPM solution. BPMS delivered on this challenge, transforming AgFirst's loan approval process in just 16 weeks. AgFirst's impressive commitment to agile working methods enabled the project to progress quickly and get results fast, delivering subsequent processes in half the time.

Whether making changes to the process flow or simply to the user interface, the ability to start small, scale fast and adapt quickly has been key to the success of the overall project. The move to BPM has transformed how the Loan Transmittal process is handled. AgFirst can now handle more loans, more accurately, whether it is from their desktop or from their mobile devices. Embedded business rules, tight integration and centralized documentation ensure that the process is regulated and streamlined. And for the first time, ACA management has the baseline metrics they need to monitor, measure and improve performance. In short, AgFirst has been able to use the BPM tool to create solutions quickly and be agile enough to customize it for their customers.

2. Overview

"Our decision to choose BPM was a strategic move to deliver agility within changing market conditions. Above all we wanted to be able to create solutions in a short amount of time. "

Bala Sivankoil, Director of Application Development

In just 16 weeks, AgFirst defined, implemented and delivered a complete Loan Transmittal process. Careful selection of the pilot project has enabled the bank to deliver value and achieve benefits fast. Second processes were delivered in half the time, and subsequent processes in a matter of weeks. Processes are consistent and streamlined: double keying of data has been reduced considerably, Key Performance Indicators (KPIs) are embedded, and a full scale rollout is under way.

This is backed by impressive dedication and strong sponsorship from AgFirst's key stakeholders. Together, its staff, management and Project Team have steered its BPM initiative through large change in record time and overcome significant cultural challenges. Now, BPM is seen as a powerful way to automate business processes.

3. BUSINESS CONTEXT

As the technology service provider for 19 different, but similar Associations, a key opportunity for AgFirst is to be able to share and reuse business solutions. For example, if an appraisal request program was created for one Association, it was very important to show others how the solution worked and to be able to quickly copy and modify the solution to meet the unique business needs of other Associations.

However, it was very challenging to share and reuse best practices when developing business solutions. For example, a solution that automated the loan transmittal for loan officers and processors would require a great deal of business logic coded in InfoPath forms. In order to share these business processes, a manual effort was required to document them using Microsoft Visio. This created two significant challenges:

1. It was difficult to ensure that the Visio document accurately reflected how the code actually worked.
2. It was a completely manual effort to reuse a business solution. This would require the developer to copy and paste code.

These challenges posed by the underlying technical platform were hampering AgFirst's ability to add value by sharing and reusing business solutions across its District Associations. Furthermore, AgFirst was unable to deliver these legacy solutions on mobile devices.

4. THE KEY INNOVATIONS

4.1 Business

BPM has "changed the game" for the AgFirst services teams. Key innovations the platform has delivered include:

- **Improved business partner engagement.** Using the BPM modeler, solution architects can collaborate with business users to design intuitive process models. These models have two significant benefits. First, they form the basis of a "self-documenting" system. The process model (the documentation) is what actually drives the system. Second, these models can easily be shared and reused when doing similar solutions for other District Associations (see figures a and b).
- **Rapid application development.** Using the BPM development tools, complex solutions can be delivered in weeks.
- **State of the art integration platform**. Since BPM tool is built on a Service Oriented Architecture, AgFirst has been able to integrate it with other back office solutions (see figure c).

- **Mobile device access.** The BPM platform features a responsive design and solutions can be delivered on mobile platforms (see figures d and e).

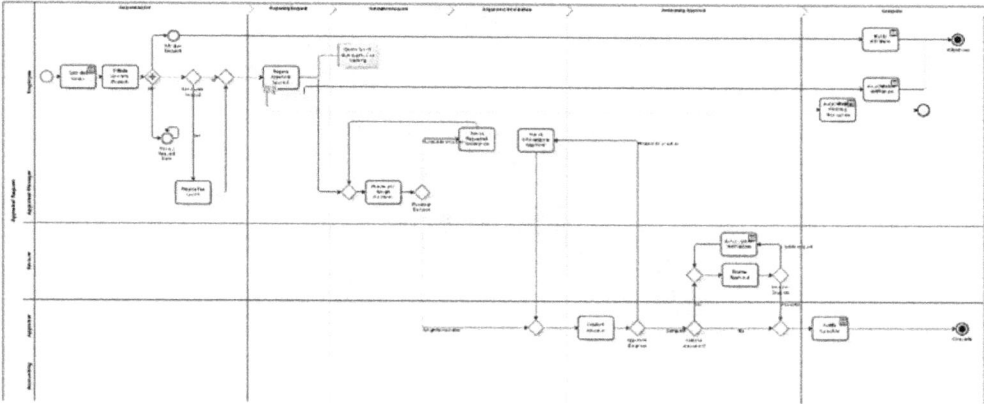

Figure a – Loan Transmittal Process

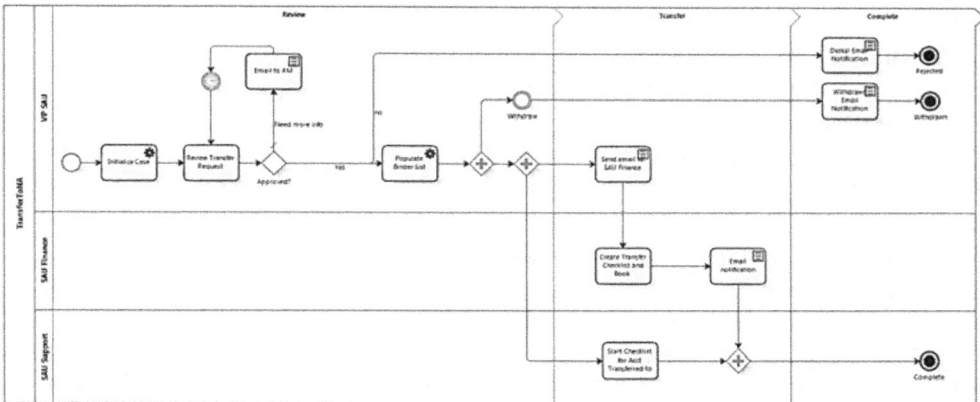

Figure b – Special Assets Management Process

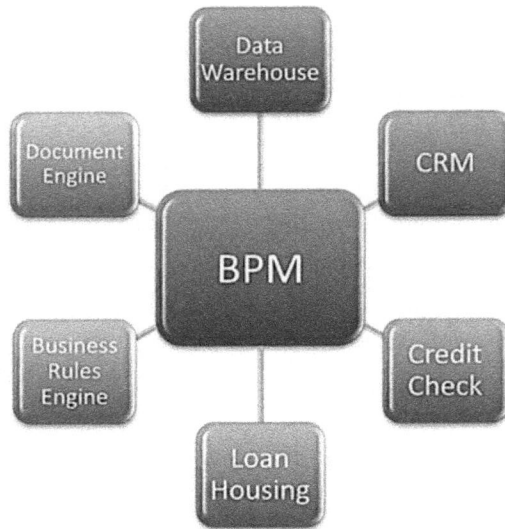

Figure c – BPM Integration with other backend systems

Other innovations that the BPM platform has delivered include:

Adaptable process model: The ability to make changes, even late in the process development, has been key to user acceptance.

"Midway through the project, our customers came to us with suggestions to change the user interface substantially. In any other system we've used, the answer would've been a definite "no way". But our solution allows us to make these changes quickly and cost-effectively."

Bala Sivankoil, Director of Application Development

Ability to add more processes quickly: the system's adaptability and reuse capabilities has enabled AgFirst to create new processes and roll them out fast. AgFirst added Assets Management, Loan Insurance Tracking and Asset Value estimation processes within the first eight weeks of implementing Loan Origination.

Mobile solution: Enabling Loan Analysts to review and approve loan applications on the move has removed bottlenecks within the approval chain. AgFirst's 75 users can now start to work more productively around the clock no matter where they are located.

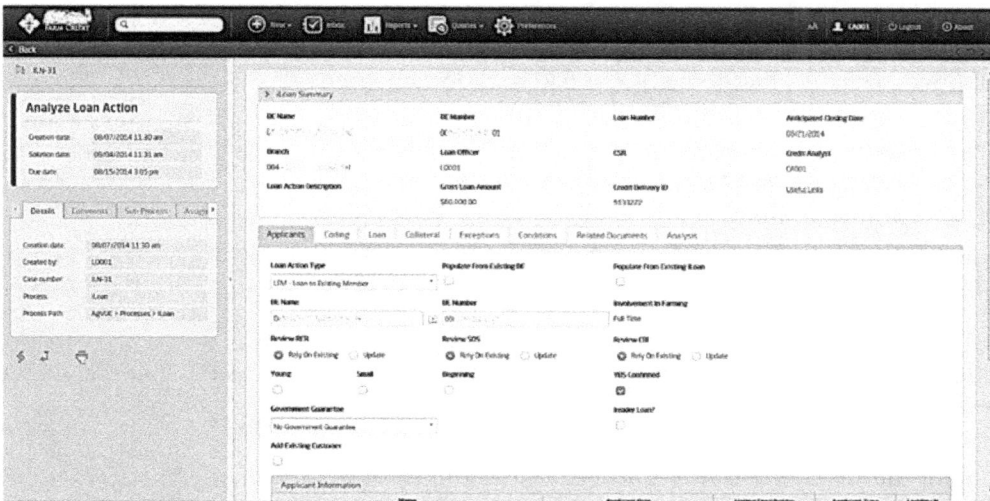

Figure d - Loan Transmittal Application using BPM Tool

4.2 Case Handling

AgFirst asked the vendor to deliver a full working Proof of Concept, which they did in one week. The next step was to define the case template. Five key stakeholders from different business roles at the ACA came together in a process workshop where process owners were appointed to manage the requirements gathering and process design.

4.3 Organization & Social

AgFirst's ACA loan officers and analysts had no previous exposure to application development using BPM tools. However, the vendor's free process modeler was critical as a medium of communication between them and the developers. Their input into the business process model and seeing it come alive in the modeler were important factors in getting their buy-in.

"The important thing for our users is that they now have everything in one place and benefit from looking at the same version of the truth."

BPM has had a positive impact at management level too. *"Committee Members are now notified when their sign off is needed and can now sign off Loan Approvals remotely either using a desktop or through their mobile devices – this gives them tremendous flexibility. And with more tech-savvy employees and customers, mobility is now a must to stay competitive."*

Bala Sivankoil, Director of Application Development

User and business acceptance has put in place the foundation for an IT Center of Excellence combining a mix of internal and outsourced staff. The vendor's training services and quality documentation have significantly lessened the learning curve, enabling all involved to build familiarity with the system and implement change quickly.

5. HURDLES OVERCOME

AgFirst's move to BPM has not been without its challenges. The leap from their current methods to a regulated administration created a few challenges for both staff and management. Their previous solution, while not entirely streamlined, afforded users to make more subjective decisions. In order to create a BPM solution, all business rules had to be quantified and documented.

These challenges have been addressed by the dedication of AgFirst's BPM Project Team. Taking time to walk staff through the interfaces has paid off, as has getting the business involved in process discussions.

5.1 Management

One of the concerns was that some of the users wore multiple hats while in some cases users within the same group worked slightly differently. This presented a challenge, which the BPMS addresses by providing a simple way to delineate roles and allowed for users to be in multiple roles. Management also saw that the process was self-documenting and enabled them to have a visual view of their Association's business process.

5.2 Business

One of the requirements in the process was to be able to measure various performance metrics that would give management an indication of how efficient the process was and how quickly the customer was being served. It was also important that such metrics would be used to improve the business process.

5.3 Organization Adoption

Right from the beginning of the BPM project, AgFirst made all attempts to get buy-in from key stakeholders at the ACAs. This helped immensely to convince all users that this was important for the whole organization to use this solution consistently.

6. BENEFITS

At time of writing, AgFirst's solution has been live for three months. The baseline metrics related to process performance are in place, and will be measured at frequent intervals. However, the specific goal of the project was not to save time or money. Instead, the focus was finding a cost-effective solution that could be delivered quickly and would increase data quality and reduce risk.

Some key metrics are:

1. Average number of loan transmittals per month – **65**
2. Average duration of closed cases is **12.5 days**. This exceeded ACA's expectation of 20 days
3. **97 percent** of the loans were analyzed within expected durations in the last three months
4. **100 percent** of the request for information from Loan Approvers was completed on time in the last 3 months.

6.1 Cost Savings / Time Reductions

The goal of the solution was to create consistent processes, reduce the risk of errors and to be able to process more Loan Transmittals without increasing staffing.

6.2 Increased Revenues

This is not a goal of the project and will not be measured.

6.3 Quality Improvements

Automation using BPM has resulted in consistent process that reduces the risk of errors by reducing rekeying of data and bringing all information necessary to make decisions in one place.

7. BEST PRACTICES, LEARNING POINTS AND PITFALLS

7.1 Best Practices and Learning Points

✓ *Appoint one of the vendor's development team to work on-site during the development stages to speed up delivery time.*

✓ *Involve stakeholders in the process discussion early and allow plenty of time for feedback*

✓ *Prepare to overcome misconceptions about KPIs; explain the benefits of process measurement.*

✓ *Ensure the solution supports single and multiple delineation of roles; this provides governance but also flexibility for employees.*

7.2 Pitfalls

✗ *BPM technology alone cannot bring fast results. Process discussions with the right people are essential.*

✗ *Don't take the vendors' word that they can do the job. A proof of concept is necessary.*

✗ *Make time to walk stakeholders and users through the interface. A visual view of processes will hugely increase their acceptance.*

8. COMPETITIVE ADVANTAGES

AgFirst's BPM solution has delivered immediate short-term advantage. In 16 weeks, the bank has transformed the quality of loan transmittals it offers to customers. The ability to define, deliver and adapt processes very quickly has allowed the momentum to continue: a third and fourth process have been deployed in 25 percent time of the first.

Longer term, AgFirst plans to "ramp it up" across several additional associations within the next six months.

9. TECHNOLOGY

- AgFirst Farm Credit Bank selected BPM platform to model and automate the business processes. They used BPM Process Modeler to design and document all aspects of the loan Approval process, BPM Studio for automating the processes and lastly BPM Engine to deploy them.
- The BPM Studio enables AgFirst to be agile and make changes fast to the unique processes of each Association. It also allows AgFirst to integrate their processes with four key IT systems including CRM, Document Management and a Credit Checking service, making full use of BPM system's powerful Service Oriented Architecture (SOA) capabilities such as web services, data virtualization and replication.
- BPM tool is an integrated Suite which enabled AgFirst to manage the complete process cycles. It is agile enough to support changes in business and market conditions and it is robust and multifunctional to support mission critical operations and organizational growth.
- The unique benefits delivered as a result of BPM tool's unique architecture enable AgFirst to process loans faster without having to increase headcount. In addition, the optimal mobility offered by BPM tool allows AgFirst Loan Officers to process loans on their mobile phones and tablets.

10. THE TECHNOLOGY AND SERVICE PROVIDERS

AgFirst selected Bizagi BPM solution to model and automate their business processes. Because the Bizagi Modeler can be downloaded for free, users at AgFirst were able to learn the system prior to embarking on the project. The Bizagi website also offers a comprehensive self-service program that includes e-learning, training courses and videos, enabling the learning curve to be significantly shortened.

Bizagi Modeler is an intuitive drag and drop application which can also be used to generate process documentation. AgFirst used Bizagi Studio to automate their processes, turning their process models into executable applications. With Bizagi it is very easy to move from process modeling to execution, without the need for technical knowledge, so the system is often used by Business Analyst and business line managers.

Bizagi offers a complete solution which includes design and implementation of the process workflow and automation of processes. As Bizagi offers an integrated BPM Suite, AgFirst was able to manage the complete process life cycle without any other additional or external tools. The platform has the flexibility and capability of integrating and automating several processes at the same time, thereby creating a robust system that can be easily adapted to business growth as more and more processes are automated.

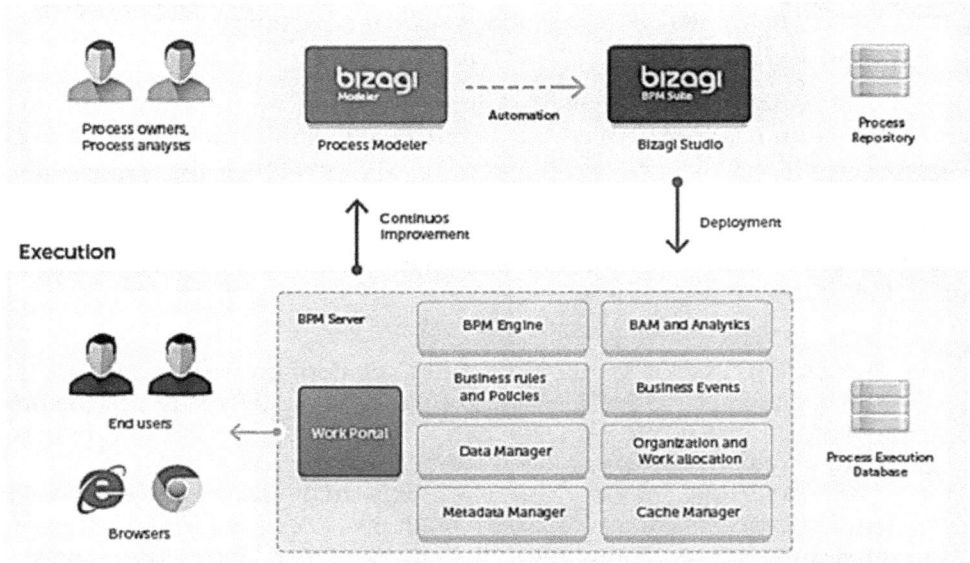

Figure e – Bizagi Platform Architecture

Bizagi BPM solution is a modern business collaboration tool for faster process automation. Its built-in functions, ease of use and flexibility makes it the ideal BPM platform to deliver faster results. The tool has most of the common and reoccurring requirements in process automation pre-built. These include:

- Control and visibility
- Alarms and notifications
- Performance analysis and reporting
- Auditing and traceability
- Workload routing and balancing
- Mobility
- Integration APIs
- Corporate features (multi-tenancy, BPMN process engine, multiple language support, time-zones, long lasting process transactions, enterprise data model, among others)

Business Partners, South Africa
Nominated by Pétanque Consultancy
South Africa

1. EXECUTIVE SUMMARY / ABSTRACT

The significance of this case study is found in this formula:

a clear vision of a desired outcome

+ *(plus)*

a strong and sustained change management campaign (people)

+ *(plus)*

clarifying what needs to happen, how, when and who the role players and stakeholders are, through a unique interactive process mapping approach (process)

+ *(plus)*

IT change (system)

= *(equals)*

improved customer experience

=> *(resulting in)*

improved profit and an improved reputation

Business Partners, a \$US342m+ risk finance lender, applied process design *and* a change management campaign to improve customer experience.

The campaign, dubbed "The Transformers" set out to:

a) Reduce approval and implementation processes, resulting in Customer Excellence;
b) Improve efficiencies and turnaround time; and
c) Increase revenue by 20 percent.

The process changes were substantial, and this required a coordinated, top management supported change management program to coincide with the process changes. Without the change management, applied weekly, monthly and quarterly for almost 18 months, the project would not have realized the substantial benefits.

a) Application-to-disbursement time was reduced from an average six to three months;
b) Costs were reduced by placing the onus of business-case build on the applicant;
c) Client experience improved;
d) Business Partners achieved lending levels not reached since the economic crises of 2008;
e) Profitability increased;
f) Clients are more satisfied, contributing to reputational improvement and more business through referral and results.

2. OVERVIEW

Business Partners is a South African financial sector business with a 268 staff complement that provides risk funding to small and medium private enterprises. Revenue is generated through interest levied on loan funding, capital returns where equity deals were structured and rental from owned properties.

The key project staff, including around 25 investment officers, engage with businesses (each has a portfolio of 10-15 businesses) that need funding. The mid-level to senior business and investment officers assess, and write the approval reports for funding. The financial team supports the investment officers and the IT team provides the systems.

The desired state was first communicated by senior management, where process design to improve customer experience along with continued change management was advocated.

Through the unique Business Destination Mapping (BDM™) and VizPro® Process Mapping methodologies the current business process that was taking on average 6 months from application to funding was mapped against a background of customer dissatisfaction with process, timing and outcomes. The new process, developed as a best practice process, was designed by the investment officers, the IT team and the finance team in a two day interactive workshop that looked to bring about radical improvement and customer delight. Efficiencies were built into the process and roles clarified. The changes were implemented through rigorous project and change management and benefits were realized from the outset by an initial focus on quick wins.

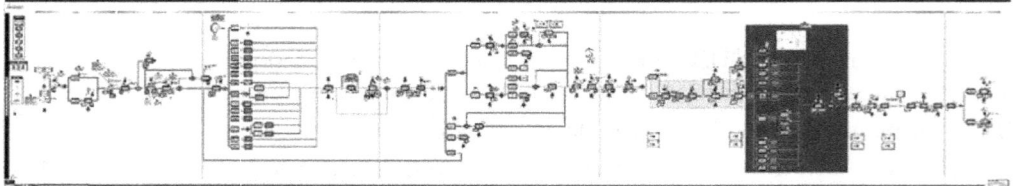

Graphic 1: The application to disbursement process that brought about improvement

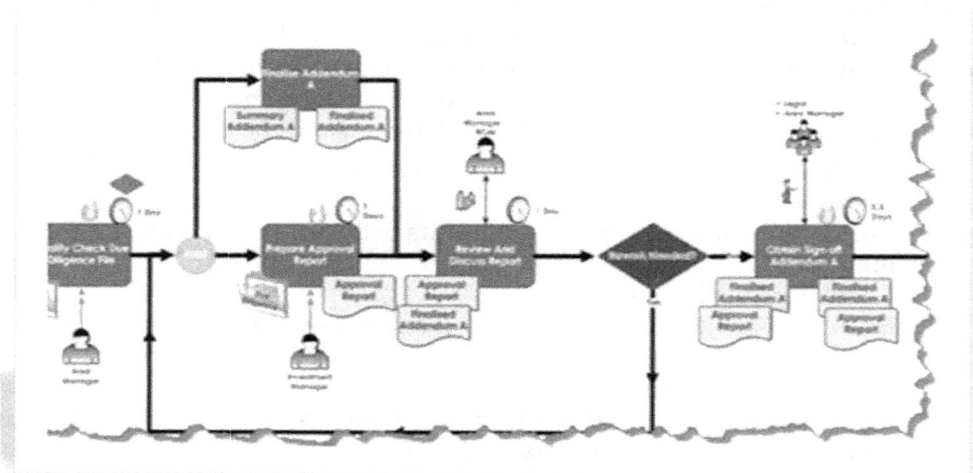

Graphic 2: Close – up snapshot of the process elements:

2.1 Benefits

Application-to-disbursement time was reduced from an average of six to a three months average:

i. Prior to the process changes, clients were annoyed with the time lag between approval and disbursement. This was caused by delays in sourcing documentation (mostly due to clients or third parties failing to submit critical documentation), resulting in high levels of re-work by the Business Partners' process role players.

ii. After the change, it was left to applicants to submit ALL client related documents as part of the application. Now the investment managers got approval reports to the approval committees much quicker.

iii. This resulted in reducing approvals from an average 60 days to 30 days. The performance indicator for the application-to-approval stage is now 30 days.

iv. Similarly, the approval to disbursement phase improved from an average 120 to 60 days.

v. In total, the duration from application to disbursement thus improved from 180 (60+120) to 90 (30+60) days.

vi. Costs were reduced by placing the onus of business-case build on the applicant and making the process transparent to clients and internal staff.

vii. By providing an easy to read-and-understand process to all stakeholders, there was a change in how staff would engage in the process. As it was clear and transparent, lower level employees also understood the "business of the business" – in all the operational hubs of Business Partners.

viii. Client experience improved, resulting in customers providing Business Partners with a 96.74 percent satisfaction rating.

Through the process improvement and implementation, supported by the ongoing change management:

i. All areas of interaction with the client were clearly defined and described, with the view of turning the process around to make engaging from the client's point of view, simpler and easier. For example, in the due diligence phase, the improvements brought about by an Outside–In (Customer Centric) view resulted in a much more focused and directed due diligence process, which significantly impacted on the speed of follow-on processes.

ii. In particular, the workshop identified bottlenecks and elements that would "delight our customers" and the team agreed on process changes that would manage or eliminate bottlenecks and bring about "delight".

Business Partners achieved lending levels not reached since before the economic crisis, and increased net profit after tax to US$14.47m in 2014 from US$11.78m in 2013.

i. Due to time delays and re-work described above, disbursements were delayed and challenging in many instances.

ii. Entrepreneurs in most instances need funding quickly and when there are delays, the impact on their businesses tends to be significant.

iii. Due to the process inefficiencies, momentum often was lost and clients were unhappy, resulting in damage to the reputation and loss of revenue.

a) Profitability increased:

    i.   Business Partners have seen an improvement in profitability.

    ii.   In comparing the cost of the same number of "deals" for the period before and during implementation of "The Transformers", profitability increased. The process efficiencies also contributed to a reduction in operating expenses year on year of US$932,000.

b)   Clients were more satisfied, contributing to reputational improvement and more business through referral and results:
There has been an improvement in client satisfaction from 93.76 percent to 96.74 percent as reflected in the client evaluation done one year after roll-out of the campaign.

2.2 Challenges

Team motivation, especially among the older team members, took a while to realize.

The existing IT system was not supporting the new process, and the challenge was how to implement process without adequate IT capability.

The existing IT system was "falling over" and it was critical to invest in "the right" system. Stand-alone legacy systems were a threat to the realization of process efficiencies.

"If we did not have early wins, the adoption and execution of the new process could have slowed down".

3. BUSINESS CONTEXT

The state of the enterprise:

3.1 Then... (the initial state)

In addition to the what-was-not-working-well aspects described in the Benefits section before, the following are note-worthy:

There was a need for
    client satisfaction
    reputation improvement
    higher revenue
    improved profit margins
    standardization: individuals performed similar tasks differently across the units. Standard practices were limited, with regional and area variations which caused for process inefficiencies;
    elimination of waste, both in terms of paper, travel, time and office space;
    effective progress tracking throughout the process;
    doing business in a new, fresh way;
    Fast-tracking new team members into the value chain and clearly understanding of roles, performance measures and areas of risk.

3.2 The transition...

www.businesspartners.co.za

ABOUT · FINANCE · INTERNATIONAL · GROWTH CENTRE · CAREERS · KNOWLE

BUSINESS/PARTNERS

What sets us apart

We are a specialist risk finance company that provides customised financial solutions, sectoral knowledge, mentorship, business premises and other added-value services for formal small and medium enterprises (SMEs) in South Africa and selected African countries. We're passionate about funding, supporting and mentoring entrepreneurs, or as we like to call them, the square pegs in round holes.

What sets us apart?

We're **'square pegs'** too.

Unlike with some risk finance companies, you the entrepreneur, are our exclusive focus.

We know that by investing in you, the entrepreneur, it will not only help with creating and building your own wealth, but also fuel the growth of the economy and the creation of jobs.

Over the past 30+ years, we have tailored every aspect of our business to ensure your success. Here are some of the ways we do this:

- Our products and services are specifically tailored to meet your unique needs.
- We don't have the same owner's capital or security requirements that many other financial institutions do.
- Our range of financing and added-value services provide an integrated solution for you, catering for all aspects of your business needs, including property broking and property management, as well as consulting and mentorship services.
- As we specialise in investing capital, skills and knowledge in entrepreneurs, our staff have in-depth knowledge of the SME sector, as well as insight into the challenges facing independent businesses.
- Our risk financing model is regarded as one of the most innovative in the world and has been internationally accepted as a working financing solution for SMEs in developing countries.
- Similarly, our due diligence process is thorough, tried and tested; therefore providing insight into the extent of inherent risk in each deal.
- Our systems and processes have earned us an ISO 9001:2008 accreditation – the first financial services company in South Africa to be accredited in this way.

The principal office is based in Johannesburg, South Africa, with investment teams, support teams and area managers in 18 branches across South Africa and support staff in African hubs.

The accounting and financial admin teams are based in Johannesburg along with the IT team. The current Managing Director commenced duties in 2012 with the mandate to improve the sustainability of the enterprise, and in particular through improved client experience.

Action	Date	Status
• Conduct process analysis	Jan 2012	Concluded
• Define specific Key Performance Areas	April 2012	Concluded
• Draft the Business Case for a Client Excellence improvement Campaign.	July 2012	Concluded
• Formulating the campaign into a project and commence with communication about the campaign internally Most impacted would be Senior Management, and a range of individuals impacted by changes	Oct 2012	Concluded
• Document internal work flow charts • Commence with weekly communication to stakeholders about the campaign, focusing on a theme related to the change per month. The focus was to be on what the changes are, how it would realize, when and celebrating results	Nov 2012	Concluded
• Engage with external vendor to deliver interactive process mapping and improvement workshop – three days • The plan: process first, then people then system change • Official launch of "The Transformers" campaign	Dec 2012	Concluded
• Pilot new process in one of the business units • Commence email communication as key change management to stakeholders • Senior Management would be change champions for their business units, translating and guiding change of campaign goals into local branches	Jan 2013	Concluded
• New process rolled out nationally, encouraging individuals to continue embracing the change and make sure the change remains beneficial and "real" • Switch to two weekly change management communication • Commence with investigations and roll-out of new IT system to support the value chain process – Microsoft Dynamics as the front-end system, integrating into the existing Microsoft back-office and other accounting systems	April/May 2013	Concluded
• Switch to monthly change management communication, reflecting on the results of a full year of change and improvement	March 2014	Concluded
• Go live on new IT system that supports the improved processes	April 2014	Concluded

3.3 Now and the future...

The number of people directly impacted in the IT, HR, management teams –198 directly out of 268 total staff complement.

"We will continue to operationalize change. The way we do business, into 2015 and beyond, is that if we see process, people or system aspects that make us non-agile, we have instilled a culture of changing what is not working, fast and effectively. We now have a quick-resolve culture when it comes to non-efficiencies" – Lionel Billing, Campaign Project Manager

Action	Date	Status
• Conclude systems' integration	Nov 2014	In progress
• Close campaign	Dec 2014	In progress

4. THE KEY INNOVATIONS

The impact that resulted from the project:

4.1 Business

The impact of the project on the way the enterprise engages its customers, partners and suppliers and other key stakeholders include:

- For clients, partners, suppliers and staff the process is clear, transparent and clients can easily follow progress, their role in the outcome and what could cause delays; in short, pretty much everyone is able to be on the "same page".
- "We have created a new culture and mind-set about communication, this benefits all areas of the business".
- Improved Client Experience was agreed to as a senior management Key Performance Indicator, leading the way to strong leadership from the top to achieve campaign success.
- Used the agreed end to end value chain process and built a workflow into the IT System.
- Applied call centre environment work flows, aligned those with the business process and created a unique financial services system that is capable of handling each particular finance application – "We regard this as innovative and leading. No one of our deals are the same, we needed to create an adaptive case environment that could be handled in the IT platform, against a standard backdrop."
- "We shifted process steps forward so as to deal with risks to speed and efficiency early on and not waste time fixing later when lots is going on."

4.2 Case Handling

"Cases" in context of this enterprise is the end to end application for risk finance. The changes effected through process, people and systems improvement, has resulted in the benefits listed earlier.

Previously, the process was not standardised, and this was often mistaken for adaptive case management with detrimental results.

With the change, actual adaptive case management now has a firm framework within which to actualise, and in particular against set and agreed to performance indicators

The following key roles are defined in the process and these were key to the change designed, agreed and effected by a core team of between 18-20 persons from the following functional areas

- o Investment teams: nationally and area managers
- o Support team members from across the country
- o Accounting, back office team – Johannesburg based
- o Two Operations focused individuals and two individuals from Investment Support, who advance the money and make sure the legal elements are taken care of
- o IT general support officers
- o Management and financial accountants
- o Executive Director
- o Head of Consulting Services, acting as the project manager.

3.3 Organization & Social

The project was driven initially by top management, and through collaborative engagement, was accepted by all.

The project was linked to a roadmap to graphically reflect progress and milestones being achieved.

Continued leadership communication embedded the goals to be achieved and victories were recognized. Not a single employee resigned due to the project, only through natural attrition was staff lost.

The campaign was labelled as "not a once off project, but as new way of doing business, the culture of how we continue to re-create ourselves, be relevant." The entire organisation was engaged, ensuring that the campaign to improve the client experience was not a management decision and initiative.

Management indeed identified the threat of becoming irrelevant, and had to convey that and secure the buy-in at every level from every staff member, that each had a role to play in doing better. This approach further broke down the traditional "us and them" stance where staff regard themselves as an opposing group to management. This campaign enabled unity and was attained by the Chief Executive's continuous, consistent and frequent communication about progress, wins and challenges.

5.   HURDLES OVERCOME

The challenges and the way in which the team addressed them, including human issues, were addressed through the innovative elements listed earlier.

5.1 Business

Early wins: "If we did not have early wins, the adoption and execution of the new process could have slowed down". In the first three weeks of the campaign, we concluded a deal in 15 days and disbursed the funds. This proved it was possible, and set a new benchmark.

5.2 IT

There was an in-house legacy system that managed the application process. This was inflexible and archaic. Together with the IT team we search for suitable off the shelf systems that could integrate the application process as well as introduce a customer relationship management element. After an assessment of various CRM software we settled on Microsoft Dynamics. A professional team was engaged to customize and implement the new system and this was done in record time with system go-live on 1 April 2014. Users were trained on the new platform and the transition was relatively painless as the user interface was familiar to all users being Microsoft based.

5.3 Organization Adoption

"We needed to deal quickly with areas of concern as the tendency is to focus on the negative. We engaged on concerns and built it into change management program as burning issues: aligning experiences with the characters in the well-known book by John Kotter, "Our Iceberg is Melting". Decisive leadership moved those with concerns along, making it clear that it is not so bad and could benefit you too if you tag along.

Once the "what-is-in-it-for-me" filtered through via the continued feedback and communication, there was sustained buy-in and support.

6. BENEFITS

6.1 Cost Savings / Time Reductions

Application-to-disbursement time was reduced from six to three months, on an average.

Costs were reduced by placing the onus of business-case build on the applicant.

6.2 Increased Revenues

Business Partners achieved lending levels last experienced before the economic crisis, increasing revenue by 13.14 percent.

Profitability increased by 13.5 percent.

6.3 Quality Improvements

Clients are more satisfied, contributing to reputational improvement and more business through referral and results.

Client experience improved, resulting in more applications and in larger funding requests.

Staff have a clear roadmap on what constitutes quality, client satisfaction and adaptive case management against agreed to performance indicators.

7. BEST PRACTICES, LEARNING POINTS AND PITFALLS

7.1 Best Practices and Learning Points

- ✓ Design the improvement project around people, process and systems
- ✓ Be clear about the destination – what are we aiming for?
- ✓ Define and obtain leadership buy-in for the desired outcome
- ✓ Design the change management plan (people)
- ✓ Engage the team in improved process design, implementation, challenges and victories (process)
- ✓ Aggressively follow the change management plan and adjust as needed.
- ✓ Align information technology to process and business needs, and ensure people support and uptake for the technology due to it enabling the desired outcome
- ✓ Communicate, communicate, communicate.

7.2 Pitfalls

- ✗ Project not embraced by all

- ✗ *No involvement or drive from executives*
- ✗ *Poor communication*
- ✗ *Them vs. us mindset.*

8. COMPETITIVE ADVANTAGES

As a financier of SMEs our success is being able to do volumes at reduced costs, which results in greater profitability. The advantage is thus to have standardized processes and systems to ensure that there is quick turnaround. This coupled with trained investment officers and back-office staff is critical.

9. TECHNOLOGY

We realized that we needed to be customer centric and thus needed the appropriate systems to assist with this. By choosing MicroSoft Dynamics we were able to implement in record time and ensure early user adoption due to the familiar interface to users.

10. THE TECHNOLOGY AND SERVICE PROVIDERS

The process mapping vendor was Pétanque Consultancy – www.petanque-c.com. They specialize in Process, Change, Business Intelligence and Project Management, making them a full service solution consultancy to take any enterprise from strategy to execution, and beyond. They use image-rich storyboarding techniques to graphically depict strategy and processes. This not only simplifies complexity, but also brings strategy alive to ensure buy in and comprehension of all involved, regardless of the level of responsibility. Speed, engagement and profit is how clients derive value.

At the initial stages of this project, the VizPro® process mapping methodology was deployed by Pétanque as a key input into the change phases.

Post Card 1:

A Process Map
Describing Reality

Telling the story of exactly how something works, with pictures. That is a Process Map. It is an image rich storyboard that defines and unpacks the detail of a process.

"If you can't describe what you are doing as a process, you don't know what you are doing."

W.E. Deming

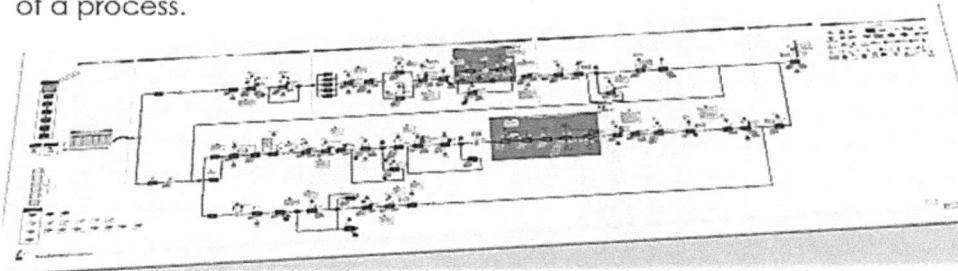

Describing your process is describing your reality. Know who needs to do what, when and how.

Pétanque Consultancy
Clearly Better

info@petanque-c.com   086-178 6783   www.petanque-c.com

A Process Map
Describing Reality

How does it work?

A Process Map is developed by talking to the people who know best – the process owners. Through intensive workshopping we ask questions, create debate and draw the picture in real time. It can take anything from a few hours to a few days to complete, depending on the complexity of the process. Printed as an A0 laminated map it can be up to 2.5 meters long.

What makes this different?

SEEING how things get done in your enterprise is more effective than reading about it. People only remember 10% of what they hear and 20% of what they read, but about 80 % of what they see and do. A visual depiction of your process reality creates an instant common understanding that bridges language, cultural and perception gaps. Our Process Maps ensure that everyone is on the same page, literally.

RISK

How can I use the Process Map?

- To train new employees.
- To create minimum standards.
- Find gaps in a process.
- Search for cost saving opportunities by eliminating waste and duplication.
- Highlight risks and see where KPI's are needed.
- Eliminate bottlenecks.
- Business improvement by starting with the current reality, then enhancing it.

info@ petanque-   086-178 6783   www.petanque-c.com

Change Management formed the framework within which the project was deployed. Although Business Partners managed the change through each of the project phases, the vendor, Pétanque ensured that it positioned its process mapping as a key element to bring about clarity about what change was needed, where in which process and who would need to make the change, who would be impacted and what the outcomes of change, as well as no-change would be.

Change Management
Looking after your Team

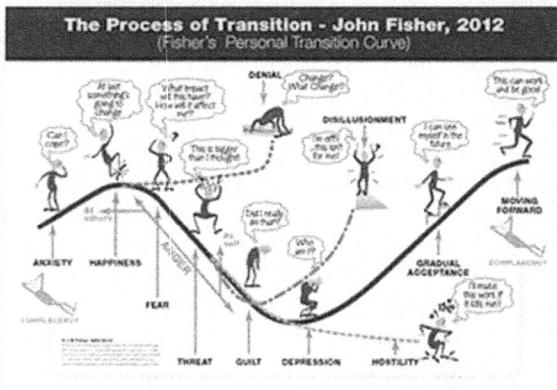

Anticipating the human response to change, to reduce resistance.

Unmanaged responses to change, if left unchecked, can seriously impact and even sabotage change initiatives.

Build change leadership skills and personal change resilience to help people move through the stages associated with responses to change.

Pétanque Consultancy
Clearly Better

| info@ petanque- | 086-178 6783 | www.petanque-c.com |

Post Card 2:

Change Management
Looking after your Team

The Process of Transition - John Fisher, 2012
(Fisher's Personal Transition Curve)

How can I use Change Management?

Myers-Briggs personality profiling studies find that 80% of people will find change difficult. That means that 8 out of 10 customers, stakeholders and people in organisations will need some change support to successfully make the changes required.

How does it work?

A Change Readiness Assessment provides valuable information on which to base a Change Management Rollout Plan. This plan integrates the management of team dynamics, mobilising leaders, getting stakeholder alignment and managing the human resources impact.

| info@ petanque-c.com | 086-178 6783 | www.petanque-c.com |

Chicago Parks District, USA
Nominated by Sofbang and Oracle, USA

1. EXECUTIVE SUMMARY / ABSTRACT

The Chicago Park District (CPD) is one of the largest municipal park systems in the US. It is responsible for more than 8,100 acres of green space, including 580 parks, 77 pools, and 26 miles of lakefront and beaches. CPD implemented an integrated custom and off-the-shelf solution to streamline operations for interdepartmental efficiency across the organization, saving costs and eliminating duplication of efforts. An integrated BPM platform enables the enterprise to work within its specific applications, such as E-Business and Enterprise Project Management products, and ensures effective collaboration across these integral departments.

The key objectives were to automate, track and share project information, automate manual processes, integrate existing systems, and accelerate mobile capabilities. The successful $3.3 million project brought together Funds & Grants Management, Project & Portfolio Management, Mobile Work Order Management, Enterprise Asset Management, and 311 Mobile Service Request into a complete seamless integrated solution. This resulted in increased productivity, accurate real-time data, and accountability and enhanced visibility for over 400 park projects annually.

2. OVERVIEW

The Chicago Park District manages 350 to 400 separate projects per year, directing the various staff members tied to each plan, allocating funding for each assignment and ensuring sound communication to avoid any workload overlap.

As one of the largest municipal park systems in the nation, the district is responsible for more than 8,100 acres of green space, including 580 parks, 77 pools, and 26 miles of lakefront and beaches. Whenever there is a repair needed or a new project in one of its parks or facilities, the Chicago Park District is in charge of developing the plan, allocating the budget and following the project through to completion.

A few years ago, the district implemented an integrated custom and off-the-shelf solution with the goal of streamlining these processes. Developed by technology consultant Sofbang, the system helps the district manage its funds, grants, projects and work orders.

"Prior to the Project Management solution, I would get 10 calls a day from project managers asking very simple questions about the status of or funding for their projects," said Elizabeth Tomlins, the district's capital projects manager. "Temporarily, we created an Excel sheet with project statuses and funding sources that all could see. But now that we've put everything into the Project Management System, it's put the responsibility in the hands of the project manager to be accountable for their work."

As a part of the $3.3 million project, the district has also restructured the way they manage grants and funding allocations. Before deploying the new solution, everything related to grant dates, requirements and deadlines was listed on a spreadsheet.

"Prior to our implementation, the district would conduct several meetings reconciling spreadsheets across six different departments," said Danny Asnani, principal of Sofbang. "This took a lot of time and cost. There were significant savings per year by reducing overtime and resource costs, reducing reconciliation time and minimizing rework and duplication of efforts."

This solution also improved communication between park staff and trade staff, such as carpenters, plumbers and electricians. Previously, park supervisors or service requesters would submit a request for a repair, and then receive a request number. Follow through was absent, however, as the requester often didn't receive any status updates on their request.

"Now, park staff can see everything they've submitted and they can see the status of their work requests in one central location," said Victoria Cordova, the district's project manager. "They can also view reasons for why something might have been cancelled. Before, they were in the dark. The trades also like it because they can prioritize their schedules and work orders. Everyone can have an even workload. It's helped productivity and it's made our staff more efficient."

In the future, the district plans to expand the service request solution as a mobile technology. The staff, in conjunction with Sofbang, is exploring tools, like rugged tablets, that can be utilized in the field by trade staff. The mobile upgrade would replace paper forms and allow for real-time project updates.

Tanya Anthony, the district's chief administrative officer, said that the new system also has the potential to support the city's transparency initiatives. The district is discussing an online function in which the public could view the number of work orders completed and each job's timeliness.

Anthony said that, thus far, the new system's biggest value has been the opportunity to collaborate.

"The communication and knowing what each division is doing has been the greatest outcome from a user perspective," she said. "From the park staff knowing the status of their work order to the project manager knowing the status of their funding, has been extremely valuable."

3. BUSINESS CONTEXT

Administratively, the CPD has over 30 departments, each with a unique mission. Many of these departments interact with each other on a daily basis and share information to coordinate operations. These departments each have specific internal requirements regarding the processing of information on a daily basis. With complex, specific business processes all managed manually on spreadsheets, the CPD was in need of an enterprise Grants, Project Management & Work Order Management system, which would facilitate cross-department coordination, automate processes and seamlessly integrate for effective communication and collaboration within the organization.

"The communication and knowing what each division is doing has been the greatest outcome from a user perspective. From the park staff knowing the status of their work order to the project manager knowing the status of their funding, has been extremely valuable."

-T. Anthony, Chief Administrative Officer, Chicago Park District

Objectives
- Automate, manage, and process information so that departments (collectively & individually) will communicate & coordinate their operations more efficiently
- Automate workflows, providing each department with the ability to efficiently track projects and share project related information

- Automate & transform several redundant manual, existing processes to improve efficiency, accuracy & eliminate delays
- Manage Funds and Grants for Capital Projects & Facilities

4. THE KEY INNOVATIONS

This was a major modernization for the CPD. It involved using new BPM/SOA and now mobile technologies to improve integration and collaboration between many systems across 6 departments.

4.1 Business

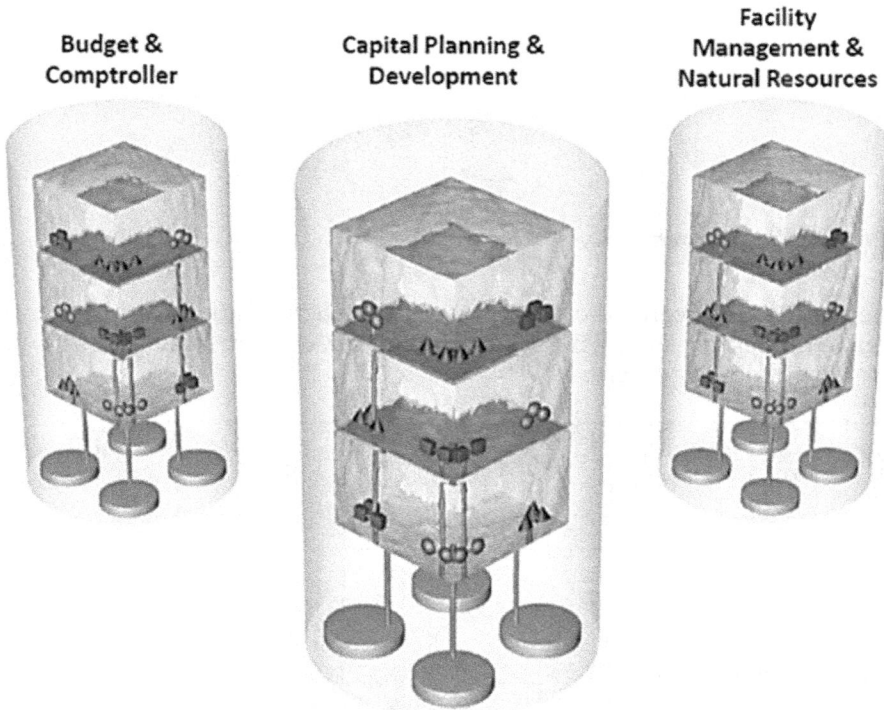

Budget & Comptroller

Capital Planning & Development

Facility Management & Natural Resources

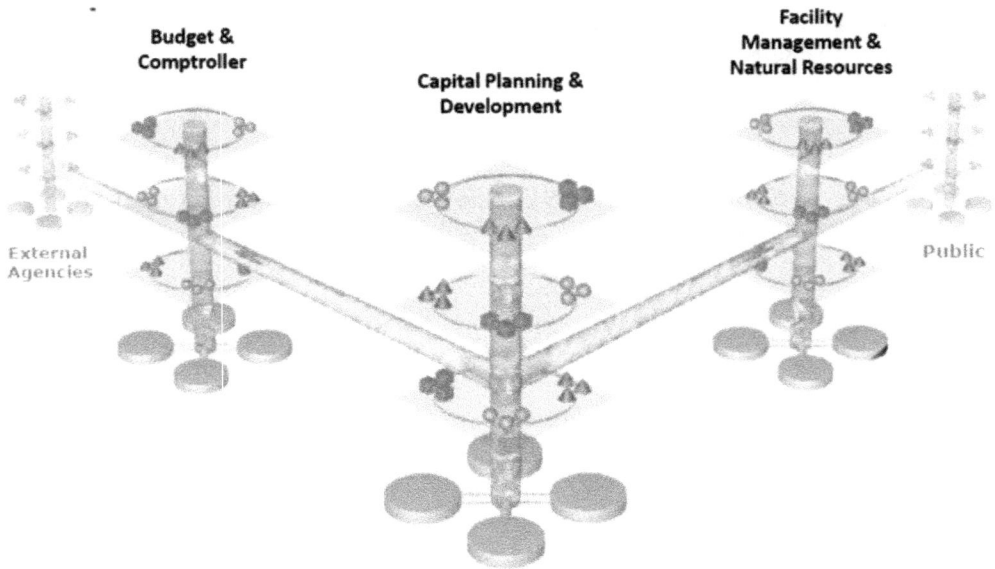

4.2 Process/Implementation

CPD implemented an integrated custom and off-the-shelf solution with the goal of streamlining these processes. The system helps the district manage its funds, grants, projects and work orders.

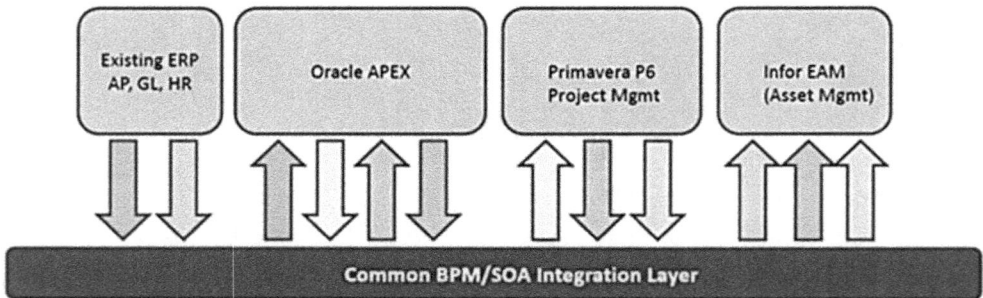

Chicago Park District (CPD): completed integrated Grants Management Module, Project/Program Management Module & Work Order Management Module* which included the:

- Business Process Analysis & Re-Engineering of six Departments
- Architecture & Installation of CPD App Dev & Integration Environment:
- Implementation of Grants Management Module, Project/Program Management Module & Work Order Management Module
- Seamless integration of the four modules
- Business Intelligence for all capabilities

4.3 Organization & Social

The first step was to spend time with the CPD stakeholders in outlining pain points, current business processes and objectives of this initiative across the various CPD departments. With an understanding of the current state, we were then able to architect, design, implement and integrate the following three modules: Oracle Primavera P6 for Project & Portfolio Management, Infor EAM for Work Order Management & a custom Oracle Apex solution for Grants, Funds & Parks Management. Sofbang then installed the BPM/SOA product stack and implemented a variety of workflows based interfaces to integrate these modules, along with CPD's ERP, for smooth exchange of data & workflow across the departments. This BPM/SOA-based implementation set the framework for future, easy-to-manage enterprise integration within CPD.

5. HURDLES OVERCOME

As the scope of our Strategic initiative was Enterprise-wide we had to ensure all our stakeholders had buy-in to our plan.

5.1 Management

This project was a major investment by CPD and was fully supported by senior management stakeholders from the COO, CAO, Chief of Staff and all the functional Directors (Facilities, Capital Construction, etc.)

5.2 Business

Administratively, the CPD has over 30 departments, each with a unique mission. Many of these departments interact with each other on a daily basis and share information to coordinate operations. These departments each have specific internal requirements regarding the processing of information on a daily basis. With complex, specific business processes all managed manually on spreadsheets, the CPD was in need of an enterprise Grants, Project Management & Work Order Management system, which would facilitate cross-department coordination, automate processes and seamlessly integrate for effective communication and collaboration within the organization.

5.3 Organization Adoption

The Organization has fully embraced the new system because it makes their lives easier and they are able to improve their service to the public. The solution spans across six departments.

"The communication and knowing what each division is doing has been the greatest outcome from a user perspective," she said. "From the park staff knowing the status of their work order to the project manager knowing the status of their funding, has been extremely valuable."

6. BENEFITS

CPD has seen significant ROI for this project and has received very positive feedback from the user community across all six departments.

6.1 & 6.2 Cost Savings / Time Reductions

CPD has seen significant cost savings, reductions in non-productive activities, and reductions in processing / activity completion times:

- Reduced overtime costs associated with time spent on reconciliation, meetings, etc.
- Reduced time & costs associated with funding source acquisition
- Reduced time & costs associated with managing projects & funds

"Prior to the Project Management solution, I would get 10 calls a day from project managers asking very simple questions about the status of or funding for their projects," said Elizabeth Tomlins, the district's capital projects manager. "Temporarily, we created an Excel sheet with project statuses and funding sources that all could see. But now that we've put everything into the Project Management System, it's put the responsibility in the hands of the project manager to be accountable for their work."

"Prior to our implementation, the district would conduct several meetings reconciling spreadsheets across six different departments," said Danny Asnani, principal of Sofbang. "This took a lot of time and cost. There were significant savings per year by reducing overtime and resource costs, reducing reconciliation time and minimizing rework and duplication of efforts."

6.3 & 6.4 Increased Revenues / Productivity Improvements

CPD is not a commercial enterprise, so it is not focused on increased revenue, but instead focused on productivity improvements:

- Accurate, Real-Time Data
- Respond & process work orders more efficiently to enhance constituent satisfaction
- Accurate data to make more sensible, informed decisions related to budget & safety
- Reduce errors and reconciliation efforts
- KPIs, Accountability & Enhanced Visibility
- Accountability for departments to respond in a timely manner electronically
- Visibility into what the workers are actually doing and associate the costs to each job
- Ability to look at struggling departments and pinpoint bottlenecks
- Track WOs and projects in a timely manner and ability to measure performance

This solution also improved communication between park staff and trade staff, such as carpenters, plumbers and electricians. Previously, park supervisors — or service requesters — would submit a request for a repair, and then receive a request number. Follow through lacked, however, as the requester often didn't receive any status updates on their request.

"Now, park staff can see everything they've submitted and they can see the status of their work requests in one central location," said Victoria Cordova, the district's project manager. "They can also view reasons for why something might have been cancelled. Before, they were in the dark. The trades also like it because they can prioritize their schedules and work orders. Everyone can have an even workload. It's helped productivity and it's made our staff more efficient."

7. BEST PRACTICES, LEARNING POINTS AND PITFALLS

7.1 Best Practices and Learning Points

- ✓ Governance includes department heads (i.e. Directors of Facilities, Capital Construction, IT, etc.), COO, CAO, Chief of Staff, etc.
- ✓ Leveraged an agile/iterative methodology, releasing incremental capabilities/functionality every 1-3 months
- ✓ Continuous improvement and enhancements to the business processes in an effort to attain further efficiencies and improvements with operations

7.2 Pitfalls

× *We worked hard to involve the user community through the process to avoid misinformation and conflicts*

× *Tackling the complexity of integrating the different systems, we leveraged the Service Oriented Approach to mitigate risks*

× *We switched from our normal waterfall development to a more Agile methodology further reduce risks to the project*

8. COMPETITIVE ADVANTAGES

In the future, the district plans to expand the service request solution as a mobile technology. The technology team, is exploring tools, like rugged tablets, that can be utilized in the field by trade staff. The mobile upgrade would replace paper forms and allow for real-time project updates.

Tanya Anthony, the district's chief administrative officer, said that the new system also has the potential to support the city's transparency initiatives. The district is discussing an online function in which the public could view the number of work orders completed and each job's timeliness.

Anthony said that, thus far, the new system's biggest value has been the opportunity to collaborate.

"The communication and knowing what each division is doing has been the greatest outcome from a user perspective," she said. "From the park staff knowing the status of their work order to the project manager knowing the status of their funding, has been extremely valuable."

9. TECHNOLOGY

Chicago Parks District has many IT capabilities to meet its needs. Included below are several views of its IT capabilities starting with its overall Reference Architecture.

Chicago Parks District Reference IT Architecture

High-Level Reference Architecture

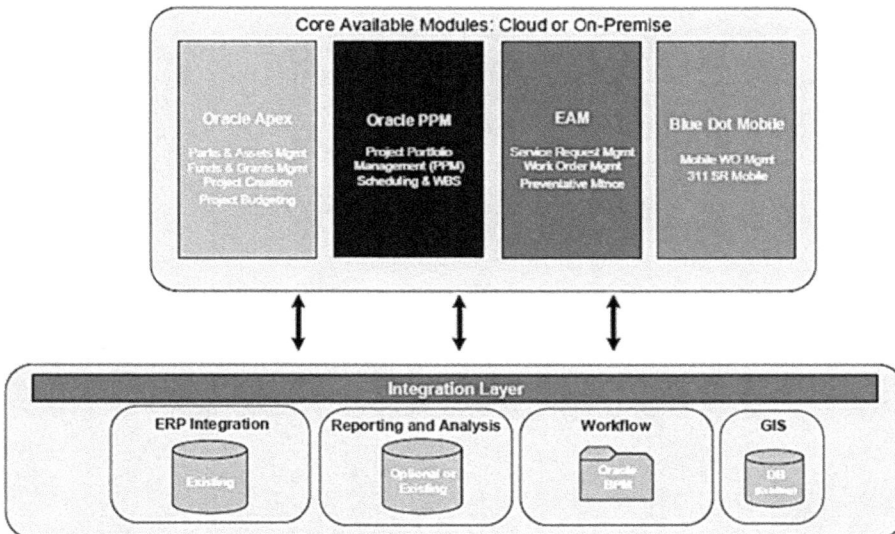

10. THE TECHNOLOGY AND SERVICE PROVIDERS

- Oracle Corporation: www.oracle.com
- Sofbang: www.sofbang.com

11. REFERENCES

GovTech Article: www.govtech.com/Chicago-Parks-District-Masters-Project-Coordination.html

www.sofbang.com/Portals/0/SofbangFiles/CaseStudies/Sofbang-CaseStudy-CPD.pdf

https://oracleus.activeevents.com/2014/connect/sessionDetail.ww?SESSION_ID=2988

Delta Lloyd, the Netherlands

Nominated by You-Get, the Netherlands

EXECUTIVE SUMMARY / ABSTRACT

Delta Lloyd Group is an expert, reliable and accessible financial services provider. We have a single goal: to offer security to our customers, now and in the future. We operate under three strong brands: Delta Lloyd, OHRA and ABN AMRO Insurance.

Our product and service offering covers the areas of insurance, pensions, investing and banking. And we do not only service consumers, but small and large companies, multinationals and pension funds as well.

Reputation

At Delta Lloyd Group, commercial success starts with sound entrepreneurship and integrity, financial solidity, a strong focus on long-term objectives and advanced risk management. In this way, we protect our good reputation and receive the trust of our customers. We aim to be transparent and ethical in all our activities, to take account of all dimensions of sustainable development and to make a responsible assessment, taking account of the interests of all stakeholders.

About Delta Lloyd NV

Delta Lloyd has been a trusted partner for insurance, pensions, investing and banking since 1807. It is our goal to offer financial security, now and in the future. We deliver clear, reliable and contemporary products and services that meet our customers' needs and create value for them, our shareholders and our employees. Our primary markets are the Netherlands and Belgium. In the Netherlands, we operate under the Delta Lloyd, OHRA and ABN AMRO Verzekeringen brands, while in Belgium we use the Delta Lloyd brand. We employ 5,135 permanent staff, of which 3,833 in the Netherlands, 1,115 in Belgium and 187 in Germany. In 2013, we achieved a premium income of € 4.7 billion and a net operational result of € 430 million. Our shareholders' funds amount to € 2.6 billion and we manage investments worth € 78 billion. Delta Lloyd is listed on Euronext Amsterdam and Brussels, and included in the AEX and Bel-20 indices.

Over the past years a number of digitization initiatives have been started within ABN AMRO Verzekeringen (part of Delta Lloyd Group). To gain greater control of these initiatives, it has been decided to combine them in a program entitled "Digitaal Verzekeren" (Digital Insurance). By managing the digitization initiatives as a coherent program, potential inconsistencies have been largely prevented. In addition, process optimization, operational excellence, output management, time and location-independent working (as well as cost reduction) support the goals and targets of the program.

In order to fulfill the strategic goals, Delta Lloyd implemented a Business Process Management (BPM). You-Get was selected as the implementation partner.

Results:

Private Persons – General Insurance Claims and Document Management processes of ABN AMRO Verzekeringen entered production successfully in early 2014.

Costs savings and reduced throughput time, although not primary goals, are a positive indirect consequence:

- 100 percent paperless working; files and dossiers can no longer get lost.

- When the Go-Live of the A&B (Underwriting & Support) and SSC (Shared Services Center) departments have been completed, a total of 160,000 cases will be processed digitally (previously postal mail documents). This concerns approximately 50 FTEs in total;
- Reduction of four FTEs out of 80 (five percent); because of digitization and process management, the roles of mail delivery to the proper department, as well as workload balancer, have become obsolete after the first go-live and this reduction will grow in subsequent go-lives;
- Processing a claim treatment (filling out the first-time-fix form) at the shared services center has been reduced by 75 percent (from 2 minutes to 30 seconds);
- Time-independent working; this concerns over 50 FTEs in total;
- Location-independent working; this concerns over 50 FTEs in total.

1. OVERVIEW

The Challenge

Delta Lloyd is a financial service provider that offers products and services in the life insurance, general insurance and asset management markets, as well as banking products and services. Delta Lloyd offers its customers greater assurance by helping them look more critically at their financials.

The core markets of Delta Lloyd Group are the Netherlands and Belgium. In the Netherlands it is operated mainly under the Delta Lloyd, OHRA and ABN AMRO Verzekeringen brands, and in Belgium under the Delta Lloyd brand. Delta Lloyd Group has over 5,300 employees and is traded on the NYSE Euronext stock exchange in Amsterdam and Brussels. ABN AMRO Verzekeringen is a joint venture between Delta Lloyd (51 percent) and ABN AMRO Bank (49 percent).

Information is essential for Delta Lloyd. It is the fuel as well as the result of the business processes. The world of information is changing and developing rapidly, however. From a paper-dominated world we are seeing a progressive shift towards a digital world in which new means of communication and information-sharing make it possible to work independently of time and place. Delta Lloyd workplaces will become places at which the proper and necessary information is always available, regardless of time and place. Delta Lloyd therefore had the requirement to meet the strategic wish and the need to implement digitization in a structured way. The company increasingly operates digitally: customers, society, ABN AMRO Bank as well as the employees require a service provider and organization that can accompany these developments.

The approach

In order to fulfill the strategic goals, Delta Lloyd decided to implement Business Process Management (BPM). BPM excels as a management philosophy in providing extensive change management in business processes, leading to continuous improvement. BPM is intended to provide a secure and location-independent workplace, as well as offering improved communication, thus raising customer satisfaction. The efficiency and reliability of the operations processes can also be raised. The IBM BPM (BPMS) software solution enables the improved processes to be automated.

Step 1 - Process Awareness

The first step taken by Delta Lloyd is the creation of process awareness (inter-departmental). The business has explored and documented the current processes jointly with both internal and external consultants. No changes to the organization have yet been executed. In parallel with this activity the consultants have set up a process architecture jointly with the architects. The process awareness has been continuously put on the agenda by both management as well as the business.

Step 2 – Search for the right BPMS

In 2012 ABN AMRO Verzekeringen conducted a successful Proof of Concept with a BPM Suite for process management. The IT staff of Delta Lloyd stated that this scenario could potentially lead to a Delta Lloyd-wide implementation. Because Delta Lloyd (Life) already used IBM Websphere Process Server (WPS) as an STP integration platform, platform integration was specified as a precondition for the final selection of a BPM Suite as the process management platform.

The technical feasibility of the integration possibilities between the BPM Suite and IBM WPS were investigated and proven. A technical design was set up to determine the costs of the scenario, and to make a global comparison with the IBM solution. A task force was set up with technology architects from both Delta Lloyd and ABN AMRO Verzekeringen to investigate the different scenarios. Finally, IBM BPM Suite was compared with the originally selected BPM Suite on the basis of criteria such as functionality, integration, support of the development and maintenance process and infrastructure.

The conclusions of the investigation were:

1. Both BPM Suites are functionally capable of supporting the business of Delta Lloyd;
2. From a technical integration perspective IBM BPM is preferable;
3. From a development and support perspective IBM BPM is preferable;
4. From an availability and scalability perspective IBM BPM is preferable;
5. From a security and integration with web / mobile environments perspective IBM BPM is preferable.

Step 3 – Search for the right BPMS implementation partner

In early June 2013 Delta Lloyd issued an RfP to select the right implementation partner for IBM BPM. The potential implementation partners were qualified on a number of criteria, such as knowledge and experience with BPM and IBM BPM, scoping, references, implementation approach, securing and transferring knowledge, willingness to take risks and responsibility, as well as matching the culture and the maturity of the organizations. After a number of selection rounds You-Get was selected.

Step 4 – Process Improvement

Investments were made with the knowledge of experiencing the benefits of a process-oriented way of working and to show how this can be applied in practice. The employees became aware of the advantages and were able to successfully implement a process-oriented way of working. The organization was at that time sufficiently aware of the proactive process improvement potential and had the proper skills. To build up this knowledge, the consultants took lean certification training and the brown paper method was implemented. The employees learned that cooperation, clear roles and responsibilities are essential in their daily job. The foundation for a process-oriented way of thinking and working was established.

You-Get supported Delta Lloyd with the process improvements. Process owners were selected in the organization. Workshops held jointly with the Business (various departments), consultants and architects led to the start of improvement cycles. The target was, and remains, to process as many customer questions as possible in the most efficient manner. By directly pinpointing firm improvement potential (based on workshops), the benefits of process-oriented working are visible right away. In order to ensure a 1-on-1 fit between the process automation preparation and the agreed technical scope, the user requirements within this scope, the possibilities within the process tool and the delivery of the required integrations from the "basis voorziening" subproject, intensive cooperation takes place (via workshops, reviews, joint project meetings and continuous control).

In order to facilitate the implementation of BPM, Delta Lloyd decided to use the "best practices" BPM approach from You-Get. Delta Lloyd and You-Get joined forces to implement BPM, with You-Get taking the lead and gradually transferring knowledge and skills to Delta Lloyd. The best practices must take into account a number of dimensions from process discovery to process implementation:

1. **Process**: parallel start with process architecture, i.e. inventory of processes and interrelations. Additionally it is required to set up the right data model as a basis for development;
2. **Strategy**: the strategy consists of the mission and vision, which are starting points (critical success indicators) to set up organization targets and goals;
3. **Culture**: it was jointly decided and documented how process working would be communicated, so employees are prepared for the production phase of the new processes;
4. **Organization**: for the training of the different skills and areas, BPM-specific training of You-Get was deployed. You-Get uses a lot of on-the-job training, so the complete analysis, design and implementation of processes with IBM BPM (BPMS) can be carried out autonomously;
5. **ICT/Systems**: determining technical demands and the new landscape. The future landscape will be determined with the appropriate integration points and adapters and applicable You-Get solutions as accelerators;
6. **BPM Organization & Governance**: setting up of a BPM organization (project manager, program manager, steering group) and Center of Excellence base with a process team for the first process.

Every dimension consists of a number of steps. Between the dimensions and the steps, as well as within and between the dimensions, there are dependencies (e.g. the relationship between the strategy and the process architecture). Subsequently the steps for each dimension and the applicable phasing are addressed in more detail. For every dimension it is important to achieve growth in maturity, which means growth in the area of business process management.

A phasing is necessary to manage the steps within each dimension. In addition, each phase concludes with a benchmark and evaluation of achieved results. This way of working guarantees optimal growth in process maturity. A big advantage of this phased approach is that steps are executed in parallel. The implementation of the technical facilities as well as implementation will be achieved very efficiently and effectively.

Step 5 – Process-focused

The next step taken by Delta Lloyd was the step towards a process-focused organization. In this step the connection between business and IT is made through the implementation of BPMS. With the support of BPMS, process improvements and process automation could be rapidly deployed and the key targets (paperless work, time- and location-independent workplace) realized. With the support of training and workshops, the organization has now changed into a transparent organization led by a process-focused way of working.

Step 6 - Process Implementation

Delta Lloyd required a proven and suitable approach for the realization and implementation of processes with IBM BPM (BPMS), including clear phasing. With the implementation of IBM BPM (BPMS) a number of dependencies can be distinguished, and You-Get works on both a top-down and a bottom-up basis. This means the process architecture plays an important role in the set-up. In addition, the application and IT architecture of Delta Lloyd are important, having regard to the current landscape. Harmonization with the program plan (or any bigger picture) is essential in the execution of a project. The performed Quick Scan is an important measurement for the project and the program.

The development projects are executed in a short cyclical and iterative way according to the Agile Scrum methodology. After the first process has gone live into production, the process can from then on be continuously improved on the basis of a number of optimization proposals. To facilitate this constant improvement cycle of the incumbent process, it was decided to combine You-Get's BPM approach with the Agile / Scrum methodology, resulting in a BPM Scrum approach.

The BPM Scrum approach describes the way of working whereby the current insurance processes are described in workshops and are analyzed, improved, automated and implemented jointly with the stakeholders of Delta Lloyd. These activities are executed by a BPM Scrum team consisting of the Product Owner (supported by consultants), a Scrum Master and a development team.

From a content perspective the product owner has ultimate responsibility for the BPM product and provides the vision for this BPM product. The consultants are responsible for the process description and documentation of the improved processes and transfer these to user stories. The development team is responsible for development, testing and implementation of the BPM Software solution. The scrum master facilitates this entire process. A project leader outside this team manages the project at the receiving (business) end.

The Delta Lloyd employees are trained and educated within the BPM Scrum team and supported by You-Get. In time the whole project will be executed by employees of Delta Lloyd. In this entire process, the emphasis is on continuous cooperation between the team itself, as well as with the Delta Lloyd organization, in order to ensure that the BPM implementation and the transition runs smoothly and without delay.

Step 7 – Innovative Process

The Private Persons – General Insurance Claims and Document Management processes of ABN AMRO Verzekeringen were taken into production successfully in early 2014. As a result of the implementation of these processes, ABN AMRO Verzekeringen is now much more flexible and efficient. All required information is constantly available in real time, allowing active management and control of these processes and enabling decisions to be taken and validated quickly. The next goal of ABN AMRO Verzekeringen is to optimize and extend the current processes even further.

Conclusion

The ultimate goal of Delta Lloyd is to transform into an Innovative Digital Insurance Company. The choice of full BPM implementation has led to the result that the targets within the "Digital Insurance" program have been more than achieved. In addition to the predefined targets, customers as well as management and end-users are experiencing a lot of positive effects. An extension to the next set of processes is therefore high on the list of priorities.

2. BUSINESS CONTEXT

Customers require and expect the following from financial service providers:

- To be reliable: they fulfil agreements and are transparent in terms of status, pricing and price structures;
- To be able to communicate through mobile and digital channels;
- To be able to respond swiftly, clearly and directly to requests and questions from customers;
- To be able to offer personal and direct contact (including by telephone) for the provision of service;
- To be able to offer customers the opportunity to be in control themselves: customers can acquire products or services themselves and report changes, when and how they want (preference channels);
- To show in their communication with customers that they understand what is important for the customer, in their particular circumstances.

Employees require and expect that the organization will offer facilities for working from home:

- Working from home in a responsible way, i.e. no confidential documents out in the open
- Working from home can be managed and monitored;
- Working from home should be as convenient as working from the Delta Lloyd offices;
- Expanding the attractiveness of Delta Lloyd Group as an employer for (new) employees;
- Enabling paperless working;
- Reducing the cost of office buildings for Delta Lloyd Group

Regulatory bodies such as AFM (Dutch Financial Market Regulator) are making higher demands of financial services providers, such as:

- Transparency (in terms of status and price structure);
- Clarity and care towards customers (duty of care, customer-focused insurance hallmark, customer interest as a main goal)
- Auditing of customer contacts.

Delta Lloyd also wants to be a "trusted insurer", because it can then demonstrate compliance with legislation and compliancy demands such as record-keeping. Delta Lloyd has the ambition to lead in the above-mentioned market developments, so as to guarantee continuity and stand out from the competition.

A number of digitization initiatives have been started within Delta Lloyd in past years. To gain greater control of these initiatives, it has been decided to combine them for ABN AMRO Verzekeringen within a program entitled "Digitaal Verzekeren" (Digital Insurance).

By managing the digitization initiatives as a coherent program, potential inconsistencies have largely been prevented. In addition, process optimization, operational excellence, output management, "Sterk Werk" (time and location-independent working as well as cost reduction), must support the goals and targets of the "Digitaal Verzekeren" program.

Targets and Goals:

- Paperless work: digitizing the 'physical' postal streams for reasons of sustainability, costs and efficient work;
- Time- and location-independent working: to enable employees to work in a controlled manner;
- Short processing time: putting the interests of the customer at the center with the processes, with fast and secure processing;
- Transparency of the process to customers and others;
- To strengthen control of the process (not only in individual cases, but also in the overall process).

3. THE KEY INNOVATIONS

3.1 Business

The implementation of the BPM solution has advantages for the customer and the operational teams as well as staff teams. Digitizing the paper postal stream is part of the sustainability drivers. The implementation of the BPM solution makes it possible to work on a location-independent basis and to work in a paperless office. Working from home can be achieved smoothly and efficiently, with the employee being supported in performing the required administrative activities. This means the employee will view Delta Lloyd as a modern employer, preventing unnecessary travel and providing greater opportunity for employees to plan their individual working hours.

BPM(S) places customer experience at the center of the processes, leading to proper and fast servicing of that customer. This means greater control of the process, and hence cost savings.

On top of that, the implemented solution offers process transparency for both customers and other parties.

3.2 Case Handling

Before the project

Before the implementation of the BPM solution, case building was carried out to a minimal extent within ABN AMRO Verzekeringen. All dossiers were physically (paper-based) managed by one person. Some departments were using a basic workflow registration system (WSR) alongside the physical files and dossiers. This was not the case with the implemented processes using the BPM solution.

After the project

For the realization of the first two processes, ABN AMRO Verzekeringen defined a client-event model. Within this model an event (e.g. an accident) can trigger one or more cases in multiple products. Every case within the event is defined as "a set of documents, information and activities related to each other and therefore treated as a unit". The client-event model is designed to support multiple cases in one event to run simultaneously and supports multiple running processes in one case as well. The result of one case can have an effect on all or one of the cases within the event and processes running in the case itself can have an effect on the other processes.

The fact that documents belonging to one specific case do not always come in at the same time needs to be taken into account during classification and indexing.

After the information has been updated, it will be checked and validated using the case identifier to determine whether or not the document belongs to an existing case / process, or whether a new process may need to be started.

If a situation arises whereby a document comes in later and belongs to a closed case (e.g. a forgotten claim belonging to an old event), a new process will be started. Depending on the process, the employee will determine which steps need to be dealt with. A closed case can be reopened again because of the document but it could also be that because of the document the case can be closed. The closing of cases is done only after all relevant triggers have been fired at other applications and a confirmation letter to the customer is received from the automated document generation application. This way the case is always complete when closed.

By using the "customer overview" screen, the employee gets into the customer screen. In this screen it is possible to look at all information related to running and closed events, cases and processes of the customer. All levels within the event: client, case, document, process, tasks etc. are visible to the employee. By using a number of selections and filters (comparable with Excel filters) in the screen, the results can be adapted. In this way the employee can easily look into one or more cases and is able to update multiple cases and can provide a customer with all relevant information in one glance, thus enabling the principle of "first time right".

Follow up actions can be chosen from this "customer overview" screen and new tasks, processes and cases can be created and assigned to all users of the BPM solution. In the current processes the choices are all pre-determined and not dynamic, but in next phases follow up actions will become more dynamic and ad-hoc. The targeted and designed end result will be a full dynamic case management solution.

3.3 Organization & Social

The impact on the operational teams is substantial. They have to get used to working in a paperless way and to be able to plan their working hours themselves, as well as taking the opportunity to work at a different location. With the BPM solution they are better equipped to do their work, since they now have one system providing them with an overview. The employees are supported in the required administrative activities by the BPM solution. With the case file implementation, there is no longer any need to look for an actual physical file or dossier, nor any need to get connected to that one specific co-worker who currently has the physical file under his or her control.

Delta Lloyd is working on setting up and securing the competence profiles. The BPM solution is a new application and is considered to be a knowledge extension (competence) on top of the existing roles and functions. Competence management ensures that knowledge and experience, as built up with BPM within the ABN AMRO Verzekeringen program, becomes transferable and reusable for other implementation projects in other business divisions of the Delta Lloyd Group. Developing BPM Competence management is a joint responsibility of all involved parties.

A BPM manual has been compiled to support the BPM project. This contains a description of the agreements and the aforementioned best practices to be used when applying BPM within the Delta Lloyd Group, and contributing to the standardization of the approach and the way of working. The broader use of BPM within the Delta Lloyd organization is picking up now, and applying this model will facilitate this almost organic growth in a pragmatic fashion.

The implementation of a BPM Center of Excellence is now ongoing on a number of levels. The establishment of a Center of Excellence is seen as a tremendous added value within Delta Lloyd.

4. HURDLES OVERCOME

4.1 Management

The commitment and the daily involvement of the management of ABN AMRO Verzekeringen and Delta Lloyd have ensured the successful implementation of this project. The management was tenacious and maintained the necessary staying power, which it also conveyed to the operational teams on the shop floor. The management has been flexible and sufficiently open for advice. In addition, the project has been sponsored by the Board.

4.2 Business

The business has at all times shown a lot of drive as well as carrying out the required daily activities. It has adapted well to the new processes. It has been a challenge for the business to critically assess what was really needed. This required the ability to let go of the "old pattern" as well as the former way of thinking. Moreover, this had to be done in a short timeframe.

4.3 Organization Adoption

Adoption within the end-user community has been incredibly high. This is because they were involved from day one and because a phased go-live approach was adopted, providing users with enough time to get used to the new solution. The use of BPMS has not been forced upon them; the business has implemented it itself. The chosen steps were validated for all those involved (including stakeholders) in a vast number of playbacks. This ensured that no one was taken by surprise and changes could be implemented on time when required. The active attitude and commitment of the project team members and the management also contributed strongly to the high level of acceptance of the solution on all levels of the business organization.

5. BENEFITS

Cost Savings / Time Reductions

Optimization of the processes leads to clearer agreements and an acceleration of the entire process. BPM leads directly to faster communication with the customer. Agreements (lead time) made with the customer are now being achieved. Regulatory and policy values concerning the lead time of communication and feedback to the customer are being fulfilled.

BPM will lead directly to a reduction of FTEs on the shop floor. Although this is not an objective in itself, it has a direct effect of increasing the profit margin.

Previously the management was only capable of managing retrospectively, because the required information was also only provided retrospectively. With the implementation of BPM there is now direct control of standards that are at risk of being exceeded, and this is now leading directly to management of the 'obstacles' in order to be more successful.

Cost savings and reduction of throughput time are not primary goals and targets of the project implementation, but they are a positive indirect consequence.
- 100 percent paperless working; files and dossiers can no longer get lost.
- When the Go-Live of the A&B (Acceptance & Support) and SSC (Shared Services Center) departments has been completed, a total of 160,000

cases will be processed digitally (previously postal mail documents). This concerns approximately 50 FTEs in total;

- Reduction of four FTEs out of 80 (five percent); because of digitization and process management, the roles of mail delivery to the proper department, as well as workload balancer, have become obsolete after the first go-live and this reduction will grow in subsequent go-lives;
- Processing a claim treatment (filling out the first-time-fix form) at the shared services center has been reduced by 75 percent (from two minutes to 30 seconds);
- Time-independent working; this concerns over 50 FTEs in total;
- Location-independent working; this concerns over 50 FTEs in total.

An even bigger gain on throughput time will be achieved when an interface is established with a VTA (Insurance Technical Application). This is planned as part of the future scope.

Increased Revenues

The implementation of this project does not have a direct impact on an increase in revenue. The target of providing the most transparent possible overall view for the customer and an increased quality of service will nevertheless make a positive contribution in terms of an increase in the overall number of customers, leading to an increase in revenue.

Quality Improvements

The biggest quality improvement is the digital case file / dossier. Physical files are no longer required and therefore can no longer get lost. There is now uniformity in processing the processes, as well as firm control of the processes. On top of that there is a demonstrable quality improvement in terms of the throughput time that ABN AMRO Verzekeringen communicates to its customers. The real-time availability of management information also contributes to this.

- Extension of management information, detailed information about a case, lead time and urgency. A file / dossier is no longer in the hands of one user, so if this person becomes inactive, the case can still continue;
- Extended file / dossier compilation. ABN AMRO Verzekeringen can now document Input and Output, together with the process steps and choices made, in the case. The file is more complete now, greatly improving the audit trail;
- Standard processes, which are better for the customer because the quality of services delivered remains the same regardless of the user.

1. BEST PRACTICES, LEARNING POINTS AND PITFALLS

Best Practices and Learning Points

- ✓ *Take small steps;*
- ✓ *Document the future vision clearly, share it and monitor it continuously;*
- ✓ *Continue to involve more people from the business, do not go for only one or two "opinions";*
- ✓ *Clearly define roles upfront: who is approving which activity or document, and who is also taking responsibility for that;*
- ✓ *All involved people need to remain engaged in an active and short cyclical manner;*
- ✓ *The purpose of the documentation must be unambiguous;*
- ✓ *Set up a clear and transparent test plan, and stick to it.*

Pitfalls

With the aforementioned best-practice approach there will be a continuous learning cycle for improvement. This can potentially lead to a number of pitfalls:

Generic

- × *Do not try to think for someone else;*
- × *Always validate the requirements with the proper responsible party;*

Governance

- × *Make sure there is the right level of connection with other running projects;*
- × *Do not only set up requirements for the current situation, but also focus on and think about the future;*

Communication

- × *The business is inclined to use the current process as a starting point;*
- × *Do not try to think about everything beforehand;*

Execution

- × *It is not only about the implementation of BPM; it is the complete transition around it. This also requires proper attention;*
- × *Do not try to start implementing as fast as possible;*

Performance

- × *Integration with other systems can be quite complex.*

6. COMPETITIVE ADVANTAGES

Delta Lloyd considers BPM tooling important in supporting the increasing demands regarding;

- Faster and first time right servicing of customers
- Compliance with internal and external policies
- Efficiency to reduce processing costs

7. TECHNOLOGY

The following principles apply to the Delta Lloyd IT and Services organization:

- Using existing standard services and technologies: reuse, before buy, before build. Delta Lloyd has a Technical Reference Architecture in which the standard infrastructure building blocks are defined;
- There is a single integrated BPM development environment for the BPM competence center: standardization of development environment, standards, guidelines and cost savings;
- Every business unit has its "own" logical BPM deployment environment: because of logical separation of runtime deployment environments, the workloads of different business units are separated and portable, and capacity and performance can be specifically allocated;
- Authentication and authorization of BPM services is handled in the generic user access environment: all BPM workflow applications and STP services are protected and secured using generic user access management tooling;
- The existing WPS services of Delta Lloyd Life are migrated to the new BPM 8.5 deployment environment: the WAS 8.5 BPM environment is the technological successor of the current WAS7 WPS environment. Maintaining old environments means extra costs (licenses, hardware, support);

- Integration of BPM with other business services is handled via Datapower: all WebServices that BPM exposes or consumes are configured in Datapower. Routing, load balancing / failover, security and logging are configured in Datapower, so continuity, security and controllability of the chain is guaranteed;
- Security with external parties is configured in TAM on the basis of mutual SSL authentication: TAM Webseal is the standard building block for authentication. Delta Lloyd delivers the client authentication certificates for the other party;
- All incoming messages are secured: securing ensures that no data is lost in the event of a technical error, and an audit trail is maintained for the source of delivered data;
- Cross-platform file integration takes place through MQ FTE: MQ FTE is the standard file transfer technology within Delta Lloyd and delivers managed transfer (monitored);
- Transport channels for data with integrity and confidentiality classifications of Extremely High Security with certificates (encryption and signing); http security through certificates and SSL encryption MQ AMS for Messaging.

In addition to these principles, a number of new challenges have arisen for Delta Lloyd:

- Multiple Process Server Runtime Deployment environments. The goal is multi-tenant (Business Unit hosting) in one generic BPM hosting environment;
- One process center environment for multiple BPM development teams. The goal is to support the new BPM development team for life insurance;
- Migration of Process Center Database to production DB2 hosting environment. The goal is to have performance optimization and meet "production-like" service levels on the data and database level;
- Multiple process integration patterns via Datapower. The goal is the exposure of BPM STP services to front-office systems and integration of DL VTA back-office systems;
- Migration of WPS on WAS7 to new BPM Advanced WAS8.5 infrastructure. The goal is to migrate and integrate the current WPS (STP) services in the new BPM Advanced processes and infrastructure.

The principles and challenges have resulted in the following overview of activities within the Delta Lloyd IT landscape:

- Documents are scanned in the Kofax scan infrastructure;
- Files / documents are offered to the BPM platform through IBM MQ FTE;
- Documents are archived and saved in the IBM Content Manager (via the IMIS interface, which is the generic BPM application);
- Cases are created in IMIS (BPM) with reference to documents in IBM Content Manager;
- IMIS (BPM) determines which sub process needs to be started.

An important guideline is that the existing infrastructure should be used for both user maintenance and support of the platform (Websphere). Another essential guideline concerns the split into different applications: one generic for the determination of metadata for each incoming document from different sources (scanned, mail, bank, web application). This initiates processes in other applications, where the business rules of that department reside.

The overall advantage of BPM for the technology (IT&S) organization of Delta Lloyd:

- Work can be picked up per role, so is automatically available to the right people;
- Working online is possible, so no physical presence is required;
- Monitoring of processes and process status is easier;
- Location and time-independent working;
- Digitization of input (scanning/email/internet);
- Making work bins and information available digitally in the workflow application;
- Optimization of workflow processes: securing processes digitally (monitoring) and configuring flexibly;
- Automation of workflow processes: automating process tasks through integration with the Delta Lloyd application landscape.

8. THE TECHNOLOGY AND SERVICE PROVIDERS

You-Get is the BPM partner for Delta Lloyd and ABN AMRO Verzekeringen. You-Get has advised and executed a BPM approach according to the 360° Business Services Approach™ developed in house.

In this approach, a clear growth path is followed via different dimensions: process management, strategy, culture, organization, ICT and BPM Governance. This BPM approach is realized through iterations with support in the form of advice, training, tools, best practice methodology and project management and has been successfully applied by You-Get on numerous occasions. In the software track You-Get has implemented the IBM BPM software with success.

IBM provided the BPMS software for the project implementation. After pre-defined blocks of the project went live, IBM was also involved in health checks of the full application, including toolkits. As part of the health checks, best-practice follow-up and generic architecture and set-up were checked. You-Get has taken the results of these health checks and incorporated them in the continuous cycle of process optimization and improvement.

Freedom Mortgage, USA

1. EXECUTIVE SUMMARY / ABSTRACT

This case study details the **Retail Title Track Rewrite Process**.

Title Ordering and Review are key components of the mortgage financing process. Title ordering and the title search process reveal the financial obligations that could potentially impact the sale of the property, including such actions such as lawsuits, liens, legal claims, etc. The mortgage lender holds responsibility for the title review process.

The change to this process impacted the Title department, closers, mortgage applicants, title providers, and FMCs management team. FMCs Title Process dramatically changed the once manually intensive title ordering/review process. The Retail Title Process Rewrite Project uses a BPM solution to modify the timing of the preliminary title review, indexes title documents to the EDMS(Electronic Document Management System), modifies the ownership of activities to make the Exception Reviewer the performer of all post-Exception Review tasks; and allows delivery of a title order cancellation event to the integrated Title Vendor terminating both the BPM and external systems' instances.

Finally, the creation of a real-time dashboard provides management with a view into task metrics (such as title ordering). As a result of this project, the speed of the Title Process increased by 51 percent, with reduction employees needed to complete the title process 52 percent. However, the most important intangible benefit was the acceptance of the BPM team into the fabric of the organization; it is now easier for the BPM team to work with business units on initiatives since the Retail Title Track Rewrite Project was a visible, well-documented success.

2. OVERVIEW

Definition of Mortgage Title and Mortgage Title Insurance

Title is the legal term used to describe the conveyance of a bundle of rights in a piece of property. Title is necessary to convey ownership of the property and is an essential part of the home purchase process. Public records, such as recording of deeds, liens, easements, and other encumbrances, provide evidence of the property's title history.

A title insurance policy is a contract of indemnity that guarantees that the title is as reported. If the title is not as described, and the owner is "harmed" at a later date, the title policy covers the insured for loss up to the face amount of the policy.

A title search and issuance of title insurance is required during the mortgage process. Title Insurance Companies issue title insurance which protects the potential home buyer against previous encumbrances not revealed through a thorough search of public records. Title Insurance insures prospective homeowners during the purchase process that they are acquiring marketable title to the property upon settlement of funds. In other words, title insurance provides insurance against title defects from past events. Title insurance provides coverage only for title problems that were in existence at the time the policy was issued.

Issuing a title insurance policy is an exacting process. Title insurance companies work to eliminate risks by performing a painstaking search of the public records, laws, and court decisions pertaining to the property and the parties to the escrow are maintained.

Freedom Mortgage orders title insurance for buyers applying for mortgage financing for the property and reviews the titles.

The "As-Is" State of the Title Process (Prior to BPM)

The Retail Title process allows for the processing of title policy orders through the Retail Call Center Operations "Title Track" process; this process is either integrated or manual. Orders with preferred vendors are handled through integration with software that enables paperless mortgage preparation and ordering of the title policy documents. Manual orders are routed to a sub-process that allows for the follow-up and tracking required for obtaining the required title policy documents.

The title documents were reviewed by the Freedom Mortgage Retail Center Operations team after the title provider renders a decision on the quality of the title.

3. BUSINESS CONTEXT

Challenges for the Title Track team include work management for title orders from preferred vendors outside of their control and the need to create a sense of personal accountability for each loan acquired by the Title Track team member to motivate employees in a tedious task. There is a need for reporting to manage title orders.

The business wanted to change the title process to move the review of the title document back to when it is first received instead of the current process timing when the decision is provided by the title provider. The decision has also been made to move to a pod-type concept where there is one Quality Assurance (QA) reviewer and a group of exception reviewers tied to each title from the time of the first review.

The goals of the To-Be state add functionality to the existing Retail Title Process:

- Modify timing of preliminary title review.
- Modify ownership of activities so that the exception reviewer becomes the performer of all post-exception review tasks.
- Enhance task presentation in the dashboard view.
- Provide management team access to the task management module.
- Index documents to an electronic database system based upon specific elements in the inbound automated title request event.
- Allow delivery of an order cancellation event from Freedom Mortgage to the integrated title vendor, terminating both the Business Process Management (BPM) and their propriety title-order software instances.
- Enhance task presentation in the manual title process,

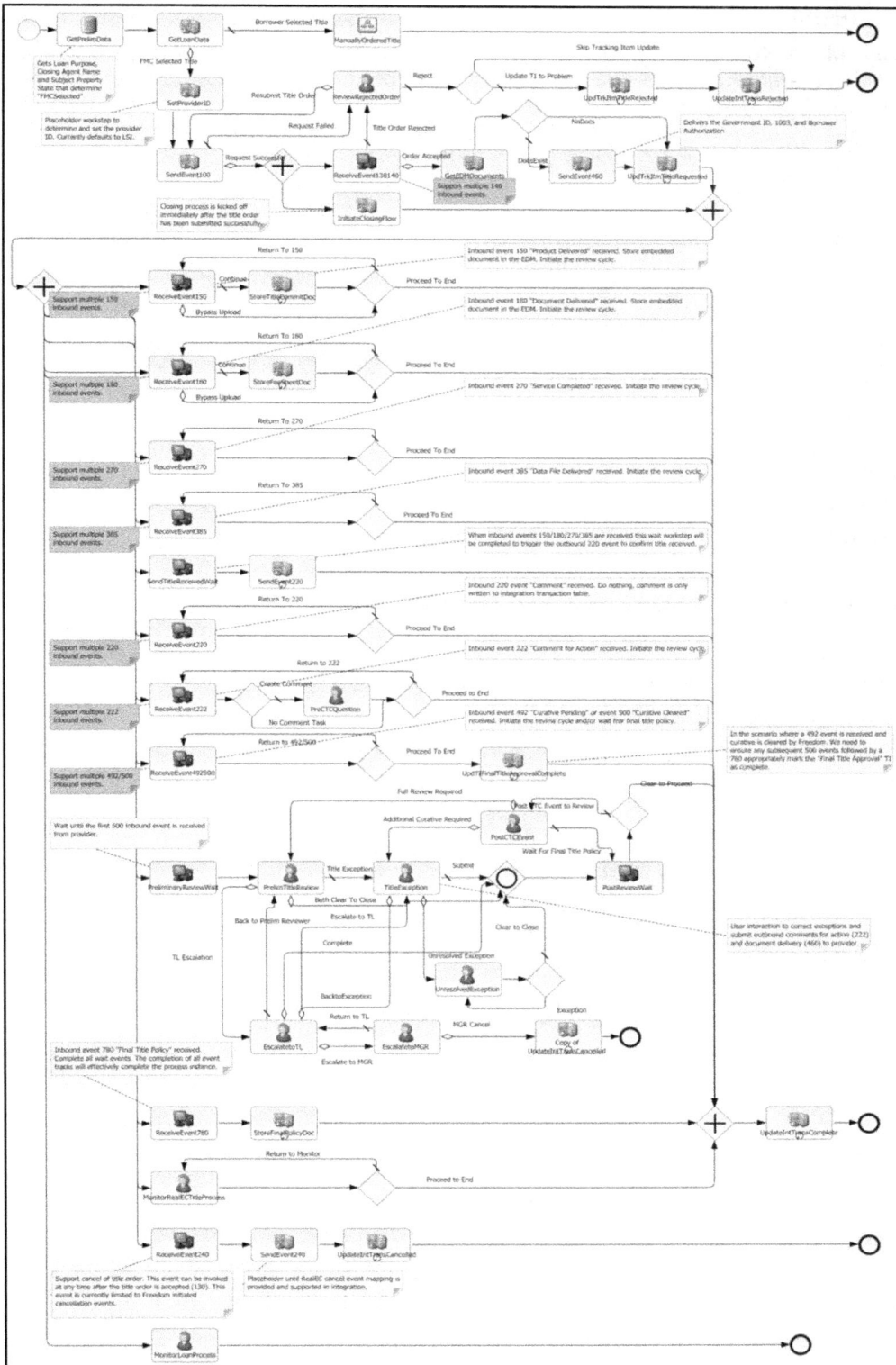

Figure 1: To Be Title Process Design

4. THE KEY INNOVATIONS

Exception Review Handling for title defects is a key innovation of the process. The newly created tab allows the user to view comments from Freedom Mortgage's proprietary Loan Origination System within the BPM, title provider review comments (if integrated) within the system, and a review checklist for the title.

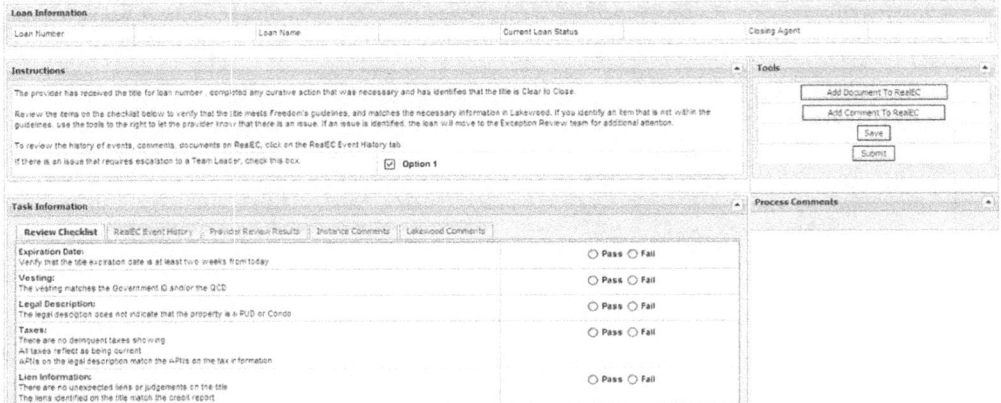

Figure 2: Exception Review of Title Process with checklist

Team Leader / Manager Question Handling allows the team lead and the manager to receive questions and review all comments/work performed on the title in one screen:

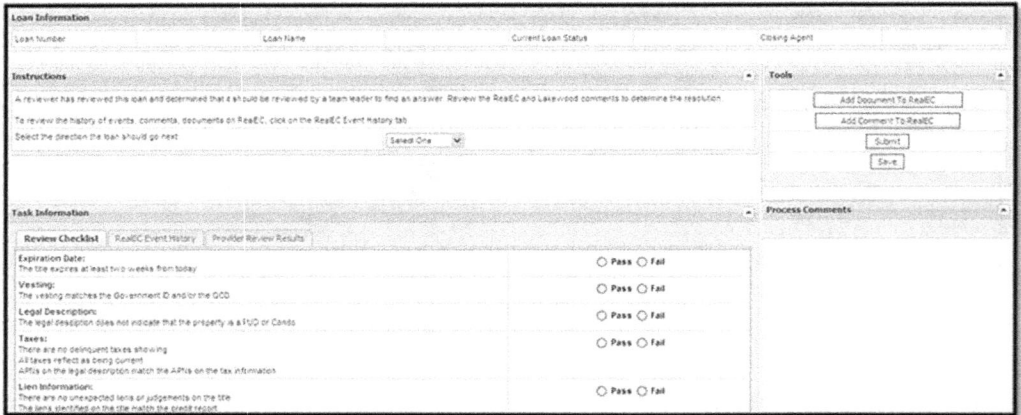

Figure 3: Team Lead Screen

Dashboard creation for individuals, team leads, and management is a key innovation in this process. The Pipeline Summary shows all of the loans with their related title statuses. The dashboard displays links to the loans, tasks the user must complete, and the name of the active work step. Moreover, the dashboard shows My Unresolved Exceptions. When an Exception reviewer completes the Exception Review work step without marking the Clear to Close indicator as TRUE, the workflow moves to the Unresolved Exception work step, and the loan is displayed in the My Unresolved Exceptions widget. The columns shown within this widget include:

- Loan Number
- Loan Name

- Last Saved/Completed Timestamp
- Instance Comment

Loan Processor Monitoring (Integration with outside title vendors) shows all posted events for the Title product based upon the Loan Number and provider review checklist. Items needing to be addressed (or cleared to close) to issue a title are clearly indicated. Comment fields capture important information.

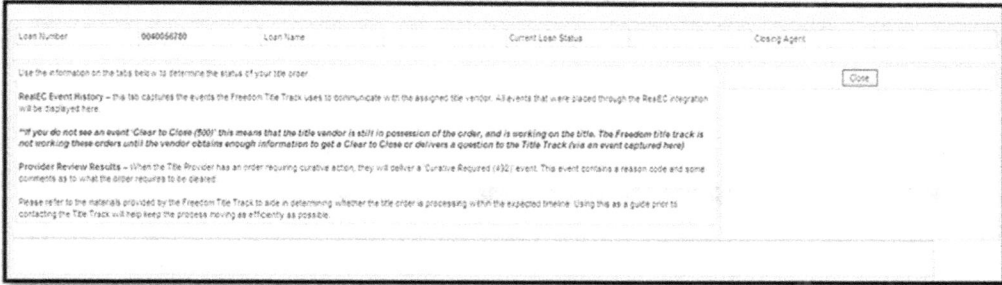

Figure 4: Event History

Dashboards indicate success with external title vendors and provide Freedom Mortgage employees a window of understanding into external vendors' work in the title process performed on Freedom Mortgage's behalf.

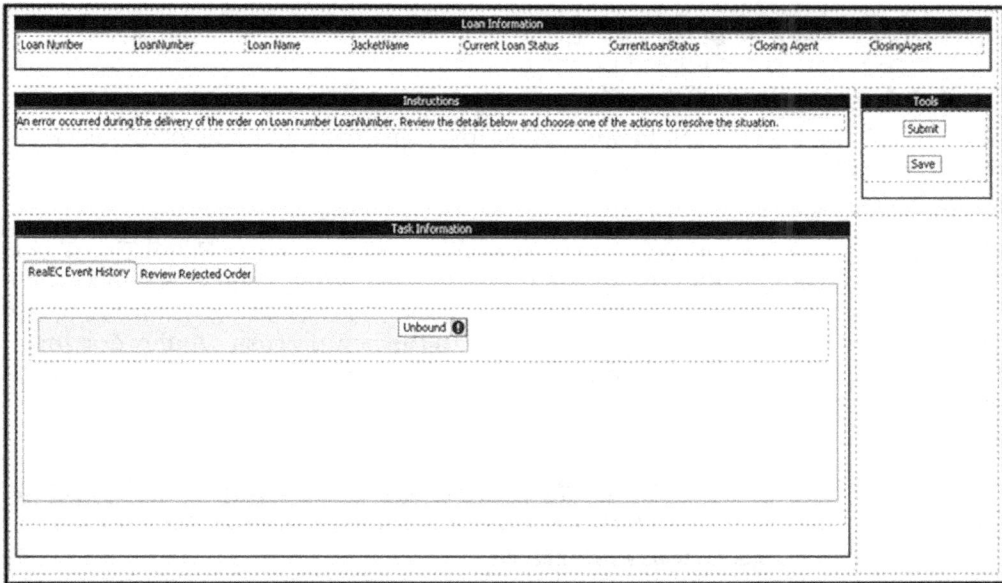

Figure 5: Integration Screen with External System Showing Error (Unsuccessful Title Request)

Clear to close issues marked as such by external vendors are clearly delineated, and the Freedom Mortgage employee can review those items and determine concurrence of the external vendor's assessment of the title issues.

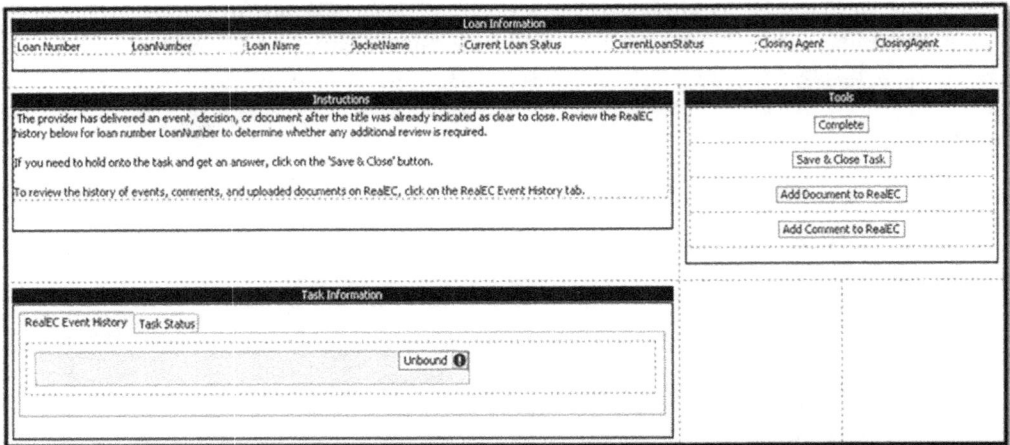

Figure 6: Clear to Close Review of External Vendor's Assessment

4.1. OBJECTIVE

4.3 Case Handling
No case management used in this project.

4.4 Organization & Social
The Retail Title Track Team is now staffed by 52 percent less employees since the implementation of this solution because of increased efficiency.

5. HURDLES OVERCOME
Management was eager to adopt new business processes in the Retail Title Track. The business users felt empowered with the clear assignment of tasks and the ability to send questions to team leads within the system. Thorough training of end users allowed the users to feel comfortable with the new process. Quality documentation of the business process and creation of job aids and process flows greatly assisted implementation of the new process.

6. BENEFITS
As a result of this project, the speed of the Title Process increased by 51 percent, with reduction employees needed to complete the title process 52 percent.

6.1 Cost Savings / Time Reductions
As a result of this project, the speed of the Title Process increased by 51 percent.

6.2 Increased Revenues
Reduction employees needed to complete the title process 52 percent.

6.3 Quality Improvements
Improved exception handling to clear title exceptions and the creation of dashboards improve the title process. However, the most important intangible benefit was the acceptance of the BPM team into the fabric of the organization; it is now easier for the BPM team to work with business units on initiatives since the Retail Title Track Rewrite Project was a visible, well-documented success.

7. BEST PRACTICES, LEARNING POINTS AND PITFALLS

7.1 Best Practices and Learning Points

✓ *Exception review handling for title best performed if the exception is made the default performer; Q_TitleExceptionReview*

　　o *If the Preliminary Reviewer has indicated that a Subordination is required, the performer is set to Q_TitleExceptionReviewSUB*

　　o *Once the task has been acquired the Performer is changed to the current user.*

　　o *The Exception Reviewer also becomes the performer for any Event questions (Event 222's) that are already in queue or received during the review period.*

　　o *Any Event 222's that are received after the review is complete are assigned to the default performer*

✓ *Agile software development methodology allowed the business users to see the new system early in the process thereby enabling the development team to loop-in their feedback for subsequent revisions.*

✓ *Robust Quality Assurance testing key to successful external/internal system integrations.*

7.2 Pitfalls

✗ *Adapters to external sources require more time than planned.*

✗ *Creating effective dashboards that meet business needs a highly iterative process.*

8. COMPETITIVE ADVANTAGES

The modified process provides dashboards for managers and employees offering real-time transparency into the title process. Integration with the vendor's systems through BPM reduces errors and increases speed.

9. TECHNOLOGY

The creation of BPM dashboards and routing of work within these dashboard queues enhanced the title rewrite process. The screens developed are streamlined and uncluttered, allowing for quick scanning of title issues, outstanding questions, and clear assignment of tasks.

10. THE TECHNOLOGY AND SERVICE PROVIDERS

RealEC® Technologies, a division of Black Knight Financial Services, is Freedom Mortgage's vendor for paperless mortgage solutions.

Aurea's Savvion BPM is one of Freedom Mortgage's BPM automation solutions, and it is the solution used in the process described in this case study.

GE Avio Srl, Italy
Nominated by EKA Srl, Italy

1. EXECUTIVE SUMMARY / ABSTRACT

In 2012 Avio SpA, now General Electric Avio, supplier of engine modules and components, started a new project to modernize the management and dissemination of quality procedures.

Promoted by the Quality Unit, this initiative involved an inter-disciplinary project team composed by several divisions (e.g. Purchase, Business, and Logistics) with the additional participation of the IT Unit and EKA Srl, in charge of IT system development.

The new approach consists of a quality system that aims to map operational processes and gathers them under a unique reference tool to all procedures.

The platform consists of a multi-language web-based solution developed by Signavio GmbH, enabling collaborative modeling and optimizing business processes according to BPMN 2.0 standard. The platform combines professional BPM with the advantages of collaboration during the design phase: a certified cloud platform that ensures the preservation of confidential avionic information.

The main benefits introduced are: structured definition of business process and rules that govern them; self-understanding of the employees' activities positioning in the corporate environment; integration of multiple document management systems into a single platform; automatic generation of official documentation and real time knowledge management of rules' updates.

2. OVERVIEW

Avio SpA, now General Electric (GE) Avio, is an important Italian aerospace company, leader in the development of engine modules and components for aircraft industry (mainly turbines and gearboxes,). The headquarters are in Italy, with divisions located in Turin, Pomigliano and Brindisi, while production plants are situated in Poland, Brazil, USA and China.

In order to improve the compliance with company procedures, GE Avio started a new project to modernize the management of quality-related procedures. The project combined two important themes: the compliance with quality standards and the Business Process Management methodology.

Due to the multidisciplinary and cross-functional context, the project involved all business units led by the Quality Unit.

The project aimed to implement a methodology and an information system, in order to enable the understanding and dissemination of operational processes among workers. An additional scope was to facilitate the creation, reviewing, and updating of quality standards by certification units. The result of this work was expected to provide a new approach in mapping operational processes and managing all quality-related documents and processes, via a unique platform called SGP ("Sistema di Gestione per Processi").

This new system provides benefits and positive results about usability, searches of quality-related information and documents by all users, and the simplification of quality procedures formalization process.

3. Business Context

In GE Avio, the update and usage of quality processes was characterized by high complexity related to: (1) dissemination and explanation of firm processes among workers; (2) creation, update and review of procedures by certification units. In fact, workers did not exhibit a good and complete knowledge of processes. Two main reasons were identified.

- The structure of quality-related procedures was characterized by a vertical and very stratified arrangement, composed of many levels: the "integrate management system" is the main quality document; processes directives or documents at a business processes level; sub-processes procedures, related with sub-process level; instructions, related with macro-activities and technical documents.
- The knowledge sharing was done with paper documents, so the users had access only to static information.

In addition, the flow for creation, modification or update of quality-related procedures was very complex: the main unit involved was the Quality Unit, which was the promoter of the formalization or updating activities. However, this unit had to interact with many different departments. In the best-case scenario, when the documents contained all the information required, the task for the Quality Unit was just to verify them. Otherwise, this unit was in charge of preparing the documentation in collaboration with the interested unit(s) and workers. This meant collecting the process description, generating the documentation, and verifying its correctness with the interested department, see Figure 1.

This flow required many information exchanges and feedbacks (by email, paper documents exchanges, meeting, etc.).

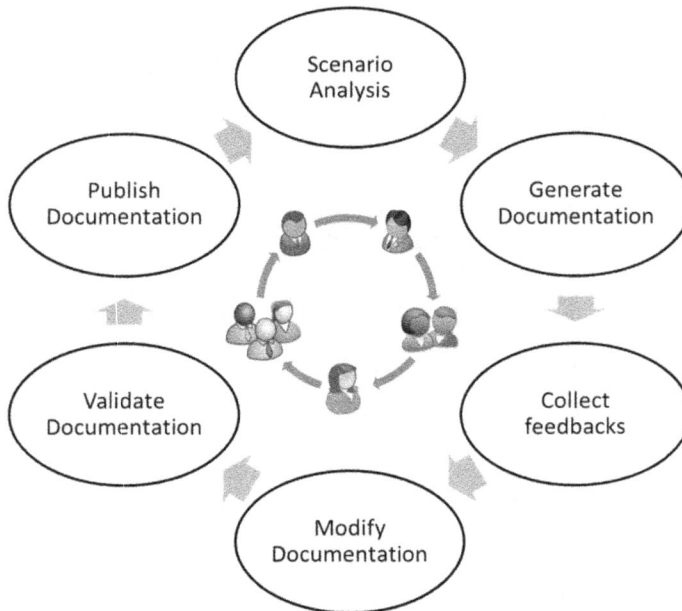

Figure 1 - Example of quality collaboration scenario.

Moreover, the system used to formalize processes and information was MS Word. To track reviews, for example, it was the used convention to underline the changes; so users focused on the changes, losing attention about the global quality scenario.

Quality documents produced with MS Word were published in the company intranet. This acted as a repository of about 1000 unlinked documents, difficult to explore and retrieve all the information required.

These reasons urged the company to have a methodology and a technological system to manage documentation. The system had to be designed as process-centric, so to facilitate the dissemination and understanding of quality processes by workers, supporting all the business units to create, review and publish procedures.

This BPM approach is in agreement with the GE Avio trend to shift from the traditional functional-view to a process-centric company view.

4. THE KEY INNOVATIONS

4.1 Business

The implementation of this BPM solution has provoked a radical transformation in the company business, because of the improved visibility of company processes. A good example of this evolution can be given in terms of internal and external company audits.

The internal audits are carried out by Quality Unit and by other units (in particular by Product Quality and Laboratories units). These audits are checklists compiled with the workers that verify, for example, if they know their duties and responsibilities, if these responsibilities are well defined, if the workers know the general principles of testing and quality, the instructions and finally if they correctly applied these instructions. For example, the results of the audits are used to review the quality management system and can lead to organizational changes (such as the reorganization of some divisions), or the calculation of quality scores for customers' satisfaction.

The external audits are carried out by customers and certification authorities. The most important external audits are conducted by the certification authority (EASA, CAA) to check the compliance of quality certifications with the standard EN9100, or to achieve additional certifications for the company processes, such as the Quality System certification according to the standard AS9110A (requirements for Aviation Maintenance Organizations). These audits also check if the documentation is incomplete, outdated, not available in the workplace or not known/implemented. Finally, the qualifications of the operating staff are also important.

For these reasons, this scenario emphasizes how important it is to have a system that allows to explore each process and sub-process in a clear way, and to easily access information and rules related to each activity. Finally, it is important for workers to understand the importance of management of processes that can bring benefit in terms of clarity and efficiency.

4.2 Case Handling

Due to transversal themes handled by the project and the involvement of multiple business areas in the quality-related processes, the project needed a multidisciplinary team. The team was formed by: experts of quality procedures and processes, the IT team, BPM technological and methodological specialists and the Quality Unit. In particular, the Quality Unit was responsible for the periodic verification of project progress and findings.

The project development has been structured in four main phases (Figure 2). Firstly, in order to understand the business context and to highlight the company needs, the team conducted an As-Is analysis, consisting of:

- interviewing key people of different business units, to discover and identify activities, actors, resources and information flow, characterizing the process of quality documentation management and to point out the actual problems;
- analysis of the quality procedures, instructions, and documents.

This phase led to the identification of two main needs: (1) facilitate the access to available know-how by workers; (2) supervise the correctness and the compliance with quality standards.

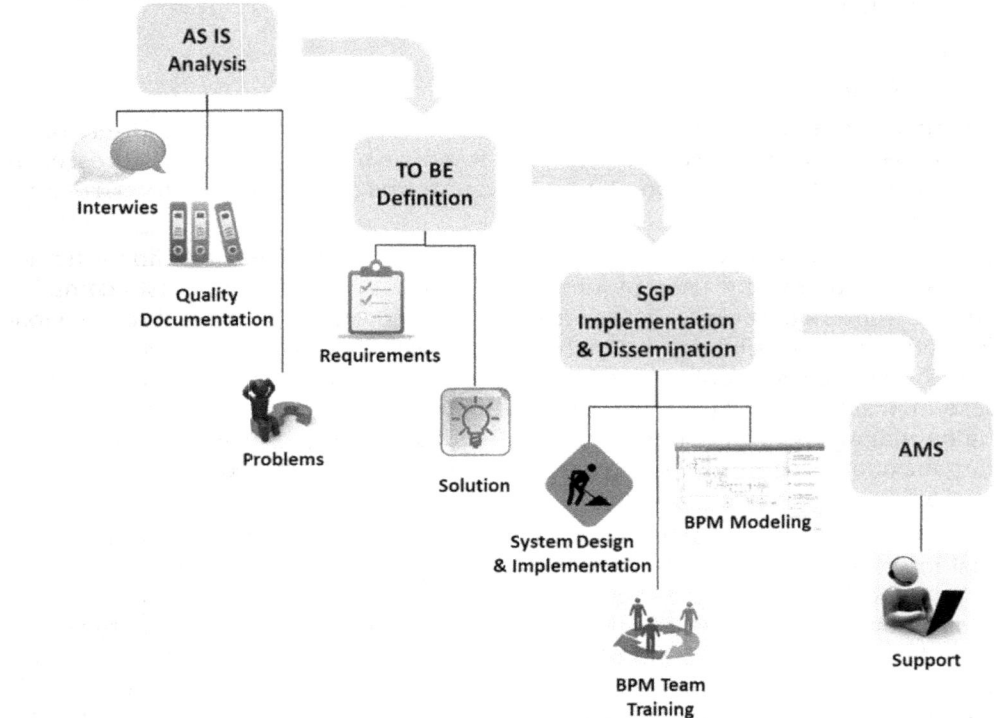

Figure 2 – SGP Project Phases.

The second step was represented by the design of the To-Be phase: the analysis of the As-Is had led to the decision to start a change management initiative to reorganize the quality management process. A new approach, methodological and technological, has been established and it is based on:

- the graphical representation of quality procedures, via BPMN 2.0 standard language, easy to understand by every company worker;
- the introduction of a BPM team in every unit;
- the design of a new information system to create, update and publish quality processes.

A benchmark among BPM tools highlighted Signavio as the best tool available for the design and publishing of quality processes. The main reasons for this choice are as follows: it is intuitive and customizable; it permits the comparison among different process diagrams; it can be integrated with MS SharePoint; it is based on a cloud architecture, so users can access to an on-line workspace, without any installation required.

The innovative approach aims to map operational processes and to gather them under a unique reference tool, for all procedures.

The SGP system, in fact, has been designed to model processes in a collaborative manner and to publish them on the intranet site. The workers are now able to browse processes and to access quality documentation.

As shown in Figure 3, the SGP system is composed of five main logical units:

- *Graphical Process Editor* that is used to create and edit a diagram, to extract reports and official documents, to publish diagrams, to define roles and rules.
- *Quick Model* that allows fast process capturing and completion by all users, without knowing modeling conventions. It enables to create diagrams through a table based modeling approach. The user inserts information by filling a table and the system automatically creates the graphical diagram representation.
- *Analytics Module* that helps the processes management and evaluation, via standard instruments and functionalities. E.g. it is possible to extract the RACI matrix (Responsible, Accountable, Consulted and Informed), used to represent individual responsibilities for the various activities.
- *MS SharePoint Process Portal* that is integrated into the intranet-site. It enables workers to browse processes, read official documents and attachments, and to search information efficiently and effectively, thanks to the search engine function.
- *Reporting documentation* that allows creating and printing the process documentation. It consists of a graphical panel, enriched by a set of custom document templates, where graphical elements and shapes can be "dragged and dropped", without prior knowledge of any programming language.

Modules in grey "next steps" area are actually available on Signavio Platform and represent future developments of the SGP Project.

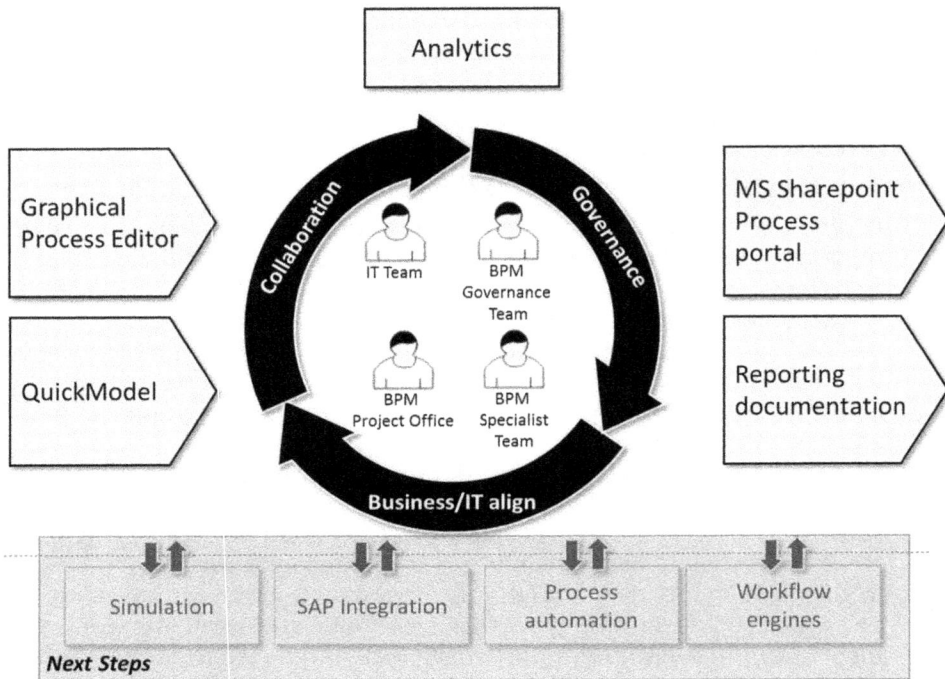

Figure 3 - SGP Project overview.

The pilot process modeled is "Procuring Materials and Services". It is a complex process, because it is characterized by many quality procedures and links between them, many actors and organizational units involved, many sub-processes and activities. Moreover, it represents a cross process impacting all product lifecycle phases. The Quality organizational unit has modeled this process with its sub-processes and activities, as well as the associated quality documentation.

Now, SGP connects over 3000 users placed in several locations (Italy, Poland, New Jersey) and involves each of these functional areas: Product Quality, Engineering, Industrial Technologies, Financial Administration and control, Human Resources, Environmental Management System and IT.

The quality procedures are divided into Development Processes and Support Processes and are modeled with different detail levels: the 0th level is represented by the GE Avio Value chain, the 1st level is the process map, etc. (Figure 4).

At present, about 70 diagrams have been re-designed and modeled, and they are divided into: 10 Support Processes and 60 Development Processes, including 30 processes which have been published and then shared on the Intranet in Italian and English version. Furthermore, the organizational structure has been modeled, and a key-elements dictionary has been created in order to easily manage them.

It is estimated to complete all business quality processes and procedures modeled by January 2015.

Finally, an Application Maintenance Support phase is guaranteed by EKA BPM experts, in order to manage new customer requirements (e.g. to configure a new users group), to inform users about Signavio's new releases and functionalities, to solve other development requests (e.g. customize a new template).

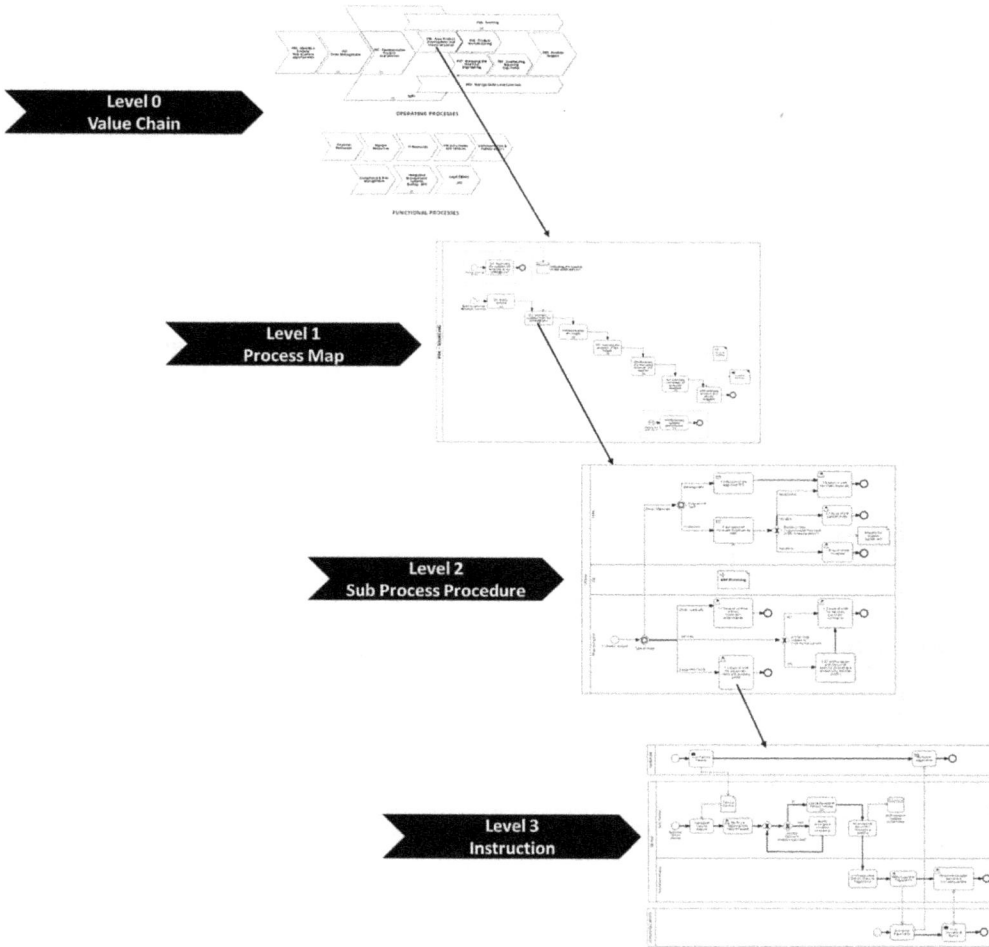

Figure 4 - Levels structure.

4.3 Organization & Social

The SGP system had a positive impact on employees' work activities.

The work of every division's employee is changed: all the organizational units are encouraged to insert their own information about the business processes.

Moreover, the use of a graphical language to represent procedures and activities' flow makes it easy for all workers to understand them.

The example below clarifies how the introduction of this system has greatly simplified the effort of the employees in keeping an updated documentation. The example also shows how the modality of searching information in the company repository system radically changed.

Search activity: before SGP system

Suppose an employee of the Logistic Unit needs to discover what processes are related to his activity, the first step is to access the intranet list of business rules (Figure 5).

Avio Aero»

PROCEDURE del SISTEMA di GESTIONE INTEGRATO

Aggiornamento del 91/07/2014

PROCEDURE SISTEMA GESTIONE PROCESSI

Processo	Numero	TITOLO	Ed	Rev	Limitazioni
Gestire le Vendite	P01 - Gestire le Vendite		1	-	N.A.
	P01.501Q - Sviluppare e mantenere le relazioni con i principali Clienti		1	-	No MR&O Civ Parti
Commercializzare Prodotti e Servizi	P02 - Commercializzare Prodotti e Servizi		1	A	No MR&O Civ Parti
	P02.501Q - Definire concept e prevenzione d'offerta		1	A	No MR&O Civ Parti
	P02.102Q - Finalizzare l'offerta commerciale		1	-	No MR&O Civ Parti
	P02.103Q - Gestire la trattativa commerciale		1	-	No MR&O Civ Parti
Approvvigionare Materiali e Servizi	P04 - Approvvigionare Materiali e Servizi		1	-	N.A.
	P04.101Q - Analizzare il fabbisogno		1	-	N.A.
	P04.102Q - Approvare Fornitore in Albo		1	A	No MR&O Civ Parti
	P04.104Q - Trattare e negoziare la fornitura		1	-	N.A.
	P04.109Q - Ricevere e gestire materiali e servizi		1	-	N.A.

Figure 5 – Intranet page with the list of all procedures.

Earlier, the employee had to locate the specific rule in the list, open the corresponding file and search in the text the info he needed. The file also included a summary table, suggesting other related procedures and resources (Figure 6).

Sometimes these resources (e.g. technical drawings) were residing on other systems. This required the employee to perform another access operation, in order to read them.

2.2	Procedure ed istruzioni associate	
2.2.1	Procedure	
	06.01Q	Valutazione e Approvazione dei Fornitori	Rev A
	06.03Q	Emissione ordini / Contratti d'Acqusito
	04.01Q	Validazione tecnologica
	13.01Q	Gestione dei materiali non conformi
	14.01Q	Azioni correttive
	16.01Q	Mantenimento delle documentazioni e registrazioni di qualità
	17.01Q	Gestione delle attività di Audit	Rev A
2.2.2	Istruzioni	
	4008Q	Dichiarazione di conformità (Certificato di conformità)
	4062Q	Modalità operative per l'approvazione dei fornitori	Rev A

Figure 6 - Manage update and link with others rules.

Search activity with the SGP system

Now employees can type a keyword, for example "logistic", into the search field in the SGP. Searching for "logistic" will deliver all diagrams having "logistic" in its title, as well as all diagrams tagged with this keyword. Therefore, the search engine operates with diagram titles, diagram meta-data, and tags. Additionally, comments, revision information and dictionary links are included in the searchable parts.

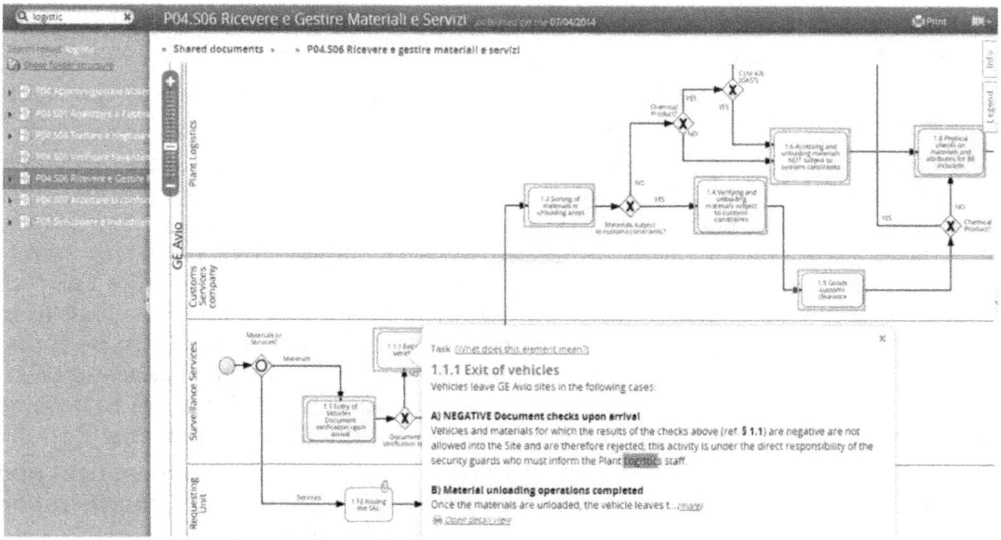

Figure 7 - Example of a search result.

In conclusion, a simple search operation allows the employee to obtain an overview of all the processes of interest.

Another major challenge was to introduce novel personnel groups in every unit.

These groups are formed by:

- IT Team, providing leadership and expertise in resolving integration design issues (e.g. solution design and architecture capability).
- BPM Governance Team that is fundamental in looking at the bigger picture and the impact on the business itself. It works at the strategic level and helps management considering how the business operations should change to deliver strategy and meet goals. It is responsible for the approval and publishing of the processes.
- BPM Project Office that has experience in building models. Its members are expert in major BPM concepts and basic application concepts. They are responsible for modeling and updating those processes.
- BPM Specialist Team that is composed of BPM technicians who understand how to set up and use the entire tool. These technicians must also understand how the system can be used and what the tool can and cannot accomplish. They manage the interaction with the vendor and address GE Avio's requirements.

In particular, the BPM Project Office was supported by introductory courses about BPMN and how-to information about the quality system.

In addition, the employee training time has been reduced considerably, because now it is delivered via videos. This video is shared in the intranet and shows the core functionality of the system and the best-practice for its usage. This is perhaps one of the most important effect of the SGP system in addition to the simplification of searching information.

5. Hurdles Overcome

5.1 Management

The project has represented a change in the management initiative and during its development some difficulties were encountered.

One of the major challenges was to modify the execution of daily work activities. The new system, in fact, has created new responsibilities. For example, the BPM Team (one per unit), is the owner of the unit processes and procedures, with the supervision of the Quality Unit. Therefore, workers had new tasks and they had to use a new methodology and information system. Moreover, some units used an internal graphical convention to model quality processes. To enable the shift from this ad-hoc methodology to a standard one, BPM training courses have been dispensed. At first, moreover, only a small fraction of the whole processes was BPM-modeled. This made the transition smoother, and permitted the users to become familiar with the new notation and to try-then-trust the Signavio benefits.

Another need was to offer BPM tools capable of satisfying the myriad changes and requirements emerging from everyday usage. In order to take into consideration future requirements, it was selected as a customizable platform.

Even the introduction of a cloud system has presented some difficulties: to overcome the skepticism of the preservation of confidential avionic information, a certificated cloud platform has been used. The update to new system releases is supported by EKA Application Maintenance service (on an average, two Signavio system releases occur within a month).

5.2 Business

No specific hurdles to overcome from the business perspective.

5.3 Organization Adoption

In the beginning, a transition phase was necessary to manage the old and the new solutions together, because there were many processes to redesign, many sources to link, many attachments to handle, etc. Another difficulty encountered was related to the adoption of a standard template for all units, and for whatever quality documentation was issued. All these problems have been overcome thanks to the sponsorship of top management and the immediate benefits perceived by users.

6. Benefits

The benefits resulting from the introduction of the SGP system derive from:
- the usage of BPM to manage the internal GE Avio regulations and
- the choice of Signavio as a standard instrument in the company environment.

Signavio was not the first company to deliver cloud-based process diagrams, but it is the first company to deliver a product that offers repository-based multi-user support, as well as analytics and simulation capabilities. Signavio producers are focused on the combination of convenience and ease of use. For example, they allow greater engagement of non-specialists in the model creation, through the Quick Model module.

In the sub-headings below, some quantitative and qualitative measures of benefits are listed.

6.1 Time Reductions

Key metrics about time reductions are listed in the table below.

Metrics description	After SGP
Time to obtain information (search)	- 40%
Time for training new workers	- 60%
Time to update procedures	- 50%
Time for comparing different revisions of the rules	- 80%
Time for drafting official documents	- 80%
Time spent in the elaboration of reports	- 40%
Integration with existing information	- 40%

Table 1 - Key metrics on time-reductions.

6.2 Increased Revenues

Business process modeling creates immediate value, because this new approach is focused on the processes and improves the quality of activities and products. This, in turn, increases customer satisfaction.

6.3 Quality Improvements

- Constant, clear communication among stakeholders: customer interactions enable knowledge increase;
- Easy audit and training;
- Better visibility and control of processes;
- Flexibility in incorporating changes in business process;
- Centralization of the information: the system maps operational processes and gathers them under only one tool, where all applicable procedures are referenced;
- Less paper, less signatures, elimination of unimportant steps in the workflow approval process;
- The project influences the organizational culture by introducing the paradigm of processes as a way of thinking;
- Clarifies the roles, responsibilities and interactions of the people involved.

7. BEST PRACTICES, LEARNING POINTS AND PITFALLS

7.1 Best Practices and Learning Points

- ✓ Use standard notation
- ✓ Use a unique platform to consult the regulations and related documentation
- ✓ Share experience and know-how
- ✓ Engage everyone involved in the process
- ✓ Define ownership as an important attribute for collaboration purposes
- ✓ Have robust control when changes are introduced
- ✓ Enable collaboration when designing the process and within the process
- ✓ Standardize documentation for all units
- ✓ Realize a detailed analysis of every process before its design.

7.2 Pitfalls

- ✗ Some processes are tedious to some users without BPM culture: these processes have been simplified

×   *Defend the new approach: avoid any trends to fall back into the old ways.*

8.   COMPETITIVE ADVANTAGES

One of the key values identified by GE Avio is the customer satisfaction. To achieve this goal, GE Avio has to maintain the highest standards of excellence regarding quality, product performance, competitiveness and service levels. In this scenario, many aspects are important: compliance with statutory requirements and standards adopted by the aeronautical industry; satisfaction of customer requirements; certifications issued by control authorities; training of human resources.

The project implementation allowed a re-design and simplification of these processes, with the final result of sharing clear procedures and official documentation. The ease of access and the readability of this information increase the know-how of the processes and consequently the quality of service. Easy update of the information ensures compliance with required quality standards. These lead to a better quality of the product and an increase in client satisfaction follows.

Finally, SGP system can be seen as a first step to enable processes automation and simulation.

9.   TECHNOLOGY

The solution adopted by GE Avio can be split into two logical components:
*   Editing module
*   Presentation module

The Editing module manages the modeling of the business processes and their changes whilst the Presentation module provides a read-only access to diagrams published within the Intranet. Read-only access is granted to every user who is able to access the Intranet through SharePoint Server.

For the first module, GE Avio selected a safe cloud-service solution. The system is hosted on the Signavio server and Signavio is responsible for the update and deployment of new versions of the software. Even the rescue operation of databases and their backup operations are dependent on Signavio.

With this "Software as a Service" (SaaS) solution, it is possible to customize the software and to take advantage of the updates as soon as they are released, without worrying about upgrading the installations. It is also possible to cut the costs related to the configuration of a deployment environment, fully internal to GE Avio.

Presentation module is based on the Signavio process portal that is directly embedded into a SharePoint environment through a preconfigured SharePoint "web part". Seamless navigation through the process landscape can happen directly within the company Intranet. This module combines both process models and documentation in one place. This allows a direct access to the documents in the Microsoft SharePoint document library.

For managing the access to data in the Active Directory domain, it is necessary to install a WebService. The Active Directory is linked to the system, only in order to verify every access to read the model diagrams via a single-sign-on.

The final architecture of the solution is shown in Figure 8.

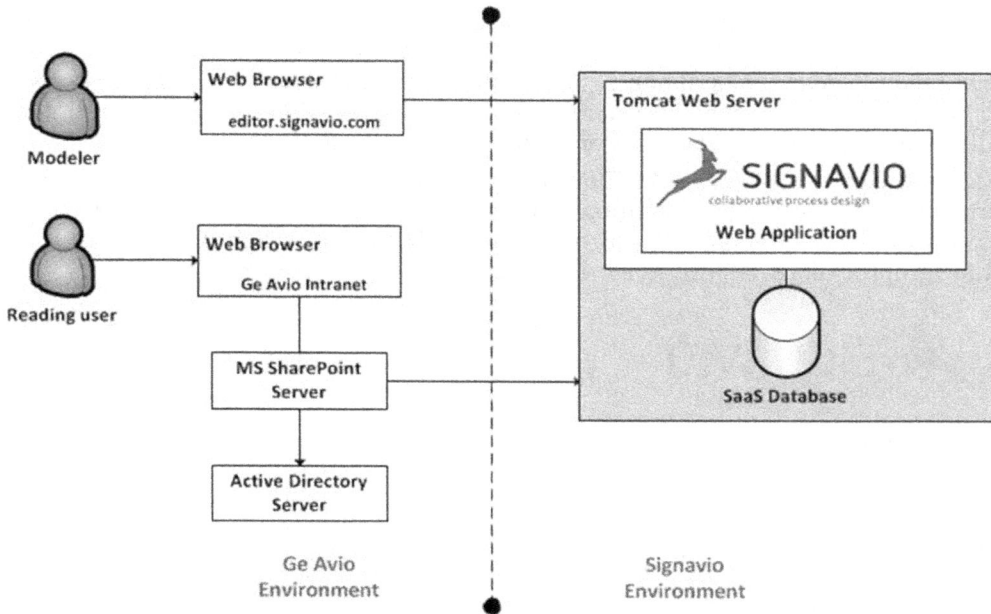

Figure 8 - Final architecture with process designer and navigation environment.

As a result, the core of the solution is the central repository managed by Signavio, where the charts of all users are stored. This allows multiple users to work simultaneously on the same diagram. These changes are made available to other users by saving diagram changes.

All process models are maintained by Signavio Process Model Editor with a complete revision control. So, models can be updated at any time without directly publishing these changes on the GE Avio Intranet. Only after its approval, the latest version of a process diagram is available to all users with access to the Intranet.

10. The Technology and Service Providers

EKA Srl

EKA is a spin-off of the University of Salento founded in mid-2010, after several years of collaboration among the University and several industrial partners involved in Regional, National and European major research projects.

With its experience on methods and tools for *Product Lifecycle Management, Business Process Management* and *Document & Content Management,* EKA's mission is to help its customers in improving their development processes along the whole product lifecycle, providing support in the usage of ICT solutions and in design and implementation of new solutions.

(Web Site: *www.eka-systems.com*)

Signavio Inc.

Signavio is a Berlin-based software company offering a fully web-based solution for business process management. Signavio meets its worldwide demand with two more offices in Sunnyvale and Singapore.

The BPM solution pioneers the field of collaborative process design by providing teams with opportunities to document and improve processes beyond departmental and organizational limits. The Signavio Process Editor is available as a safe cloud solution, as well as on-premise, and helps cover BPM initiatives throughout all stages of process modeling, from process design to optimization.

Signavio combines a powerful BPM tool with an extremely user-friendly working environment. Signavio's solution allows even those without any BPMN 2.0 knowledge to record table-based processes within a lightweight version, and produce graphic displays with just one click.

(Web Site: *www.signavio.com*)

Generali CEE Holding B.V.,
Central and Eastern Europe
Nominated by Bizagi, United Kingdom

1. EXECUTIVE SUMMARY / ABSTRACT

Generali CEE Holding[1] (Generali) is a leading insurance group in Central and Eastern Europe with total assets under management of €14.8 billion and more than 11 million clients.

In 2011-2014, we embarked on "Project Puccini," a large-scale initiative to significantly boost process visibility, productivity and efficiency in the area of Corporate Risks underwriting[2] for 10 countries throughout Central and Eastern Europe.

We needed to support the most complex insurance processes in a multi-company, multi-language environment. Potential systems were assessed on their ability to deliver strong case management, analytics and workflow through the whole corporate insurance policies lifecycle.

BPMS was chosen over in-house development and an Out of the Box Policy administration system for the costs saving, functionality and ease of integration.

Following deployment and delivery, Project Puccini has come to life and matured into full policy administration; and today, BPM extends beyond Corporate Insurance.

In March 2011, after three months of development, the first version of the company underwriting process was delivered in two member companies. Since then, its scope has widened significantly to include the whole lifecycle of insurance policy and far more complex deployments in our largest member country, Ceska Pojistovna in the Czech Republic. To date, 51 processes have been delivered in four countries in five languages. Our BPM solution has proven cost-effective, scalable & highly functional, delivering agility within our constantly-shifting regulatory environment.

2. OVERVIEW

Generali provides know-how, professional and operational support for insurance companies in 10 countries – Bulgaria, Croatia, Czech Republic, Hungary, Montenegro, Poland, Romania, Serbia, Slovakia and Slovenia. The Corporate Insurance departments of all Generali member insurance companies create on average 4,000 insurance offers (quotes) per month, which materialize into over 7,000[3] policies per year. The work involved is complex, based on staff experience, with policies tailor-made for specific clients' needs. Large risks exposure is often covered by the insurance company in partnership with other co-insurers and re-insurers.

Generali CEE Holding Corporate Risks Department initiated Project Puccini in order to provide member companies with a corporate insurance processes support

---

[1] Generali CEE Holding is joint venture of Generali Group (holds 76 percent of the joint venture), the 6th biggest insurance company in the world with total assets under management of almost €480 billion and 65 million clients worldwide and CEE Group which is one of the largest investment and finance groups in Central and Eastern Europe.

[2] Corporate insurance covers five Lines of Business (Property, Liability, Engineering, Marine, Special)

[3] This figure includes only marine insurance cover policies. Marine insurance declarations (+10 000 pieces) are not counted as individual insurance policies in this figure.

system. The solution needed to support all the activities of Corporate Risks Department including:

- Underwriting and policy administration processes (including related co-insurance and re-insurance)
- Sales activities planning (Pipeline management)
- Other related areas (Loss Control, Re-insurance Specialists).

Corporate Insurance policies form a specific subset of the overall insurance portfolio. On the one hand, these policies consist of complex insurance relationships, with very high level of risk exposure (sums insured) and complex policy administration processes; while on the other, there are relatively small number of policies per year (7000 of corporate policies compared to 2-3 million of annual retail policies in Generali CEE Holding). Therefore Generali CEE Holding was looking for an agile, robust and cost effective solution with the best value for money ratio.

Major factors were considered in the solution selection, including: multi company and multi-language features, workflow process management, document management, the ability to create policy and print quote templates, and to provide reports with strong analytical capabilities. Integration with existing assets such as policy administration systems became high priority requirement in Ceska Pojistovna - the biggest Generali member company. All these factors had to be met within a modest budget[4]. The more detailed solution selection is discussed further in Section 9: Technology.

All the above challenges have been addressed by the projects, as explained below. In addition, it enforces high standards and encourages best practice sharing across the business and with member companies[5].

3. BUSINESS CONTEXT

The corporate risks underwriting process is one of the most complex in the insurance industry. In some cases, we have one or more offers being prepared simultaneously or consecutively, which will end up incorporated into one insurance policy, or conversely, one offer can end up split between multiple insurance policies.

In the area of corporate risk insurance, the insurer forms a group of experts with unique know-how to maintain a dedicated client approach. The process itself consists of detailed risk assessments, preparation of tailor made offers and negotiation with brokers, other insurers and re-insurers.

Operations of the Corporate Risks department were mainly "paper-based" with underwriters spending a lot of time accessing policy administration systems internally, but lacking real-time access to the data once the case left the department. Duplicate data entry was also a known problem. In addition, question marks over productivity and quality were being raised, due to lack of process visibility.

Initial business requirements were defined as follows:

Workflow support
- Enforce underwriting guidelines (offer & policy preparation, pricing)
- Enable process flexibility and parallel quote preparation

---

[4] Application development team consisted initially of 3 people and later was strengthened to 6.

[5] Recently, a new business area of Life Insurance has been added in Generali Czech Republic with medical risks examination process developed and deployed to full production within 3 months.

Experience- and Facts-based Underwriting
- Easy access to previous quotes, quotation history, templates, reports, questionnaires, historical policy data (e.g. loss history)
- Deliver all relevant information from multiple systems from single queries

Pipeline Management
- Support planning and record keeping of the business opportunities
- Provide queries and reports for management on several levels
- Measure/graphically illustrate business performance of individual Brokers

Duplicate Request Management
- Effectively manage duplicate requests (duplicate request to quote for the same client) within each company and across all member companies

It was necessary for the selected solution to offer multi-company and multi-language support as well as integrate with administration systems of other member companies, as the solution needed to be deployed across all member companies in 10 countries.

4. THE KEY INNOVATIONS

Previous paper-based processes lacked visibility, structure and transparency which put underwriters at risk of not making the right decisions or failing to spot mistakes. Key innovations came with structured processes including case management, tailor-made business features and real time managerial reporting based on structured shared business entities/data model.

Structured Underwriting process including Case Management:
- Automated workflow across several member company departments as well as within Generali Corporate Risks department
- Underwriter manages the underwriting case where he assigns the work, checks progress and obtains specific deliverables for quote preparation
- Real time business context of the case available for all to view e.g. underwriting experience/observations, client, policy and quote documents

Tailor-made business features:
- Use of previous offers – copy quote functionality including copy from current policy administration system
- Automated printouts of quotes, policies, authorization reports, surveys
- Detailed historical policy data
- Business relationship/offer histories with clients and brokers
- Real time data queries providing data both from the new system and from other integrated systems, user's data sets available to export for analysis.

Managerial Reports and Queries
- Process analytics real time and historical performance
- Business analytics for Sales production, Underwriters production, Policy history, Loss history, Quotation history, Broker history

3.1 Business

All three major groups of stakeholders i.e. shareholders, customers and regulators were impacted positively:

Generali CEE Holding:

Gained the ability to view the process in real time, and to better manage processes according to company standards. Business processes involved are specified on the following page.

Customers, Sales Force and Brokers:

The ability to view, at a glance, all the opportunities in the sales pipeline and to initiate business directly from the process:

- Easy to use, real-time reports
- Integration with the brokers' portal
- Ability to see who has made the same request for the same client

Supervision, audit and compliance:

- Support for referrals' activities from member companies to Generali CEE Holding Underwriters
- BPMS provides detailed activity log making clear who made what, and when.

Figure 1: Reports enable sales management to glance at all the opportunities in the sales pipeline and to initiate business action directly from the process

Figure 2 – Quote process covers risk evaluation and quote preparation, authorization, issuing quote for the broker/client and finishes with issuing insurance policy

The functions and steps covered by the Underwriting Process include:

Register Request

- Search and define client & Check for duplicity
- Specify broker(s) and brokerage, Line of Business, working team

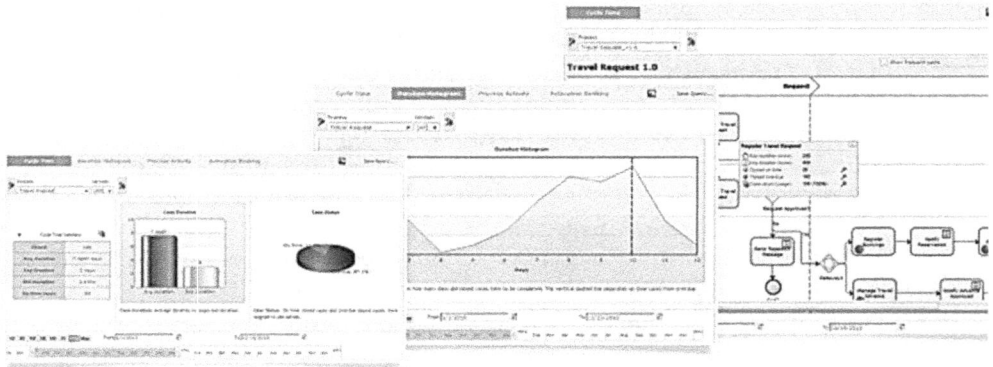

Prepare Quote

- Specify coverage (Risks, limits, sum insured, premium, rates, PML...)
- Outline insured items & define insured locations (address, territory)
- Specify reinsurance and coinsurance structure (shares, fees, roles...)
- Upload & generate XLS/PDF/RTF/HTML documents from templates
- LCE/Risk management workflow: risk grading & reports, site visits, MFL
- Pricing - import of calculations done by MS Excel based pricing tool

Authorize Quote

- Self-Authorization & Generali CEE Holding Authorization
- Intra-company authorization according to authority level
- Board of directors override

Issue Quote

- Issue official quotation to client; check delivery and acceptance
- Adjust the quote according to broker/client feedback

Issue Policy

- Specify premium installments calendar

- Specify policy data such as dates, policy number, various attributes
- Modify coverage (automatically transferred from quote)

Process Architecture

We used process design principles based on RIVA method[6] with BPMN 2.0 as the implementation standard. The RIVA method identifies processes as lifecycles of essential business entities.

Our Process Architecture consists of:

Process Entity	Process (Entity life cycle)	Collaborative Processes
Coverage request	Manage Underwriting	Quote, Manage Opportunities, Manage Partner Account
Quote	Quote	Evaluate Quote, Authorize Quote, Issue Quote
Policy	Issue Policy	Quote, Finalize Policy
Insurance Partner	Manage Partner Account	Manage Underwriting, Quote, Finalize Policy
Insurance Opportunity	Manage Opportunities	Manage Underwriting, Manage Partner Account
Product	Prepare Product Quote	Quote
Document	Manage Documents and Communications	Manage Underwriting, Quote, Finalize Policy

BPMN 2.0 allows business needs to be captured and processes to be executed according to desired behavior. The process/application design and implementation consisted of six definition/implementation steps:

- Process maps (51 processes, 713 process elements implemented)
- Data models (218 master entities, 209 parameterizations)
- User interfaces (2300 user forms including sub forms)
- Business Rules (6100 business rules and expressions)
- Participants (21 business roles, 11 user skills, 28 user groups and 27 locations)
- Integrations (12 interfaces)

Maintaining the process lifecycle

We use an agile approach to capture and implement user needs. This enables continuous process improvement and helps to close the user feedback loop. The automated deployment features are used for production deployments on a weekly basis.

Process cloning

During the course of the project we discovered that processes designed for one Generali member company were too complex to adopt for other members. By cloning these processes, reusing the shared data model and localizing the process, we were able to quickly develop tailor made processes that better suited different members. For example, the first bespoke quote preparation processes were produced within the first month of implementation.

Run time adaptability

Using BPMN features such as standalone sub processes triggered by events parallel to main process flow, we are able to provide users with high degree of runtime flexibility. The same applies for the Case Management features described below.

---

[6] See e.g. the book *Ould, Martyn A.: Business Process Management: A Rigorous Approach.*

3.2 Case Handling

During implementation, it became obvious that some of the user requirements were hard to handle with a "fixed workflow" approach. These were requirements like:

- Underwriters' ad-hoc decisions to involve other participants in the case
- Ability to assign several team members to the case and allowing them to work on the same activity at a time of their choice
- Multi-level authorization (=supervising + approving) activities e.g. within an insurance company, within Generali CEE Holding Corporate Risks department, within teams dedicated to a particular insurance line of business

The advantage of the selected BPMS is that it is fully data-centric[7]; business entities and their relationships are defined and stored in common Entity Relationship fashion (we work with MS SQL Server and Oracle). Within this environment, Case Management was implemented via standard BPMN building blocks, such as inclusive gates, signals and standalone sub processes (see figure 3).

Cases handling: before and after

Before the project, the underwriting process was mostly manual: MS Office/email-based. These processes lacked visibility, structure and transparency.

The organization now benefits from process automation, including offer & policy preparation, pricing and business rules (underwriting guidelines) enforcement. BPM captures most of the business logic including case management, which has impacted the following areas:

- **Processes connected across several departments and authorization levels:** The underwriting process is managed through an automated case; items flow across several company departments within a particular member insurance company (Underwriters, Loss Control Engineers, Reinsurance Specialists, and Product Experts) as well as within Generali CEE Holding Corporate Risks department.
- **Support for parallel offer preparation:** offers can now be prepared in parallel via multiple sub processes, each part being prepared by specialized underwriter. Once the quote preparation process is complete and the clients' business requirements have been set up, one or more quotes can be merged into one or more insurance policies. Alternatively, offers can be split into multiple policies (i.e. "policies" sub processes) through automated procedures.
- **Broker portal integration:** This capability is in production in Generali Hungary. Broker staff (1000+ insurance brokers) are able to prepare "Request for Insurance coverage" directly from a web portal integrated with Pipeline Management and Underwriting processes. A quote prepared by the underwriter is delivered directly into the broker's case folder which can then be managed in a fully automated manner; a huge leap from the previous MS-Office/email "Case management".

---

[7] Data centricity is key feature enabling for case management. See figure 13-3 and its description in the book *Swenson, Keith D.: Mastering the Unpredictable: How Adaptive Case Management Will Revolutionize the Way That Knowledge Workers Get Things Done*

Edit	Task Type	Task Status	Task Requester	Task Assignee	Creation Date	Solution Date	Description	Process ID
Edit	Prepare Property ▼	Active ▼	GHU_UserDev2	GHU_UserDev2 ▼	04.08.2014	10.08.2014	Renewal of 2013 policy	7010
Edit	Prepare Liability ▼	Active ▼	GHU_UserDev2	GHU_UserDev2 ▼	04.08.2014	14.06.2014	New Request for Coverage	7011

Delete	Product	Default	Business Line	TSI (Property) or SI e.e.o. (Liability)	SI aggr. (Liability)
☐	Fire	Yes	Named perils	100.000.000,00	
☐	Burst Pipe		Named perils	10.000.000,00	
☐	Storm		Named perils	25.000.000,00	
☐	Glass		Named perils	1.000.000,00	
☑	Burglary		Named perils		
☑	Robbery		Named perils		

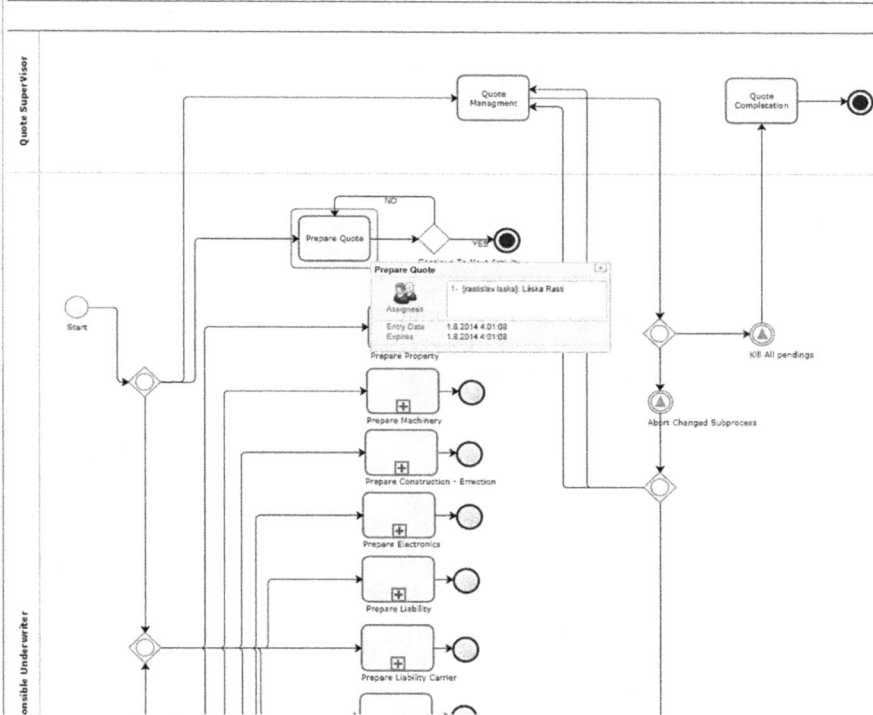

Figure 3: Quote preparation Case Management process.
Insurance products can be assigned to dedicated users.
Senior underwriter – Case Owner decides to accept selected product quoting delivery and/or finish quoting, if required.

3.3 Organization & Social

Operations

The impact of moving from paper based systems to automated and efficient processes has made employees more involved and productive.

Prior to implementing BPMS, individual member companies' practices were mostly local. Now, this information is made available centrally, enabling business people in different countries to learn from each other and share know-how.

BPM Central Team

To support reuse and best practice sharing, we formed a central BPM team consisting of six people. This team is responsible for project management, business analysis and application implementation and maintenance.

5. HURDLES OVERCOME

4.1 Management

During the whole course of the project there has been strong management support and commitment.

4.2 Business

The project was delivered alongside daily business activities. This required dedication from business people as in addition to their standard tasks, they also got involved in the project roll-out; creating time pressures on business staff involved.

4.3 Organization Adoption

The project team has adopted an agile approach to get maximum use of business people engagement and to create the best feedback loop for progression.

6. BENEFITS

5.1 Cost Savings / Time Reductions

BPMS has enabled Generali CEE Holding to completely transform manual processes resulting in significant operational risk reduction:

- Workflow automation across company departments as well as within the Generali Underwriters Department.
- Structured processes for pricing, policy preparation and decision making
- Elimination of data entry and duplication into several applications
- **Quote/offer preparation time reduced by 30-40 percent** in Generali Slovakia
- The most complex policies (50+ coverages, 100+ insured locations) renewal required **more than one day** to enter all data. With full integration to the legacy system and with tailor made business logic support, the renewal time was cut to one to three **hours** in Ceska pojistovna.
- Complex offers can now be prepared in parallel; merged and split; all of which improves customer response times
- Real time check for Quote duplicity
- Real time business portfolio snapshot available
- Simple and well-structured business portfolio reporting
- Brokers portal integration in Generali Hungary allows brokers to instigate new business

Cost savings gained specifically as a result of choosing our BPM solution include:

- Reuse, enabling cost effective deployments into member countries
- Competitive pricing: chosen BPMS initial cost was 50 percent of competitive offerings; a figure likely to rise to 90 percent cost savings as more member companies use the platform.

Savings within internal IT department

The nature of the solution means there is far less burden on IT to spend time and money on system maintenance:

- User requirements can be conveyed quickly & process changes made instantly

- Reusable elements mean that processes can be quickly adapted to fit the needs of other member groups, with minimal programming or IT involvement.

5.2 Increased Revenues

Increasing revenue was not the primary goal. However increased revenues are expected to come from enabling underwriters to focus on more value added activities e.g. client support, risk assessment etc. which currently can't be quantified.

5.3 Quality Improvements

- *Increased productivity:* Data duplication eliminated while automation enforced structured processes for pricing, policy preparation and decision making.
- *Case Management:* Implemented case management capabilities allow for business aligned automated process support, such as several levels of authorization.
- *Compliance & audit:* Documents are now tightly tied to the process, making them easy for employees to access and search. The process audit is now fully automated.
- *Pipeline management:* Is now fully integrated with the Underwriting process. In Generali Hungary, where 95 percent of corporate business is managed by brokers, the ability to view the pipeline from the online portal brings competitive advantage.
- *Improved business insights:* Business data is available in real time which gives more control to employees and allows for better process management and improvements, using the out-of-the-box reports and KPI metrics.
- *Improved access to insurance "know how":* A central knowledge repository provides real-time access to all insurance experience data, as well as a full log of the client/broker business relationship, enabling junior underwriters to benefit from their colleagues' experience. There is also a centralized view of offers history.

7. BEST PRACTICES, LEARNING POINTS AND PITFALLS

6.1 Best Practices and Learning Points

- ✓ *Use BPMS & BPMN to capture business logic including Case Management*
- ✓ *Keep user forms manageable & simple, to avoid complex adjustments later*
- ✓ *Develop dedicated forms for each insurance product to increase user satisfaction*
- ✓ *Take the agile approach rather than Waterfall methodology*
- ✓ *Put the integrated data model at the heart of the process*

6.2 Pitfalls

- ✗ *Don't underestimate the number of people you need to interact with e.g. to capture requirements and to perform user tests and training.*
- ✗ *Don't invent new processes at the same time as building the application*
- ✗ *Don't assume one process will fit all; the difference in business logic between our companies was only 10-20 percent, yet one process was too complex to manage.*
- ✗ *Consider building dedicated clones of the process while sharing the data model since this will significantly reduce the complexity and simplify management.*

8. COMPETITIVE ADVANTAGES

The immediate competitive advantage comes from the automation of our highly sophisticated business processes. The level of process automation and flexibility we have achieved can't be easily matched by any Out of the Box Insurance solution available. Our typical Time to Market is now below one month. Over time, the process design will evolve for collection and accumulation of underwriting experience within the system as well as developing more tailor made features (e.g. Offers and Policy printout templates) which will significantly help to share best practices among Generali CEE Holding member companies.

9. TECHNOLOGY

We selected Bizagi BPMS to model, automate and execute our business processes.

Infrastructure

The solution is built upon Bizagi BPM Suite Enterprise.NET 9.1.8 running in virtualized cloud environment. The underlying infrastructure is formed by MS Windows 2008 R2 Server, IIS 7.0+.NET 2.0 and MS SQL Server 2008 R2. The layout of the production environment is two 8-core Windows + IIS application servers backed by one SQL server.

Integrations

Our solution is integrated with several other internal IT systems including existing policy administration systems within companies, registry of corporate entities, and database of country addresses. Our project makes use of BPMS integration capabilities including web services, data virtualization/replication, email support, LDAP, Component Library, just to name a few:

- Replication and virtualization of data entities enables us to integrate historical insurance policies data into the application
- The historical policies are fed from flat files via SFTP batch job into the source databases
- Consuming various Web Services exposed via participating insurance companies' ESBs
- Java EE component running in JBoss AS 7.1 container connecting to Lotus Notes application via N-RPC/DIIOP interoperability protocol
- Online connection to the national corporate entities registry in particular country via HTTP protocol and XML messages
- Access to third party geocoding (addresses, flood zones) database

Data-centric system

Selected BPMS architecture delivers full data access across applications and processes. This allows us to retain our core business logic and quickly adapt it for the localized needs of member countries. In addition, we also make use of its data virtualization capabilities. Once the external data gets virtualized, that data can be handled as if it was local, meaning that users don't need to become pre-occupied with physical data locations. This way data and the process are linked together. It is this data centricity that delivers business agility for the development and allows for case management.

10. THE TECHNOLOGY AND SERVICE PROVIDERS

Selection process

Potential options were assessed on their ability to deliver process support, analytics and workflow through the whole corporate insurance lifecycle. We did not initially pursue BPM as an option. We considered an Out of the Box solution but that did not offer the integration capability, while the in-house solution was expensive to adopt for multi-company and multi-language.

We downloaded Bizagi's modeling and automation tools for free, and found them easy to use. In fact we were using it within the business in just two days. We asked Bizagi to deliver a proof of concept for an underwriting process, which they did in three weeks. Bizagi was half of the price of the other systems we evaluated.

Business Process Management System

Generali CEE Holding selected Bizagi (bizagi.com) for the implementation of the BPM initiative. In Bizagi, most of the common and re-occurring requirements in process automation have been pre-built. These refer to:

- **Control and visibility**: graphical real-time monitoring (who, what, when, where)
- **Alarms and notifications**: generated by exceptions to SLAs or non-compliance
- **Business data design**: enterprise class modeling, reusable across applications and processes
- **Performance analysis and reporting**: graphical reports with deep insights into operational performance by process and activity
- **Process versioning including sub-process:** activity forms versions and support for process clone and copy
- **Auditing and traceability:** who changed what and when
- **Workload routing & balancing**: graphical editor to define work allocation rules
- **Business rules**: graphical design of business vocabularies and policies
- **Web Portal**: customizable, multiple languages and multiple time zones
- **Corporate features**: .Net or Java, multi-tenancy, BPMN process engine, long lasting process transactions, enterprise data model, among others.

InComm, USA

Nominated by Whitestein Technologies
North America, USA

1. INTRODUCTION

InComm is an innovative market leader in payment technologies and solutions. It has grown from a garage-based company to a world-class enterprise with an international footprint in just over twenty years. InComm has more than 450,000 points of distribution, 500 brand partners and 1,800 employees globally. To support an acceleration in growth of the pre-paid gift card market, InComm focused on increased operational efficiency through improved information management and automation. This approach effectively eliminated dependence on labor-intensive, error-prone manual processes.

To address its operational objectives, the InComm Market Solutions department selected Whitestein Technologies' Living Systems® Process Suite (LSPS), an intelligent Business Process Management Suite (iBPMS), to transform processes that support the planning and delivery of products to retail outlets. The solution manages and automates the complex process of launch planning and product development using a data-driven, case management-based approach. Further, the application integrates with existing master data systems that provide product data, retailer data and validation services. Robust support for web and mobile users, integrated Business Intelligence (BI), outcome-driven workflows and a standards-compliant technology stack were key features that contributed to InComm's decision to deploy a LSPS based solution.

This case study is structured as follows – first, it provides additional contextual background and understanding of the goals InComm and the project team set out to achieve. Details of the Agile methodology vision and roadmap for the solution are then presented. The discussion is followed by an examination of the three-phased transitional macro-process diagrams that illustrate the evolutionary approach taken to deliver solution capabilities while minimizing the interruption of on-going operations. The benefits from the solution implementation are then covered. The final section concludes with a summary of lessons learned.

2. BACKGROUND

Since its inception in 1992, InComm has grown to become the world's leading provider of stored-value gift and prepaid products, services and technologies. InComm's retail network features premier brands in the big box, grocery, convenience, chain drug, discount, electronics and office supply categories. The organization scaled its operations using readily-available Commercial Off-The-Shelf (COTS) productivity tools, including spreadsheets and e-mail.

Recognizing the long-term impact of the existing infrastructure, processes and tools, InComm continued its pursuit of process improvement and automation throughout the enterprise. In an effort to mitigate the risks associated with the operational shift and deployment of a new system requiring widespread adoption, InComm leadership promoted the institution of Agile software development methodologies.

InComm's primary business goals included the following:

- Process optimization and automation of product launches
- Improved interdepartmental communications and workflows
- Legacy and third-party systems integration
- Automated notifications and task escalation
- Automation and prioritization of work assignments
- Establishment of Master Data Management (MDM) services as the authoritative source of key data, including merchant and product information
- Decision support utilizing BI reports, dashboards and near real-time monitoring
- Remote access for sales and product teams to perform reviews and approvals

One of the project's primary aims included a reduction in manual activities and methods (e.g., e-mail, phone calls and file sharing) that support information flow and status of specific projects and tasks. After careful consideration of multiple implementation proposals, InComm selected LSPS as the solution platform and Modus21 as the implementation partner.

The project implementation team followed industry-recognized Agile design and development best practices. This approach included the iterative deployment of production-quality software and user-acceptance testing.

The solution, named LaunchIT, was delivered for production use following nine months of the project development and jointly transitioned to full InComm operational ownership six months thereafter. During the project, the team delivered demonstrable product increments to the client every two weeks for review and managed three major releases and three minor releases into production. Additionally, more than 400 users on five continents were trained and an internal team of four support resources were trained and mentored to provide on-going support. InComm's LaunchIT solution was subsequently honored at the 2014 Global Awards for Excellence in Business Process Management and Workflow sponsored by the Workflow Management Coalition (WfMC) and BPM.com.

3. PLATFORM AND PARTNER SELECTION

Living Systems® Process Suite (LSPS)

Whitestein Technologies LSPS is a robust development environment that offers all of the advantages of a flexible, custom application development platform, without the limitations and encumbrances of conventional, proprietary tools. Due to the cyclical nature of InComm's launch processes, it was determined that a phased Agile development approach offered the best delivery model. LSPS allowed the implementation team to enhance existing workflows with new features, while minimizing disruption to mature operational areas.

One of the keys to success for the LaunchIT solution was its ability to integrate with existing and emerging InComm systems. MDM services, offering enterprise-wide authoritative data services, were seamlessly integrated with LaunchIT through its rich set of Application Programming Interfaces (API's). The open, flexible nature of LSPS greatly simplified this effort and played a major role in the platform's selection.

Modus21

Based on a combination of an industry reputation as a leader in Agile development of BPMS solutions and proven success with the LSPS tool, Modus21 was chosen to lead the development and implementation of the LaunchIT solution. Previous projects led by Modus21 highlighted their ability to deliver solutions of this magnitude as well as the ability to understand and tailor solutions based on the intricacies and complexity of rapidly changing business requirements.

4. SOLUTION DELIVERY

To successfully implement the LaunchIT LSPS solution, joint leadership defined a phased implementation plan. The plan transitioned actively executing product launch cycles to the newly optimized process models, while not interrupting day-to-day operations and peak operational periods. Associated with the phased deployments was a strategy to on-board InComm development resources, to enable full ownership for the continued operations and sustainment of the LaunchIT system.

The team utilized Agile road-mapping and release planning activities to establish feature epics targeted for each of the phases. This was followed by progressive collaboration throughout the course of the project to define workable user stories for the development team. The Agile approach allowed the team to adjust its trajectory and keep key stakeholders aware of the trade-offs in continuously shifting priorities.

Agile Implementation

The Phase 1 workflow implementation of LSPS, shown at a macro-level in Figure 1, targeted a change in the approvals and management operations of the Launch Management process, addressing several of the common themes arising from user groups' primary requirements. A subset of the full user base would be first to migrate their processes into the system, including Product Managers, Merchant Account Managers, Channel Managers, Finance and Launch Managers. Several supporting processes would remain external to the system, with those respective users continuing to manage work in isolated 3rd-party tracking tools.

Approvals from managers representing their associated merchants and product partners, formerly captured in spreadsheets, would be tracked in an auditable, collaborative workflow in LaunchIT. Features included the enablement of research and retrieval of product and merchant information from MDM services, expedited creation of new launches, reporting on approvals required and communication and negotiation between role-based participants.

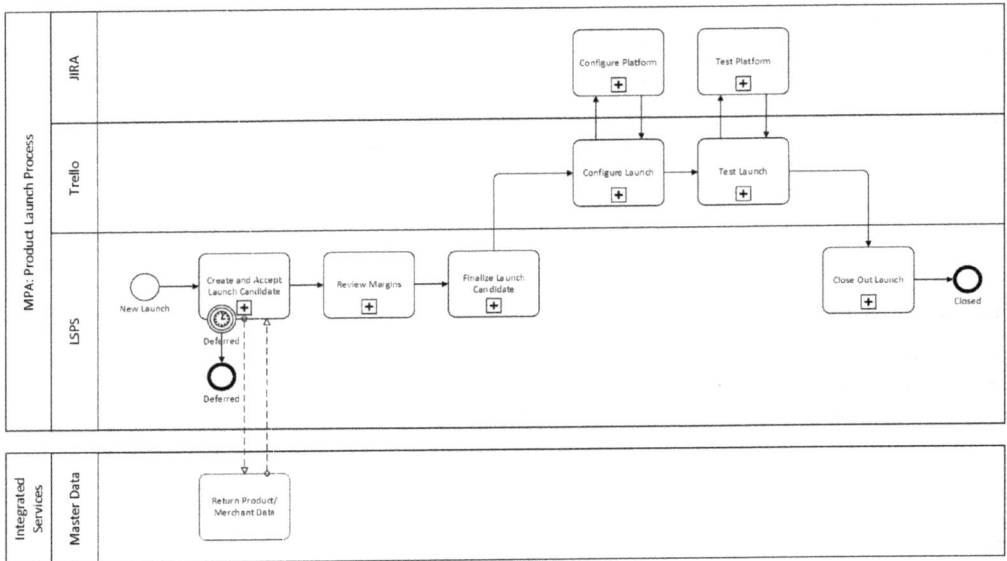

Figure 1: Phase 1 Macro-Level Product Launch Process

To enhance and transform current operational capabilities, features were added to empower Launch Managers to render decisions on late product additions to product launches. Merge algorithms were developed to allow projects created later for the same merchants to be evaluated for inclusion with other launches already in flight, with proper management approval. This sophisticated feature enabled flexibility while maintaining accountability. Put another way, product data specific to one workflow instance (launch A) could be systematically inherited by another workflow instance (launch B) at a different stage in its dynamic life cycle, while also forcing launch A's products to align to those in launch B.

Another important element of the LaunchIT solution dealt with the support of workflow managed by Launch Managers, based on the flexible manner in which these knowledge workers performed.

To address this unique requirement, the team developed a product-level LSPS signaling model, which allowed information to be communicated by launch processes to its counterpart product processes. The team further utilized the LSPS Maintain Goal structure, to create a triggered set of behaviors in the supporting goals and workflows.

Figure 2 is a screen capture from the LSPS Process Design Suite (PDS). The diagram depicts the system's Goal-Oriented Business Process Modeling Notation (GO-BPMN), an extension of BPMN 2.0, that intelligently manages the selection of LaunchIT workflow plans. Each of the workflow plans (BPMN fragments) may represent one to many steps in a workflow. LSPS uses two distinct goal-types in the GO-BPMN structure to manage workflow activity coordination: Achieve Goals and Maintain Goals. Achieve Goals stay active until a specific condition is met, in order to achieve a desirable business outcome. Maintain Goals carry out their underlying workflow plan(s) to restore a given business state, when conditions in the enterprise warrant execution.

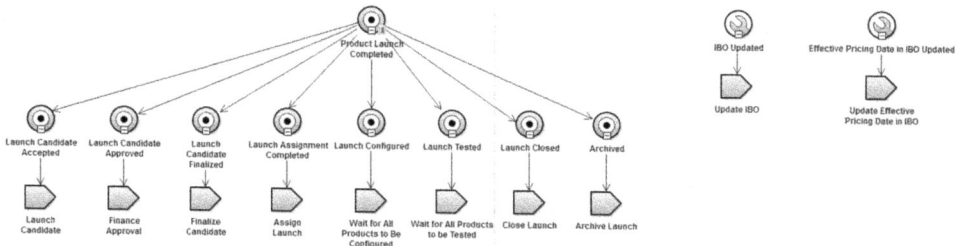

Figure 2: LaunchIT GO-BPMN Goal Structure

By establishing Maintain Goals for each possible state of the flow products must follow, and modeling the associated product-level process as a signal driven mechanism, a structure where products could dynamically flow through the process was developed. In short, an active Maintain Goal in this case represents a work item that must be completed as long as at least one product is in the state respective to that Maintain Goal. Figure 3 displays a subset of the full workflow that each product may dynamically follow as a member of a launch. This solution, something uniquely achievable using LSPS constructs, has eliminated the constraints of a standard BPMN process model and replaced it with a signal-driven outcome-based model.

Similar workflow was also created in order to track product test results and adjudicate failures when products undergo one or more types of testing. To summarize, each launch is merchant-centric and associated with one to more products. Those member products will undergo different types of tests to ensure they are properly configured for the respective merchant locations. Goal-Oriented BPMN makes this multi-layered, dynamic scheme possible.

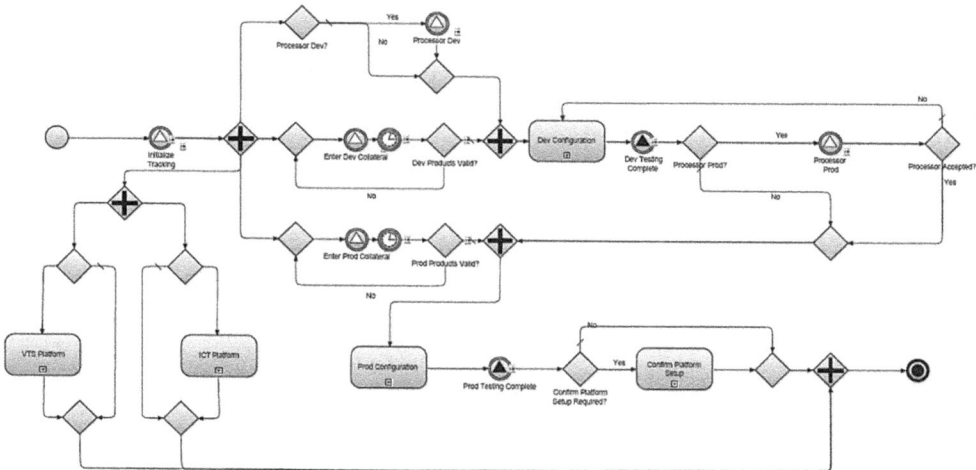

Figure 3: LaunchIT Product Level BPMN Workflow

In order to deliver a dynamic dashboard for end-user landing pages, rich composite interfaces and interactive monitoring tools were constructed using LSPS web form controls and widgets. The end-user, depending on the role configured in LSPS, is provided a Home landing page with BI widgets that show status and health metrics for the launch portfolio.

The dashboard includes a filterable list of launch projects to which the end-user is a stakeholder, as defined by rules and associations served by enterprise data sources. Work that is specifically the responsibility of the current user is separated to a secondary Worklist page. Figure 4 shows an example of the integrated dynamic user interface:

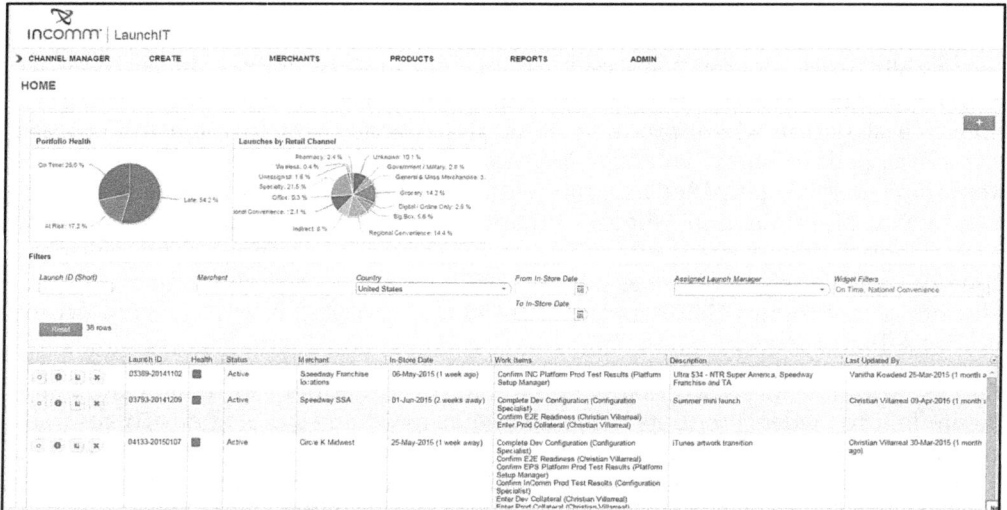

Figure 4: LaunchIT Channel Manager Home Page

Workflow transformation

An example of the extent of process transformation within this effort was the transition of the Configuration Solutions team workflow and data entry processes to LaunchIT. Configuration Solutions handles the testing of new or changed products for InComm. Figure 5 shows the Phase 2 workflow implementation of LSPS.

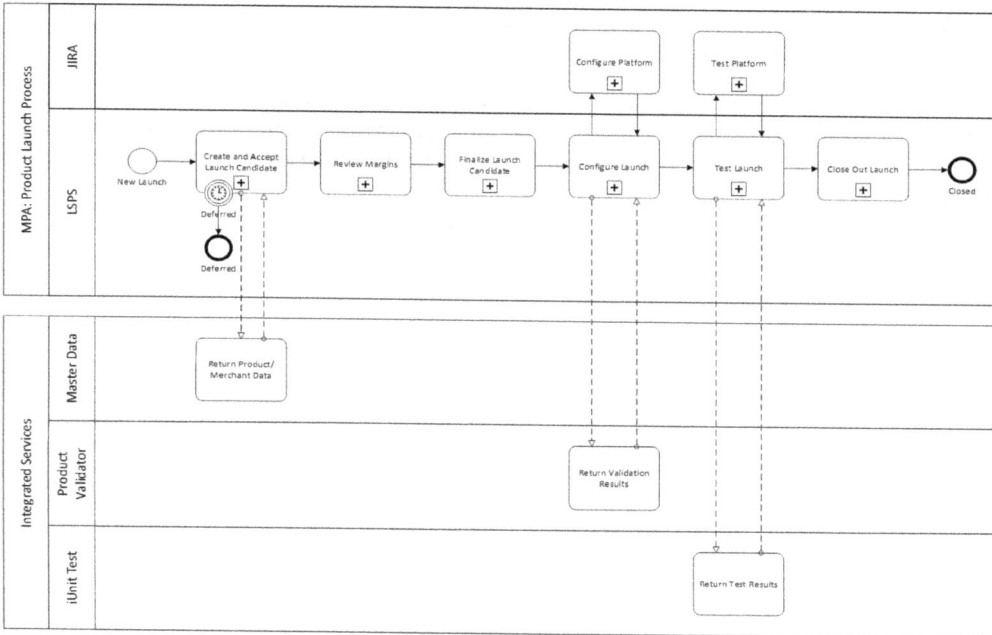

Figure 5: Phase 2 Macro-Level Product Launch Process

Users are no longer required to export data via reports or other means for input into the proprietary validation and test services. Rather than manually entering results data, the workflow now focuses on results review following the automated test and validation services execution, providing pass/fail results with drilldown explanations and historical auditing views. Based on service results, users can determine appropriate action for additional processing or may follow defined escalation paths.

Through the integration of the internal services and additional business rules that determine routing of products via the dynamic workflow previously described, a substantial portion of products previously sent to the Configuration Solutions team were now automated through a large portion of Goal-Oriented business objectives and supporting workflow. By running validation services while the launch was still in the ownership of the Launch Manager, the Configuration Specialists receiving vetted product test data, drastically reducing the risk of additional review and processing cycles.

Organizational Change

The project phased implementation of additional user types into the tool as a part of change control. Of particular note was the addition of platform Managers and InComm Digital Services. Both user bases had separate manual tracking systems for their portions of overall launch responsibilities, limiting transparency to information while launches remained in those stages. Figure 6 shows the final transition from disparate tracking mechanisms.

Rather than tasking Launch Managers with offline follow up to personnel managing setup of merchant-associated hardware for entry into the workflow, with those personnel tracking their tasking via other methods, personnel work was merged into the LaunchIT application. Each unique process now is triggered, within the dynamic Maintain Goal workflow structure, based on the requirements indicated in the merchant profile and user selection.

InComm's digital services, which support merchants with an online presence, follows a two-stage process rather than a singular end-to-end process to launch products. Design, development and implementation of these separate but related processes were added very quickly, based upon re-use of existing patterns.

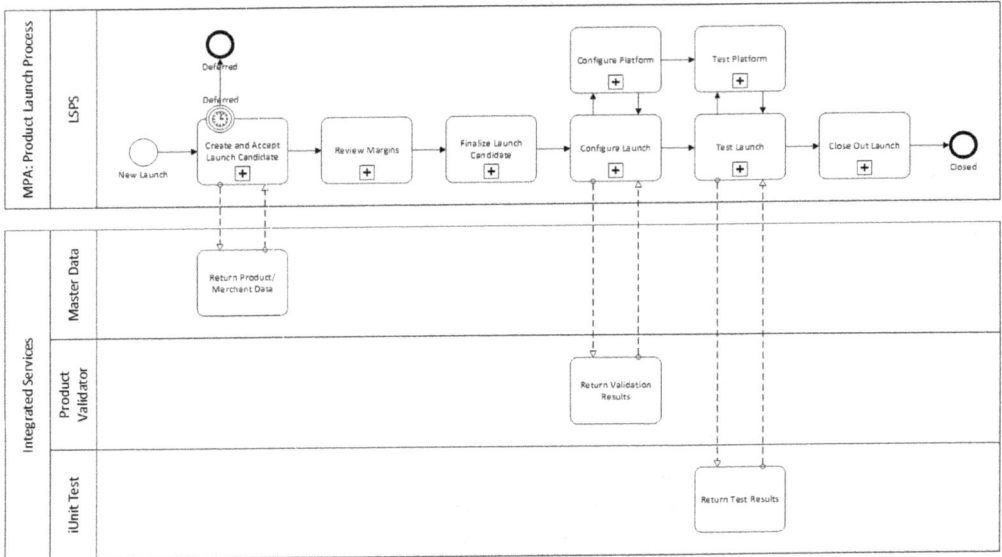

Figure 6: Phase 3 Macro-Level Product Launch Process

5. CONCLUSION

The LaunchIT solution went live in late March of 2014, with Phase 2 deployed in July and Phase 3 in October of the same year. To date, over 450 users have been on-boarded to the system. This user base is spread across the US, Canada, Puerto Rico, the UK, Australia and Japan, representing merchants from an even broader regional spread on five continents. The system also supports merchants with a solely online presence.

LaunchIT has provided a variety of benefits for InComm, which will increase as users continue to adopt the system and the InComm team continues to deliver new features and enhancements. To summarize these benefits, both realized and anticipated:

- Single source of data means one version of the truth and confidence that the data is current;
- Reduced rework in creation of launches; the right product and merchant information is used the first time;
- Visibility into the cause of bottlenecks, as key stakeholders have direct insight into process state.
- Automated escalations provide reminders and health calculations provide a focused method for prioritization of work;

- Reduced risk of incorrect billing and impact on customer relationships based on insertion of Finance users into the process with collaboration built into their portion of the workflow, ensuring financial data is accurate before a launch proceeds;
- Speed of creation based on application features expedites conceptualization phase for front-end users;
- Ability to do research - users can search on products and merchants to identify potential matches that meet all of their criteria before even starting the process;
- Business rules ensure the right group has the right data at the right time via validations and gateways, reducing rework;
- Integration of services means less time finding and managing exceptions by pushing those exceptions to the right person in the process; and
- Rather than a person managing a significant part of the process, the system is managing the process, also lending to scalability.

In addition to these benefits provided by the application, there are also several specific to LSPS platform:

- Additional goals may be added at any time that govern the process or portions of the process without impacting existing workflows; and
- Powerful ability to propagate new workflow changes to running instances ensuring that as business processes change, items in-flight do not need to be recreated or handled with external monitoring to be sure they meet the new process requirements.

As is standard with Agile, the Modus21 team held a retrospective at the conclusion of the engagement. Among the large number of lessons learned were several that are applicable to any BPMS implementation:

- A paradigm shift from nearly limitless flexibility (and opportunities for errors) to rules and workflow will be met with marked user resistance
- A reports-last mentality during road-mapping will not get senior leaders on board; leadership needs visibility and transparency built into the solution from the start
- Users do not blame bad data, they blame the system; therefore, establishing clean and verified master data up front can help preserve goodwill and minimize user frustration.
- Stretching BPMN to support multi-level flows created unintended consequences, requiring additional analysis and optimization time; leadership and stakeholders must be aware of potential risks when implementing new technologies and directives

InComm's success with LaunchIT is rooted in their commitment to innovation and the outsourcing of solution development that complements existing expertise and competencies.

Both Whitestein Technologies and Modus21 share a similar commitment to innovation, demonstrated by LSPS comprehensive, standards-based feature set and Modus21's proven Agile BPM implementation approach. LaunchIT is the result of a cooperative effort among partners committed to a shared vision. The end result is that InComm may continue to grow and expand with the knowledge that the automation and visibility provided by LaunchIT is powering productivity and scaling with continued organizational growth.

Author:
- Dan Reagan, Mr. Reagan served as Project Manager and Lead Analyst for Modus21's implementation of the InComm LaunchIT LSPS solution.

Contributors:
- David Gruber, Vice President Market Solutions, InComm
- Byron Glueck, Lead Architect, Whitestein North America

Melitta, Brazil
Nominated by Lecom S/A, Brazil

1. Executive Summary / Abstract

Melitta of Brazil, a unit of the German multinational coffee giant, Melitta, found operational barriers that impacted their costs and their agility. Therefore, the intention to improve their business routine was to break barriers between their locations, eliminating the circulation of papers, reduce the number of licenses used for approvals in ERP, integrating legacy systems and thus speed up the execution time of processes.

After studying the scenario of Melitta, flows that met these needs were created and the result was the highlight for the reduction of cost and time.

2. Overview

Melitta of Brazil, a unit of the German multinational, was in a situation where they could not find the center point which delayed their organizational reasoning processes. In order that the flow of activities within the organization ran better, Melitta sought help with a process consultant to see where the problem was. After identifying operational barriers that impacted on their costs and their agility, it became clear that the requirement was to improve their routine was to eliminate the circulation of paper, reduce the number of licenses used for approvals in ERP, integrating legacy systems and thus expedite the runtime processes.

Accordingly flows that met these needs were created. With approvals in the process, the costs of approvers in ERP licenses were eliminated and using digital certificates about the legality, integrations with the financial area and others became more agile and safe.

The result was the highlight to reduce costs by eliminating the circulation of papers by the company; the decrease in purchases of ERP use licenses; the decrease in annual interest expense and penalties with late payments; minimizing the occurrence of withdrawal of damaged goods in the market; decreasing the time and cost of execution of processes; and elimination of spending on archiving documents, once the information is being digitally signed and archived.

3. Business Context

Melitta found itself, in 2006, at a strong level of growth, with strategic projects in progress and going through major revisions in their internal business processes and workflows.

In that period of growth, as you might expect, it became extremely strategic to achieve cost optimization, as well as the centralization of areas, functions and responsibilities, and a great commitment towards streamlining internal processes and greater control (monitoring capability and management) of the process.

The strategy adopted was the implementation of an IT solution to act directly within Business Process Management. It was selected to fulfill the following functions:

1. Streamline / automate processes: steps to guide their decision points.

2. Integrating IT tools: allow information transit between different systems (Oracle and SQL), with access to databases and attaching files.

3. Reduce the number of ERP (approvers) users by enabling only authorized decision makers.

4. Freedom in using the tool; vendor independence; transfer of know-how to design new flow models.

5. Facilitate geographic independence; ability to approve steps remotely on the web platform.

6. Reduce traffic generation / paper; documents in digital form; safe and legal signature; sustainability objectives of Melitta.

7. Centralize processes / flows; designed and made feasible flows in a single platform; monitoring, communication, knowledge management, evaluation and consultation.

8. Generate performance statistics; Detailed Monitoring, identifying "bottlenecks", reworks, unproductive steps, exceptions, etc.

9. Print the legality Approvals; Approvals of flows should have legal value.

Other issues have become strategic in realizing the project, as the solution has competitive value to achieve the goals in a relatively short time. The term, although short, encompasses the issue of transfer of knowledge and training on workflow process management.

4. THE KEY INNOVATIONS

4.1 Business

The four initial flows deployed include distinct areas, bringing benefits to different audiences. Suppliers, for example, have benefited from the reduction, to almost zero, of late payments. Already the internal audience could view more agility and efficiency in matters that concern the IT sector of Melitta. Thus, the changes were accepted easily by the company, which quickly felt the business evolution as a result of new flows.

4.2 Process

SCP: Request for payment

- Creation of Documents
- Approval Hierarchy
- Accounting verification
- Signature Certified
- Integration with ERP
- Control Notices / Emails, Times, Statistics, etc.

Volumes:

- More than 50,800 cases
- More than R$ 3.6 billion in payments

Fluxo SCP - Solicitação de Pagamento

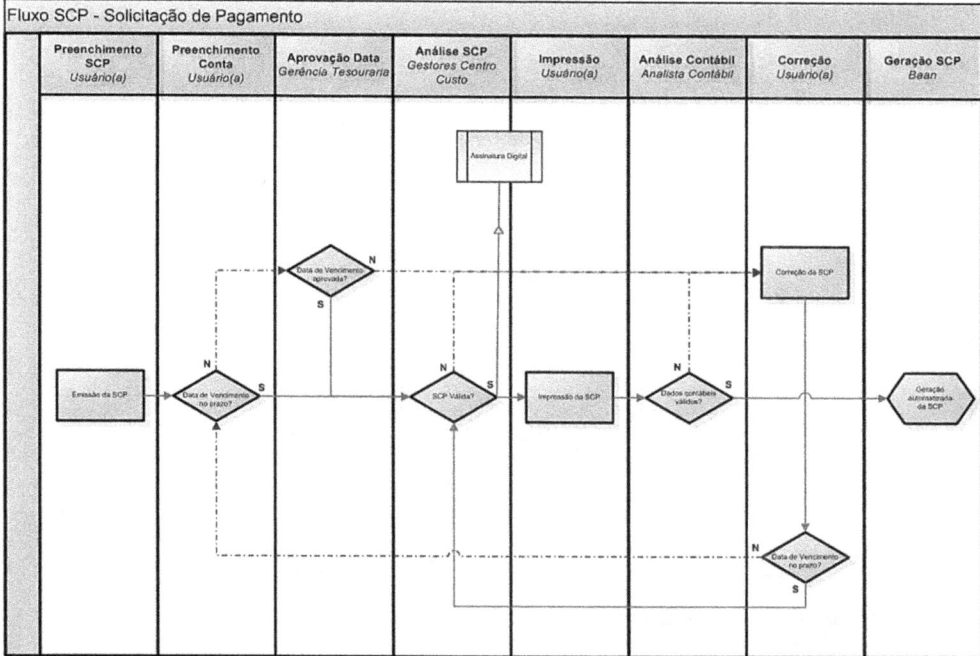

EVM: Funding Amount Marketing Effort

- Creation of Documents
- Approval Hierarchy
- Control Language Available
- Accounting Verification
- Integration with ERP
- Control Notices / Emails, Times, Statistics, etc.

Volumes:

- More than 22,000 processes
- More than R$ 268 million in payments

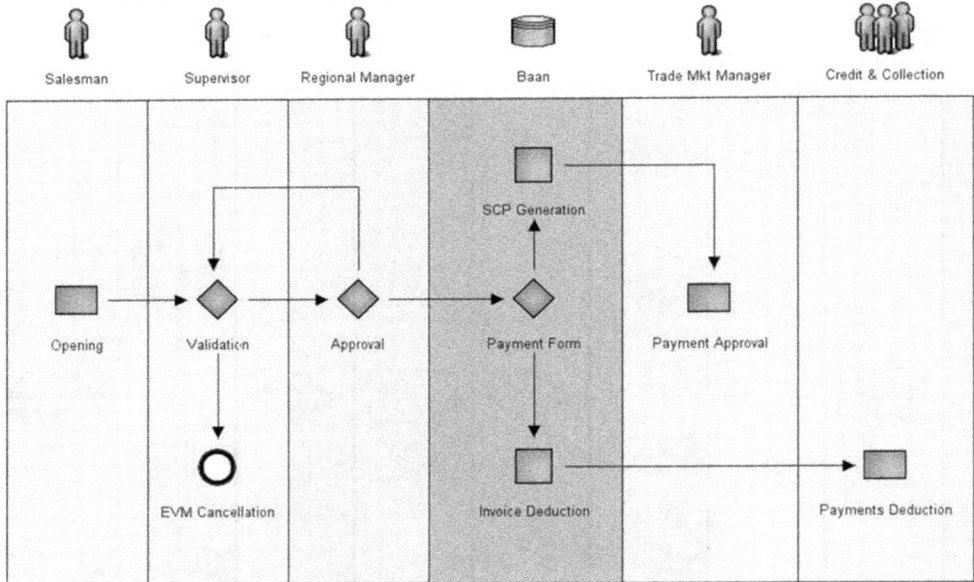

Salesman | Supervisor | Regional Manager | Baan | Trade Mkt Manager | Credit & Collection

Opening — Validation — Approval — Payment Form — SCP Generation — Payment Approval

EVM Cancellation — Invoice Deduction — Payments Deduction

RMD: Return of Returned Goods

- Creation of Documents
- Approval Hierarchy
- Better Control of Monitoring Results
- Visualization of Processes for everyone involved:
    o Sales
    o logistics
    o fiscal
- Credit Billing / Accounts Payable
- Integration with ERP
- Control Notices / Emails, Times, Statistics, etc.

Volumes:

- More than 25,000 processes
- More than R$ 1.8 million in payments

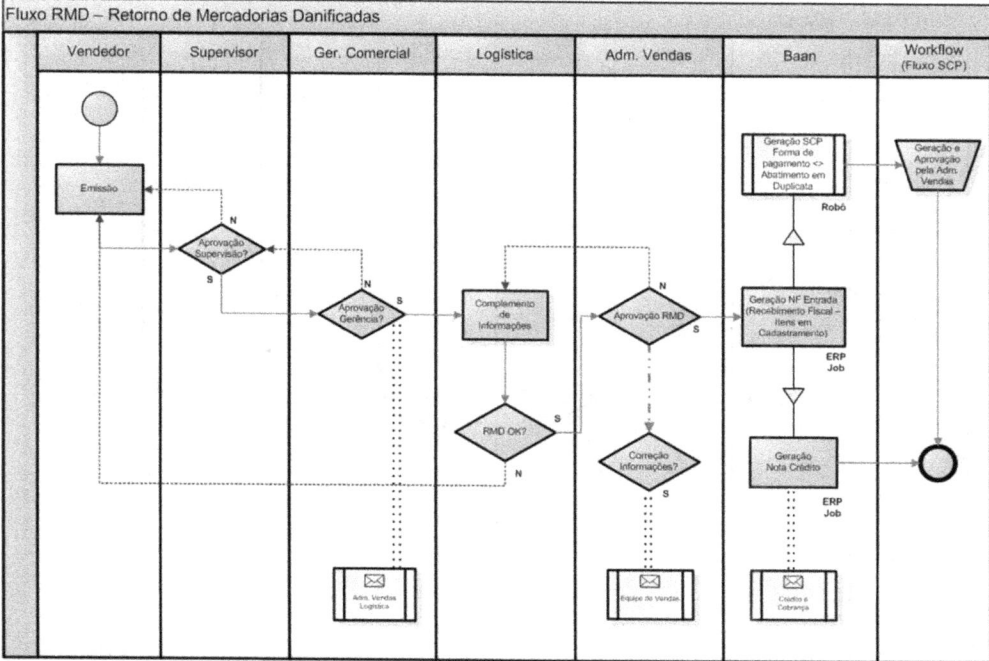

Fluxo RMD – Retorno de Mercadorias Danificadas

Sasti: Request Access and IT Services

- Creation of Documents
- Approval Hierarchy
- Better control of requests / service
- Compliance with Standards
- Integration with Service Desk / AD

Volumes:

- More than 480 processes

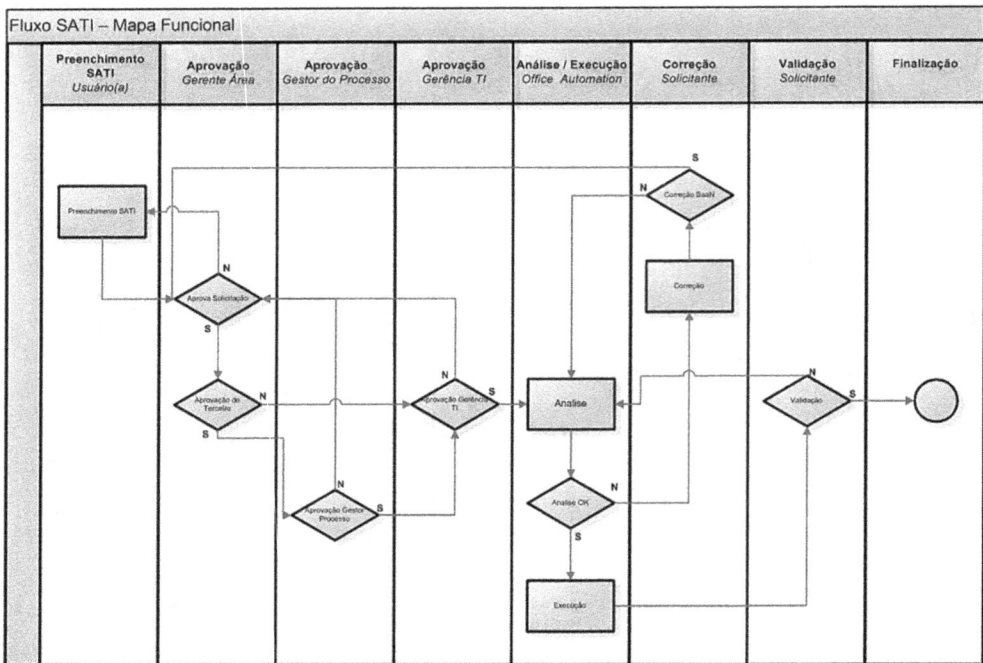

Fluxo SATI – Mapa Funcional

4.4 Organization & Social

As the benefits of the flows were quickly sensed and since different areas have been covered, the employees of Melitta easily accepted the proposed changes.

Before the implementation of the flows, there was a feeling that something was wrong, but they could not tell exactly what hindered them. After mapping problems and the deployment of streams, disorganization ceased to exist and the routine business flowed smoothly without bottlenecks.

5. HURDLES OVERCOME

There were no major issues to be corrected along the way. As the planning was very well designed and mainly aligned with the client, the expectations of both sides were met with ease. At all points, discussions were held before, during and after the implementation. Currently, any issue that arises is quickly resolved; but in general, these are simply technical issues.

6. BENEFITS

The main qualitative gains were:
- Flexibility and transparency
- Anticipation of problems (eg. accounting, payment term, taxes)
- Process execution in the proper sequence
- Facility Management / Approvals
- Management / monitoring / optimization process
- Increased agility and planning activities.
- Greater agility in the processes
- Higher gain: compliance management and governance
- Better Control of documents / payments
- Better Control of Funds by Area, Product Structure and Sales
- Better Planning

- It allowed analysis of the key causes, and action taking scenarios
- Perfect Traceability
- Reduction of Manual Controls
- Reduced Risk of Fraud
- Reduction of time allocated to RMDs
- Reduction in printing costs

Quantitative benefits include:

- Reduction in delays of payments:

  2003: 6.87 percent

  2011: 0.55 percent

- Fall in annual interest expense and penalties in the range of R$ 65K +
- Reduction of Events / costs

  2010: 1250 hits / month - R$ 82K / month

  2011: 700 hits / month - R$ 61K / month

  2012: 280 hits / month - R$ 6K / month

7. BEST PRACTICES, LEARNING POINTS AND PITFALLS

7.1 Best Practices and Learning Points

✓ *The approach Lecom with Melitta greatly facilitated the relationship*
✓ *Flows well-defined previously, facilitated the adoption of the company*
✓ *Planning was very well-drawn before the start of the project and could be followed to the letter throughout the process*
✓ *The initial alignment with the client was quite clear, so that the expectations of both sides were met*

7.2 Pitfalls

✗ *We had no negatives in this project due to the initial alignment within the organization.*

8. COMPETITIVE ADVANTAGES

The application provided rapid absorption of culture processes in the company;

- Easy navigation and use of the tool;
- Objective and flexible solution to suit the specific demands of the business environment and fully integrated IT Solution Melitta;
- Partnership relations, with the teams of the two companies committed to the successful outcome of the project;
- Proximity to the customer: Lecom availability of staff in-tending to the client when requested;
- Fast process automation, providing agility to processes of Melitta;
- Parameterizations / agile and independent customizations;
- Simplicity and speed of deployment;
- 100 percent web solution, eliminating the geographic barrier between business units and the location of its employees;
- Developed in Java and can be used in multi-platform and ATMs;
- Integration with Active Directory;
- EDM: Electronic Document Management;
- KPI: Management Productivity Indicators;
- Signature Integrated digital and legal value;
- Management and analysis of reports obtained from the tool itself;

- Centralization and monitoring information and procedures.

9. TECHNOLOGY
   - Application developed in Java using the APIs:
   - Hibernate to connect to the database;
   - jQuery to build dynamic layouts;
   - FusionCharts to generate charts.

10. THE TECHNOLOGY AND SERVICE PROVIDERS

The AtosBPM is a tool for automation and productivity processes with BPM, Electronic Document Management (EDM) and Management of Productivity Indicators (KPI) features. It enables the monitoring of all stages of the process, detects unproductive tasks and identifies trouble spots (so-called "bottlenecks"), resulting in much faster outlets and rational decision.

Melitta of Brazil: http://www.melitta.info/laenderportrait_brasilien_en.html

Lecom S/A, Brazil: http://www.lecom.com.br

South East Water
Leak Allowances
Nominated by South East Water, Australia

1. EXECUTIVE SUMMARY / ABSTRACT

South East Water (SEW) credited customers with $3,500,000 in allowances for unexplained high usage and leaks that occurred on their properties in the 2012/13 financial year.

It was projected that it would credit customers with $4,400,000 in the 2013/14 financial year.

A project was launched to reduce this amount substantially. It involved 17 teams from across the organization, ranging from customer service teams to plumbing services, debt management, legal and IT.

Through changes in policy and process, and with significant change management efforts, the project delivered $1,140,000 for the financial year, which equated to $1,500,000 on an annualized basis.

2. OVERVIEW

As a customer-service gesture, the water industry provides allowances to customers for water and sewerage costs associated with leaks that occur within their properties. There is no current government legislation on leak allowances; however, there are guidelines developed by the state water industry.

SEW had been following the guidelines, but over time, had shifted towards a more generous interpretation.

SEW credited customers with $3,500,000 in allowances for unexplained high usage and leaks that occurred on their properties in 2012/13.

Based on trends from the last five years and a significant price increase in July 2013, it was anticipated that we would credit customers with $4,400,000 in the 2013/14 financial year.

The goal of the improvement was to reduce the amount credited to customers by $1,300,000 without transferring costs to other areas e.g. credit management.

The anticipated outcome was that SEW would have a more tightly controlled leak allowance program with increased revenue benefits.

The internal Business Improvement team facilitated the delivery of the project.

The processes that were reviewed and improved included the actual leak allowance application process, the inputs to it, such as the call centre high bill/high usage call and the leak test call and the downstream processes, such as complaints and dispute resolution.

The project resulted in benefits to the organization of $1.14m for the 2013/14 financial year and $1.5m on an annualized basis. This was a combination of a reduction in money credited back to customers, resulting in additional revenue, offset by additional costs for plumbing inspections that form part of the new process.

3. BUSINESS CONTEXT

The water industry in the state of Victoria is wholly owned by the government. South East Water is one of 17 water retailers within the state, each of which is a monopoly for its defined region. Many employees have been with the organization or the previous board of works structure for their whole working lives. As such, there was a strong resistance to change and a lack of a competitive business mind-set. There was also a strong culture of customer service for the individual customer and a culture of avoidance within the organization.

At the start of 2013/14, there was a significant price increase of 44 percent at the lower tiers of usage. This resulted in more customers being able to detect a change in their water usage (via higher bills) and, therefore, more requests for assistance.

At the same time, there had been scrutiny from the Board of Directors regarding the amount of debt the company had from customers and there was pressure on the credit management team to keep the >90 day debt under control.

4. THE KEY INNOVATIONS

The changes that were implemented included:
- An adjusted leak allowance policy with tighter rules on the circumstances in which customers are eligible for allowances
- New processes with supporting scripts and procedures within the Call Centre when handling High Bill/High Usage queries, which often lead into leak allowance applications
- New processes with supporting procedures and system changes for handling leak allowance applications, which included plumbing inspections to check the eligibility of the leak and to ensure that the leak has been repaired
- New processes with supporting scripts and procedures to handle disputes and complaints
- Clear information on the company website as to what could cause a high bill, what to do if a customer suspects a leak, the eligibility requirements around leak allowance applications and the application form.

4.1 Business

There has been a shift in mindset with regards to dealing with customers on leak allowances. During the transition period, the plumbing inspection works coordinators handled most of the incoming applications and contact with customers. They had a greater commercially focused mindset and were able to impart some of this change to the customer services team.

4.2 Case Handling

Applications were previously received via mail and email. Both types were handled by the team leader and delegated to team members to process. There was little transparency to the rest of the organisation as to where the applications were in the process nor the history of the applications following a resolution.

The applications are now handled as cases in the customer relationship management (CRM) system. They start in a queue, which can be reported on, and can be delegated to individual queues, which are also transparent to others.

The application cases have fields specific to leak allowances, which helps to provide clarity to customer facing staff, such as call centre operators, who may field calls relating to the status or result of an application. These fields also enable reporting for performance management as well as for other impacted teams/processes, such as credit management and ombudsman's complaints.

The queues have enabled easy changes to the process and responsibilities. After a review and refinement of the process, responsibility for the start of the process moved from one team to another. The only system change required was to change the security access to the queue to enable the transition.

4.3 Organization & Social

Due to the clarity provided upfront to customers on what they must provide to support their applications, there has been a large reduction in non-value added work done by the customer services team in chasing information. This enables them to concentrate on assessing the validity of the claims.

There were also clearer instructions and rules to enable a customer to determine for themselves if their application will be successful.

5. HURDLES OVERCOME

4.1 Management

There were significant challenges faced by the team from management.

The main sources of resistance were:

- Competing KPIs – as the process impacted on many different parts of the business, they each were concerned with the effect any changes may have on their own KPIs. For example, the call centre was concerned about more upfront explanations during the phone conversation resulting in longer call times; credit management was concerned about the impact of less money being written off resulting in an increase in >90 day debt. Each team was supported in its concerns by the management of that area.
- Lack visible sponsorship – initially, there was a reluctance shown from senior leaders to voice their support of the project and the direction it was taking publicly.

4.2 Business

There was also significant resistance from some staff from the floor, who felt that they were advocates of customers who had been placed in a position of financial difficulty. They felt that even though the pipes within a property were the customer's responsibility, if they had a leak, the customer should be helped out. They were focused on the outlier cases, e.g. where a 90-year old woman without any family or community support lived in a dilapidated house.

There was a culture of ensuring customer received their full entitlements ("customers are entitled to an allowance regardless of circumstance") and a culture of avoidance (if a customer complained enough, the costs would be written off) as opposed to a focus on customers taking responsibility for maintaining their properties and SEW assisting those who genuinely had a spot of bad luck.

4.3 Organization Adoption

The strategies and tactics used to drive organizational adoption included:

- Bringing together the managers of the various areas – the management team was brought together and each areas key drivers were acknowledged. Agreement was reached as to the overriding goals and direction. The management team then presented their vision as a united team to all of the teams.
- Status reports were released on a weekly basis initially as implementation started and many activities were underway. They were then released on a fortnightly and then monthly basis as the majority of solutions were in place. This helped to keep the momentum going in the implementation teams.

- The KPIs were tracked for a 12-month period and reported on a monthly basis to all stakeholders. Aside from informing people of the results, it also let the teams doing the work know that their outputs were being monitored and reported at the highest levels. This helped to embed the changes in those teams. The other benefit of the long reporting period was that the effect of the changes on other KPIs, such as >90 day debt was tracked and shown to stabilize, not spiral out of control, as initially feared.
- Review of processes several times through the implementation period. Additional data was collected and brainstorming sessions held to refine the processes after initial implementation. This acknowledged that the design may not be perfect and gave the teams a chance to air their issues and provide input into making the processes better.
- Constant reinforcement through communications by managers and the project team as to the mindset change required of the operational teams.

6. BENEFITS

Qualitative benefits included:
- More transparency & clarity
- More consistency in the information being provided to customers
- A fairer leak allowance policy for customers who are taking responsibility for their properties and doing the right thing
- A level of confidence that enough information is being collected for larger value claims that will help defend against potential complaints
- Opportunities for referrals to the plumbing service for additional revenue to the business
- A feedback loop for customers and inspectors on the process to continuously improve.

6.1 Cost Savings / Time Reductions

The cycle time for application processing was supposed to reduce due to more up-front awareness from the website and call centre for customers on what was required. They would have a standard application form with required fields and a list of required supporting documents they would need to provide.

However, initially, post implementation, the turnaround time for applications was much higher than pre-project levels, with the use of the plumbing inspection team adding on additional time.

The process was reviewed after data was collected over the first three months. The rules around inspections were relaxed, which reduced the number of inspections done, which reduced the cycle time.

The process was reviewed again at the six-month mark and changes made to reduce the cycle time again. This resulted in the cycle time dropping below pre-project levels, as originally desired.

Each time, the review included data analysis to ensure that changes to process did not negatively impact on the benefits.

6.2 Increased Revenues

The forecasts for leak allowance credits were projected based on the historical trends for the previous five years, adjusting for the substantial price increase at the start of the 2013/14 year.

Credits and inspection costs were compared against the forecast monthly to determine the benefit from the project.

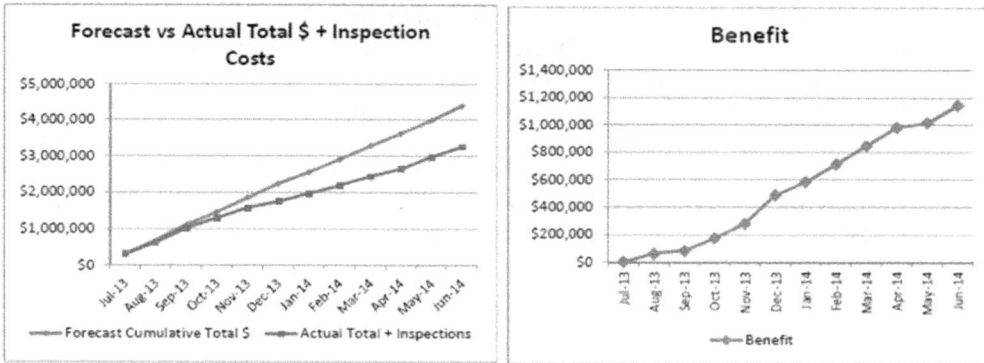

The benefit was a combination of a reduction in credits given back to customers against an increase in inspection costs, which resulted in net additional revenue of $1,143,000 for 2013/14.

As the implementation occurred from June through to November 2013, this period resulted in lower benefits as the policy and processes were embedded in the organization. December 2013 to June 2014 saw a stabilization of the process and this period was used to calculate an annualized benefit of $1,500,000.

6.3 Quality Improvements

Implementation of quality checks was part of the project with the quality team doing monthly, random checks of cases. This has helped to improve the consistency of processing and decision making.

7. BEST PRACTICES, LEARNING POINTS AND PITFALLS

7.1 Best Practices and Learning Points

✓ *Change management – there is no silver bullet. Time and persistence is required to change ingrained behavior.*

✓ *Strong Sponsorship – changes that stretch across an organization require very strong and visible sponsorship from senior management.*

✓ *Changes in policy – when it is official, staff are much more likely to conform to what is required.*

✓ *Tracking of metrics over a long period of time – these prove whether benefits are being achieved, costs and other agreed metrics are under control.*

7.2 Pitfalls

✗ *Starting a project without strong Sponsorship – with competing priorities and KPIs for different teams, time and energy will be wasted if there is not a clear direction given by senior leadership.*

✗ *Early identification of all key stakeholders and their issues – not getting a clear understanding of the drivers for key stakeholders will result in resistance from them and potential sabotage of the project.*

8. COMPETITIVE ADVANTAGES

This is not applicable as the organization operates as a monopoly within its region.

9. TECHNOLOGY

Case management was handled via the SalesForce CRM platform from the initial application from the customer, through to requests for plumbing inspections and back to the customer support team for financial adjustments and responses to the customer.

The benefits of using the case management process within the CRM system were:

- it kept all of the internal and external correspondence and results in one place, which allowed staff checking quality and handling complaints to access everything they required
- individual and team queues allowed staff to manage their backlog of work
- reports from the system showed management the status of the work and allowed them to manage the performance of their team
- other teams, such as credit management, could access information on applications quickly and easily to manage their work

Plumbing inspections were handled via the internally developed works management system.

The benefits of using the works management system were:
- the inspections were treated in the same way as any other plumbing job, which meant little training was required for staff to get up and running

Integration between the two systems is planned for future rollouts to allow data to flow directly through instead of having manual data transfer. Due to time constraints, this was not done as part of the initial project.

Smart pdfs were used for the application forms. This enabled customers to type directly into fields within the form and to send the forms in by email. The benefits of using the smart pdfs were:
- they reduced the opportunities for error in reading handwritten applications
- applications were received more quickly, instead of waiting for forms to be sent through the mail
- the emails and attachments were able to be pulled through automatically into cases in the CRM, reducing manual handling

Again, enhancements are planned for the applications to be handled directly through the company website, which would feed straight into the CRM, eliminating the need for manual data entry.

10. THE TECHNOLOGY AND SERVICE PROVIDERS

- All technical development was undertaken by the SEW internal IT development team for both the SalesForce and internal works management systems.
- The Enterprise Process Centre system was used for process mapping.
- Minitab was used for trending and data analysis.

Section 3
Appendix

WfMC Structure and Membership Information

WHAT IS THE WORKFLOW MANAGEMENT COALITION?

The Workflow Management Coalition (WfMC), founded in August 1993, is a non-profit, international organization of BPM and workflow vendors, users, analysts and university/research groups.

The Coalition's mission is to promote and develop the use of collaborative technologies such as workflow, BPM and case management through the establishment of standards for software terminology, interoperability and connectivity among products and to publicize successful use cases.

WORKFLOW STANDARDS FRAMEWORK

The Coalition has developed a framework for the establishment of workflow standards. This framework includes five categories of interoperability and communication standards that will allow multiple collaboration products to coexist and interoperate within a user's environment. Technical details are included in the white paper entitled, "The Work of the Coalition," available at www.wfmc.org.

ACHIEVEMENTS

The initial work of the Coalition focused on publishing the Reference Model and Glossary, defining a common architecture and terminology for the industry. A major milestone was achieved with the publication of the first versions of the Workflow API (WAPI) specification, covering the Workflow Client Application Interface, and the Workflow Interoperability specification.

In addition to a series of successful tutorials industry wide, the WfMC invested many person-years over the past 20 years helping to drive awareness, understanding and adoption of XPDL, now the standard means for business process definition in over 80 BPM products. As a result, it has been cited as the most deployed BPM standard by a number of industry analysts, and continues to receive a growing amount of media attention.

Workflow Reference Model

The Workflow Reference Model was published first in 1995 and still forms the basis of most BPM and workflow software systems in use today. It was developed from the generic workflow application structure by identifying the interfaces which enable products to interoperate at a variety of levels.

All workflow systems contain a number of generic components which interact in a defined set of ways; different products will typically exhibit different levels of capability within each of these generic components. To achieve interoperability between workflow products a standardized set of interfaces and data interchange formats between such components is necessary.

A number of distinct interoperability scenarios can then be constructed by reference to such interfaces, identifying different levels of functional conformance as appropriate to the range of products in the market.

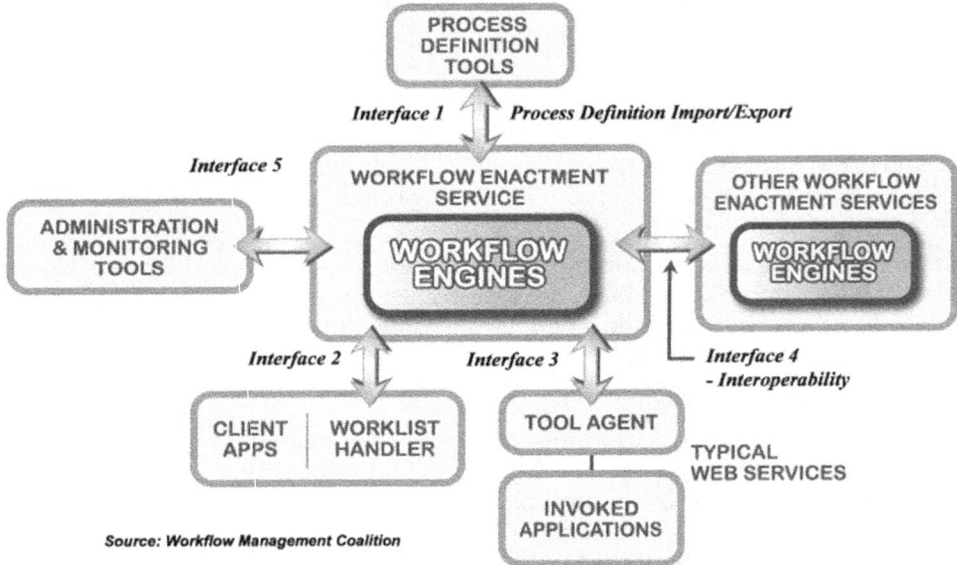

Source: Workflow Management Coalition

WORKFLOW REFERENCE MODEL DIAGRAM

XPDL (XML Process Definition Language)

An XML based language for describing a process definition, developed by the WfMC. Version 1.0 was released in 2002. Version 2.0 was released in Oct 2005. The goal of XPDL is to store and exchange the process diagram, to allow one tool to model a process diagram, and another to read the diagram and edit, another to "run" the process model on an XPDL-compliant BPM engine, and so on.

For this reason, XPDL is not an executable programming language like BPEL, but specifically a process design format that literally represents the "drawing" of the process definition. Thus it has 'XY' or vector coordinates, including lines and points that define process flows. This allows an XPDL to store a one-to-one representation of a BPMN process diagram.

For this reason, XPDL is effectively the file format or "serialization" of BPMN, as well as any non-BPMN design method or process model which use in their underlying definition the XPDL meta-model (there are presently about 60 tools which use XPDL for storing process models.)

In spring 2012, the WfMC completed XPDL 2.2 as the *fifth* revision of this specification. XPDL 2.2 builds on version 2.1 by introducing support for the process modeling extensions added to BPMN 2.0.

BPSim

The Business Process Simulation (BPSim) framework is a standardized specification that allows business process models captured in either BPMN or XPDL to be augmented with information in support of rigorous methods of analysis. It defines the parameterization and interchange of process analysis data allowing structural and capacity analysis of process models.

BPSim is meant to support both pre-execution and post-execution optimization of said process models. The BPSim specification consists of an underlying computer-interpretable representation (meta-model) and an accompanying electronic file format to ease the safeguard and transfer of this data between different tools (interchange format).

Wf-XML

Wf-XML is designed and implemented as an extension to the OASIS Asynchronous Service Access Protocol (ASAP). ASAP provides a standardized way that a program can start and monitor a program that might take a long time to complete. It provides the capability to monitor the running service, and be informed of changes in its status.

Wf-XML extends this by providing additional standard web service operations that allow sending and retrieving the "program" or definition of the service which is provided. A process engine has this behavior of providing a service that lasts a long time, and also being programmable by being able to install process definitions.

Awards

The Workflow Management Coalition sponsors three annual award programs.

1. The **Global Awards for Excellence in BPM & Workflow**[1] recognizes organizations that have implemented particularly innovative workflow solutions. Every year between 10 and 15 BPM and workflow solutions are recognized in this manner.
   WfMC publishes the case studies in the annual Excellence in Practice [2] series.

2. WfMC inaugurated a Global Awards program in 2011 for **Excellence in Case Management**[3] case studies to recognize and focus upon successful use cases for coordinating unpredictable work patterns. Awards are given in the category of Production Case Management and in Adaptive Case Management which are both new technological approaches to supporting knowledge work in today's leading edge organizations. These awards are designed to highlight the best examples of technology to support knowledge workers.
   Several books[4] have been published recognizing the winning teams. In 2013, WfMC updated the program to "WfMC Awards for Excellence in Case Management" to recognize the growing deployment of Production Case Management.

3. The **Marvin L. Manheim Award For Significant Contributions** in the Field of Workflow is given to one person every year in recognition of individual contributions to workflow and BPM standards. This award commemorates Marvin Manheim who played a key motivational role in the founding of the WfMC.

---

[1] BPM Awards: www.BPMF.org

[2] *Delivering BPM Excellence:* Published 2013 by Future Strategies Inc. http://futstrat.com/books/Delivering_BPM.php

[3] Case Management Awards: www.adaptivecasemanagement.org

[4] *Empowering Knowledge Workers:* Published 2013 by Future Strategies Inc. http://futstrat.com/books/EmpoweringKnowledgeWorkers.php

How Knowledge Workers Get Things Done. Published 2012 by Future Strategies Inc. http://www.futstrat.com/books/HowKnowledgeWorkers.php

Taming the Unpredictable: Published 2011 by Future Strategies Inc .http://futstrat.com/books/eip11.php

The Workflow Management Coalition gives you the unique opportunity to participate in the creation of standards for the workflow industry as they are developing.

Your contributions to our community ensure that progress continues in the adoption of royalty-free workflow and process standards.

THE SECRETARIAT

Workflow Management Coalition (WfMC)

www.WfMC.org

Author and Contact Appendix

LINUS CHOW

Enterprise Architect, Solution Engineering, Salesforce.com

Linus Chow is an Enterprise Architect focusing on Salesforce customers' adoption of cloud and mobile capabilities in complex hybrid architectures. Mr. Chow has over 20 years of experience bringing together people, process and technology for innovative and impactful large-scale solutions around the world and across industries. He is a published author and speaker with over 50 articles and engagements; including authoring over 25 customer award-winning nominations (e.g. CIO100, ComputerWorld, Gartner, OMG, WfMC, etc). A decorated former US Army Officer, Linus has an MBA, a MS in Management Information Systems, and BS in Mathematics; and is a Certified BPM Professional.

THOMAS COZZOLINO

Principal Architect Evangelist, Salesforce.com

Thomas Cozzolino is a Principal Architect Evangelist, focusing on the success of salesforce customers. With over 30 years of experience in industry and consulting, Mr. Cozzolino has successfully designed and deployed solutions based on next-generation cloud, social and mobile architectures across a range of industries. A pioneer in Internet, web and mobile strategies, he is a published author and speaker with over 50 journal articles, book chapters and industry interviews.

LAYNA FISCHER

Publisher, Future Strategies Inc

Ms Fischer is Publisher at Future Strategies Inc., and also Awards Director of the annual WfMC Awards programs. She was previously Executive Director of WfMC and BPMI (now merged with OMG) and continues to coordinate with these organizations to promote industry awareness of BPM and Workflow.

Future Strategies Inc. (www.FutStrat.com) specializes in publishing in-depth content about BPM, business architecture and associated technologies for business and executive management readers. As such, the company works closely with individual authors and corporations worldwide. The company manages the prestigious annual *Global Awards for Excellence in BPM and Workflow* and the annual *Global Case Management Awards*, publishing the winning case studies in the annual *Excellence in Practice* series.

Future Strategies Inc., also produces the business series *New Tools for New Times* and the *BPM Handbook* series, published in collaboration with the WfMC. Ms. Fischer was previously senior editor of an international computer publication and has been involved in international computer journalism and publishing for over 20 years.

PETER FRANZ

Co-founder and joint CEO, BPM-D

Peter Franz has been working at the forefront of Business Process Man-agement (BPM) for many years as part of a 30-year career with Accenture. He has a deep understanding of the application of Business Process Man-agement discipline to drive real business results.

His career includes education and experience in the use of Information Technology and thus understands the Business / IT interaction from both sides and can help bridge this divide. He is passionate about BPM and its application to real business challenges.

HARTMANN GENRICH

Consultant, Process Analytica, Germany

Hartmann Genrich worked for Gesellschaft für Mathematik und Daten verarbeitung (GMD), the German National Research Institute for Information Technology. He holds a Dr. rer. nat. in Mathematics from University of Bonn and published various papers on the mathematics of Petri Nets. Later he got involved in the modeling, simulation and analysis of workflow systems. He retired from GMD in 2001 and works as a consultant to North American and German companies.

DAVID GRIMM

Director Global Enterprise Architecture, Salesforce.com

David Grimm has over 25 years experience focusing on the architecture of business systems and complex technology solutions across a range of industries. He has built, grown, and led global pre-sale architecture practices at multiple companies. His area of expertise is in global strategy, methodology, enablement, and operational execution as it applies to Enterprise Architecture.

MATHIAS KIRCHMER

Co-founder and joint CEO, BPM-D

As innovative CEO and Managing Director at BPM-D, Accenture, and IDS Scheer, Dr. Kirchmer has worked successfully in an international environment across various industries. He has combined his broad practical business experience with his extensive academic research. This systematic integration has led to pioneering management approaches that have proven to be both sustainable and provide immediate benefits.

Dr. Kirchmer is visionary leader, thought leader and innovator in the field of Business Process Management (BPM). He is an affiliated faculty member at the University of Pennsylvania, published six books as well as numerous articles and shares his insights regularly in presentations around the world.

DEREK MIERS

Transformation Program Design, Structure Talent Ltd, UK

Derek focuses on the methods, approaches, frameworks, techniques, and technologies of business architecture, transformation and target operating models. His deep competence is around BPM, business process improvement and organizational change.

He places a special emphasis on an outside-in, outcome-based, customer-focused approach. His engagements usually focus on helping major organizations charter and establish their change programs, ensuring the change has the best chance of success.

Prior to joining Structure Talent, Derek spent 5 years at Forrester Research working in both research and consulting. He led the Business Architecture research practice for 2 years, before which he focused on BPM, Case Management and Organizational Transformation. While at Forrester Derek published over 60 different research reports exploring these themes.

Prior to Forrester, Derek worked as an independent Industry Analyst for 18 years where he established an international reputation in BPM and organizational transformation. He has worked in the process arena for more than 25 years, dealing with major brands, governmental organizations, and nongovernmental organizations (NGOs).

Derek is a well-known keynote speaker and chair of major BPM conferences. As co-chair of BPMI.org, he helped merge the organization with the Object Management Group (OMG). Derek completed the Early Growth Executive Program at London Business School.

NATHANIEL PALMER

Vice President and CTO, BPM, Inc., BPM, Inc.

Rated as the top Most Influential Thought Leader in Business Process Management (BPM) by independent research, Nathaniel is recognized as one of the early originators of BPM, and has the led the design for some of the in-dustry's largest-scale and most complex projects involving investments of $200 Million or more. Today he is the Editor-in-Chief of BPM.com, as well as the Executive Director of the Workflow Management Coalition, as well as VP and CTO of BPM, Inc.

Previously he had been the BPM Practice Director of SRA International, and prior to that Director, Business Consulting for Perot Systems Corp, as well as spent over a decade with Delphi Group serving as VP and CTO. He frequently tops the lists of the most recognized names in his field, and was the first individual named as Laureate in Workflow. Nathaniel has authored or co-authored a dozen books on process innovation and business trans-formation, including "Intelligent BPM" (2013), "How Knowledge Workers Get Things Done" (2012), "Social BPM" (2011), "Mastering the Unpredictable" (2008) which reached #2 on the Amazon.com Best Seller's List, "Excellence in Practice" (2007), "Encyclopedia of Database Systems" (2007) and "The X-Economy" (2001).

He has been featured in numerous media ranging from Fortune to The New York Times to National Public Radio. Nathaniel holds a DISCO Secret Clearance as well as a Position of Trust within the U.S. federal government.

ROBERT SHAPIRO

Chairman, ProcessAnalytica, Process Analytica, USA

Robert Shapiro is chairman of ProcessAnalytica. He founded CapeVisions and developed Analytics and Simulation software used by FileNet/IBM, Fujitsu, PegaSystems and Global360/OpenText.

Prior to CapeVisions, he founded Meta Software Corporation and developed graphical modeling and optimization tools for business process improvement. These tools were used by BankAmerica, Wells Fargo, JPMChase and other banks to optimize check processing and LockBox operations. As Technical Committee chair of the WfMC, he plays a critical role in developing international standards for workflow and business process management. He has been instrumental in the creation and evolution of XPDL and BPMN. He is currently co-chair of The Business Process Simulation Working Group developing standards to support sharing of simulation input and output data for process models based on BPMN and XPDL. The workbench includes Process Discovery capabilities which create BPMN models from system event logs and restructure models to improve performance and understandability.

In his recent work he has created a workbench for process optimization, using Visual Analytics and 'hypergraphics' to integrate process modeling, simulation, analytics and optimization.

Award-winning Case Studies

NOMINEE ORGANIZATION:

Company: Admin Re, United Kingdom

NOMINATED BY:

Company: Corporate Modelling Services Limited
Website: www.corporatemodelling.com

NOMINEE ORGANIZATION:
Company: AGESIC Uruguayan Agency for eGovernment, Uruguay

NOMINATED BY:
Company: INTEGRADOC
Website: www.integradoc.com

NOMINEE ORGANIZATION:
Company: AgFirst Farm Credit Bank, USA

NOMINATED BY:
Company: Bizagi Ltd
Website: www.bizagi.com

NOMINEE ORGANIZATION:
Company: BusinessPartners, South Africa

NOMINATED BY:
Company: Petanque Consultancy
Website: http://petanque-c.com

NOMINEE ORGANIZATION:
Company: Chicago Park District, USA

NOMINATED BY:
Company: Sofbang
Website: www.sofbang.com

NOMINEE ORGANIZATION:
Company: Delta Lloyd, Netherlands

NOMINATED BY:
Company: You-Get
Website: www.you-get.com

NOMINEE ORGANIZATION:
Company: Freedom Mortgage Corporation, USA

NOMINATED BY:
Company: Freedom Mortgage Corporation
Website: www.freedommortgage.com

NOMINEE ORGANIZATION:

Company: GE Avio S.r.l, Italy

NOMINATED BY:

Company: EKA S.r.l.
Website: www.eka-systems.com

NOMINEE ORGANIZATION:

Company: Generali PFF Holding, United Kingdom

NOMINATED BY:

Company: Bizagi Ltd
Website: www.bizagi.com

NOMINEE ORGANIZATION:

Company: InComm, USA

NOMINATED BY:

Company: Living Systems Technologies
Website: http://livingsystemstech.com

NOMINEE ORGANIZATION:

Company: Melitta of Brazil, Brazil

NOMINATED BY:

Company: Lecom S/A
Website: www.lecom.com.br

NOMINEE ORGANIZATION:

Company: South East Water, Australia

NOMINATED BY:

Company: South East Water
Website: www.southeastwater.com.au

HOW TO WIN AN AWARD

The annual WfMC **Awards for Global Excellence in BPM** are sponsored by WfMC.org and BPM.com. The prestigious annual Awards are highly coveted by organizations that seek recognition for their achievements. These awards not only provide a spotlight for companies that truly deserve recognition, but provide tremendous insights for organizations wishing to emulate the winners' successes.

General information and guidelines for submissions are at www.bpmf.org.

Index

Additional Reading and Resources

NEW E-BOOK SERIES (RETAIL $25.00)

Download PDF immediately and start reading. **Only $9.97 each**

- Introduction to BPM and Workflow
  http://bpm-books.com/products/ebook-series-introduction-to-bpm-and-workflow

- Financial Services
  http://bpm-books.com/products/ebook-series-financial-services

- Healthcare
  http://bpm-books.com/products/ebook-series-bpm-in-healthcare

- Utilities and Telecommunications
  http://bpm-books.com/products/ebook-series-utilities-and-telecommunications

NON-PROFIT ASSOCIATIONS AND RELATED STANDARDS RESEARCH ONLINE

- AIIM (Association for Information and Image Management)
  http://www.aiim.org
- BPM and Workflow online news, research, forums
  http://bpm.com
- BPM Research at Stevens Institute of Technology
  http://www.bpm-research.com
- Business Process Management Initiative
  http://www.bpmi.org *see* Object Management Group
- IEEE (Electrical and Electronics Engineers, Inc.)
  http://www.ieee.org
- Institute for Information Management (IIM)
  http://www.iim.org
- ISO (International Organization for Standardization)
  http://www.iso.ch
- Object Management Group
  http://www.omg.org
- Open Document Management Association
  http://nfocentrale.net/dmware
- Organization for the Advancement of Structured Information Standards
  http://www.oasis-open.org
- Society for Human Resource Management
  http://www.shrm.org
- Society for Information Management
  http://www.simnet.org
- Wesley J. Howe School of Technology Management
  http://howe.stevens.edu/research/research-centers/business-process-innovation
- Workflow And Reengineering International Association (WARIA)
  http://www.waria.com
- Workflow Management Coalition (WfMC)
  http://www.wfmc.org
- Workflow Portal
  http://www.e-workflow.org

THRIVING ON ADAPTABILITY: BEST PRACTICES FOR KNOWLEDGE WORKERS

http://futstrat.com/books/ThrivingOnAdaptability.php

ACM helps organizations focus on improving or optimizing the line of interaction where our people and systems come into direct contact with customers. It's a whole different thing; a new way of doing business that enables organizations to literally become one living-breathing entity via collaboration and adaptive data-driven biological-like operating systems. ACM is not just another acronym or business fad. ACM is the process, strategy, framework, and set of tools that enables this evolution and maturity: *Surendra Reddy, Foreword*

EMPOWERING KNOWLEDGE WORKERS: *NEW WAYS TO LEVERAGE CASE MANAGEMENT*

http://futstrat.com/books/EmpoweringKnowledgeWorkers.php

Empowering Knowledge Workers describes the work of managers, decision makers, executives, doctors, lawyers, campaign managers, emergency responders, strategists, and many others who have to think for a living.

These are people who figure out what needs to be done, at the same time that they do it, and there is a new approach to support this presents the logical starting point for understanding how to take advantage of ACM

Retail #49.95 (see discount on website)

TAMING THE UNPREDICTABLE

http://futstrat.com/books/eip11.php

The core element of Adaptive Case Management (ACM) is the support for real-time decision-making by knowledge workers.

Taming the Unpredictable presents the logical starting point for understanding how to take advantage of ACM. This book goes beyond talking about concepts, and delivers actionable advice for embarking on your own journey of ACM-driven transformation.

Retail #49.95 (see discount on website)

HOW KNOWLEDGE WORKERS GET THINGS DONE

http://www.futstrat.com/books/HowKnowledgeWorkers.php

How Knowledge Workers Get Things Done describes the work of managers, decision makers, executives, doctors, lawyers, campaign managers, emergency responders, strategist, and many others who have to think for a living. These are people who figure out what needs to be done, at the same time that they do it, and there is a new approach to support this presents the logical starting point for understanding how to take advantage of ACM.

Retail $49.95 (see discount offer on website)

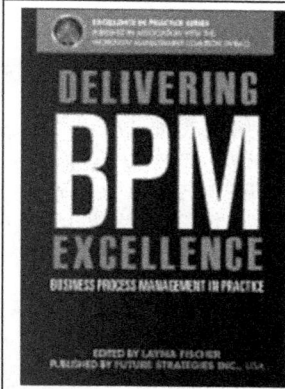

DELIVERING BPM EXCELLENCE

http://futstrat.com/books/Delivering_BPM.php

Business Process Management in Practice

The companies whose case studies are featured in this book have proven excellence in their creative and successful deployment of advanced BPM concepts. These companies focused on excelling in *innovation, implementation* and *impact* when installing BPM and workflow technologies. The positive impact includes increased revenues, more productive and satisfied employees, product enhancements, better customer service and quality improvements.
$39.95 (see discount on website)

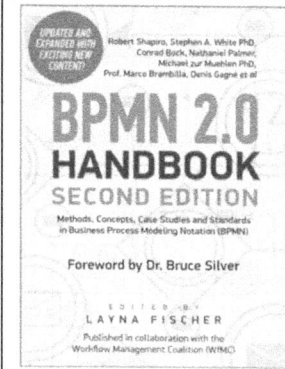

BPMN 2.0 Handbook SECOND EDITION

(see two-BPM book bundle offer on website: get BPMN Reference Guide Free)

http://futstrat.com/books/bpmnhandbook2.php

Updated and expanded with exciting new content!

Authored by members of WfMC, OMG and other key participants in the development of BPMN 2.0, the BPMN 2.0 Handbook brings together worldwide thought-leaders and experts in this space. Exclusive and unique contributions examine a variety of aspects that start with an introduction of what's new in BPMN 2.0, and look closely at interchange, analytics, conformance, optimization, simulation and more. **Retail $75.00**

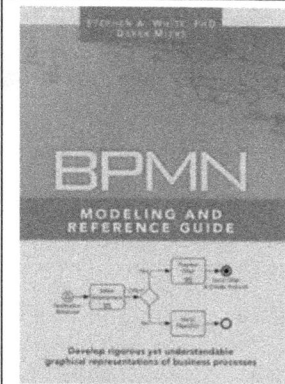

BPMN MODELING AND REFERENCE GUIDE

(see two-BPM book bundle offer on website: get BPMN Reference Guide Free)

http://www.futstrat.com/books/BPMN-Guide.php

Understanding and Using BPMN
How to develop rigorous yet understandable graphical representations of business processes.

Business Process Modeling Notation (BPMN) is a standard, graphical modeling representation for business processes. It provides an easy to use, flow-charting notation that is independent of the implementation environment.
Retail $39.95

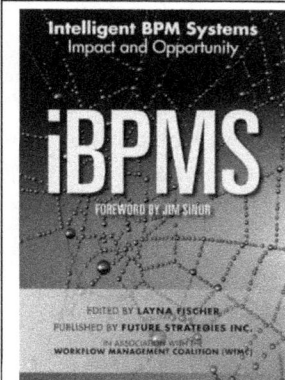

iBPMS - INTELLIGENT BPM SYSTEMS

http://www.futstrat.com/books/iBPMS_Handbook.php

"The need for Intelligent Business Operations (IBO) supported by intelligent processes is driving the need for a new convergence of process technologies lead by the iBPMS. The iBPMS changes the way processes help organizations keep up with business change," notes Gartner Emeritus Jim Sinur in his Foreword.

The co-authors of this important book describe various aspects and approaches of iBPMS with regard to impact and opportunity. **Retail $59.95 (see discount on website)**

Social BPM

http://futstrat.com/books/handbook11.php

Work, Planning, and Collaboration Under the Impact of Social Technology

Today we see the transformation of both the look and feel of BPM technologies along the lines of social media, as well as the increasing adoption of social tools and techniques democratizing process development and design. It is along these two trend lines; the evolution of system interfaces and the increased engagement of stakeholders in process improvement, that Social BPM has taken shape.

Retail $59.95 (see discount offer on website)

BPM EVERYWHERE

Internet of Things, Process of Everything

http://www.BPMEverywhere.com

We are entering an entirely new phase of BPM – the era of *"BPM Everywhere"* or **BPME**.

This book discusses critical issues currently facing BPM adopters and practitioners, such as the key roles played by process mining uncovering engagement patterns and the need for process management platforms to coordinate interaction and control of smart devices. BPME represents the strategy for leveraging, not simply surviving but fully exploiting the wave of disruption facing every business over the next 5 years and beyond.

PASSPORTS TO SUCCESS IN BPM

http://bpm-books.com/products/passports-to-success-in-bpm

BPM projects fail more often as a result of missed expectations than inadequate technology. In this book you will learn how to create and present a credible business case and plan for success, starting with the chapter "BPM Success Manifesto."

In addition to the highly insightful and instructional white papers contributed by industry thought leaders, this book provides compelling award-wining case studies written by those who have been through the full BPM experience.

www.ingramcontent.com/pod-product-compliance
Lightning Source LLC
Chambersburg PA
CBHW051409200326
41520CB00023B/7173